广东省“211工程”三期重点学科建设项目

主编 徐真华

全球化背景下的外国语言文学研究丛书

翻译家林语堂

LIN YUTANG AS AUTHOR-TRANSLATOR

褚东伟 著

上海外语教育出版社
外教社 SHANGHAI FOREIGN LANGUAGE EDUCATION PRESS

图书在版编目（CIP）数据

翻译家林语堂 / 褚东伟著.
—上海：上海外语教育出版社，2012（2013重印）
（全球化背景下的外国语言文学研究丛书）
ISBN 978-7-5446-2540-1

Ⅰ. ①翻… Ⅱ. ①褚… Ⅲ. ①林语堂（1895～1976）—翻译理论—研究
Ⅳ. ①H059

中国版本图书馆CIP数据核字（2012）第226381号

出版发行：上海外语教育出版社
（上海外国语大学内） 邮编：200083
电　　话：021-65425300（总机）
电子邮箱：bookinfo@sflep.com.cn
网　　址：http://www.sflep.com.cn　http://www.sflep.com
责任编辑：许进兴

印　　刷：上海信老印刷厂
开　　本：890×1240　1/32　印张 9.125　字数 270 千字
版　　次：2012 年 8 月第 1 版　2013 年 7 月第 2 次印刷
印　　数：1 100 册

书　　号：ISBN 978-7-5446-2540-1 / K・0067
定　　价：35.00 元

全球化背景下的外国语言文学研究丛书

编委会名单

总序

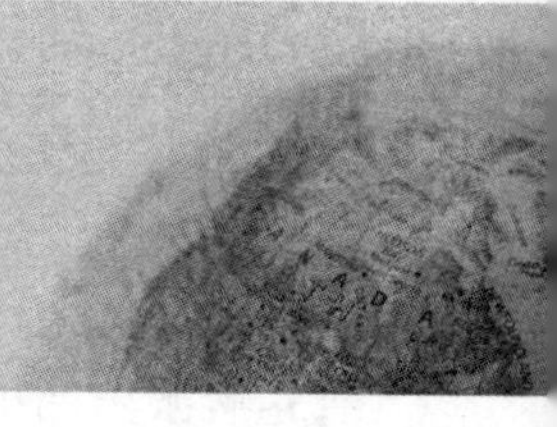

外国语言文学学科的发展是与国运衰微、西学东渐、现代大学勃兴紧密联系在一起的。随着1840年鸦片战争的爆发,东西方文明在古老中国不断冲突、碰撞、磨合以及融汇,其剧烈之程度在中国对外交往史中前所未见。西方列强的坚船利炮使东方老大帝国的羸弱暴露无遗。清政府内洋务派为了挽救清廷的统治危机,主张引进、仿造西方的武器装备和学习西方的科学技术,兴办洋务,创设近代企业,将发展重点放在"器物"层面,"师夷长技以制夷"。1894年,中国在甲午海战中惨败,民族危机空前深重,引起思想文化教育界强烈震动,"中学为体,西学为用"受到空前挑战,"制度"革新摆上核心日程,变法维新运动持续高涨。

此时,时代需要中国与西方之间的"翻译者",从一开始,外语就承担了读懂历史变迁、推动民族奋起自强的重任。中国一批最早接受西方思想的知识分子,如魏源、郑观应等,为译介西书和传播西方的政治体制、科学知识,发挥了很大的作用。1862年,被誉为近代第一所国立外国语学院的京师同文馆应运而生,恭亲王奕訢等人在给清政府的奏折上阐明了建馆的意图:"欲悉各国情景,必先谙其言语文字,方不受人欺蒙。"作为清代最早培养译员的洋务学堂和从事翻译出版的机构,同文馆为推动中国近代化作出了积极而重要的尝试。此后,得益于外语的译介作用,西学在中国的发展步伐不断加快。曾负笈海外的严复翻译了一批重要的西方著作,他的译著(如亚当·斯密的《原富》、斯宾塞的《群学肄言》、孟德斯鸠的《法意》,尤其是赫胥黎的《天演论》,以"物竞天择"、"适者生存"、"优胜劣汰"的生物进化理论阐发救亡图存的观点)启蒙与教育了一代国人,产生了振聋发聩的影响。戊戌变法之年,中国第一所国立综合性大学——京师大学堂创立伊始,即开设英、法、德、俄、日五个语种的课程。1902年,京师大学堂复学,且随即合并了京师同文馆,次年更名为译学馆。随着现代高等教育在中国的兴起,外语专业作为一门独立学科在我国建立并逐步发展。揭橥"民主"和"科学"两面旗帜的"五四"新文化运动,为外语学科的发展增添了动力和活力。

适值“三千年未有之大变局”,以促进中国近代化为宗旨的海外留学热潮激情涌动。1872 年到 1875 年间,由近代中国留美第一人容闳提议,清政府先后派出四批共 120 名幼童赴美国留学。这些留美幼童是中国历史上最早的官派留学生。此后,旨在寻求真知的官派和自费留学逐波激荡。这些留学生归国后分布在政界、军界、实业界、教育文化界等各个领域,不少人成为中国近代历史上的知名人物。及至民国时期,一批既饱览西学又具有深厚国学根底的“海归”执掌大学外文系或者从事外文教学研究工作。作为“睁眼看世界”的文化精英,他们学习和借鉴西方先进的理念、模式和方法,制订学术范式,建立课程体系,名师俊彦辈出,学术声誉远播。从当年北京大学、清华大学、西南联大等高校外文系的一流学术阵容可见一斑。在外文界,前辈不懈开拓进取,后学奋力继承创新,学术薪火相传,在短短数十年内为外语学科奠定了较为厚实的基础。1949 年以后,由于国内、国际形势的嬗变,外语学科的持续发展受到很大干扰和破坏。1978 年中国实行改革开放政策,长期以来对外封闭的坚冰开始消融,外语学科又受到重视,得以焕发新的生机和活力。

近 30 多年来,科学技术迅猛发展,社会思潮与思想观念更趋丰富多元,学科既深度分化又高度综合,这些变化既拓展了外国语言文学的外延,又深化了其内涵。尤其是 20 世纪 90 年代后,全球化趋势深入发展,国与国之间的相互依存明显增强,对人类社会的影响涉及经济、政治、教育、社会及文化等各个领域,为外国语言文学创设了新的发展环境和条件。在这个进程中,我国外语界就全球化背景下外国语言文学的使命和责任、外语教育规划、外语学科发展路径、外语人才培养模式等理论和实践问题进行了积极的探索,为推动我国经济社会发展、促进中外文化交流、培养高素质国际化人才作出了重要贡献。在全球化背景下,我们面临进一步提升高等教育国际化水平、繁荣发展哲学社会科学、扩大中国学术的国际影响力和话语权、增强国家文化软实力、增进国际理解的艰巨任务。哲学社会科学要繁荣发展,既要“请进来”,也要“走出去”,对本国传统文化精髓,既不狂傲自大,也不妄自菲薄;对外国优秀文明成果,既不全盘照搬,也不一概否定。在纵横捭阖的大时代面前,我国学术发展更需要世界眼光、国际视野和“海纳百川、有容乃大”的广阔胸怀。面对新形势、新任务,外语院校和外语系学科有独特和不可替代的优势,有责任、有义务、有能力推进内涵发展、质量提升、品牌建设,服务于整个国家学术的发展,服务于国家外交战略能力的大幅提升。

国学大师、清华研究院"四大导师"之一陈寅恪先生曾经说,"读书必先识字",他自己就精通梵语、英语、法语、德语、巴利语、波斯语、突厥语、西夏语,还修习过中亚古文字和蒙古语。时至今天,要了解古希腊、古埃及、古印度、古巴比伦文明的历史,要感受罗马帝国的辉煌和文艺复兴的灿烂,要领略工业革命和西方哲学的魅力,要把握当前国际社会发展的律动和人类进步的脉搏,外国语言文学仍然是一种十分重要而必不可少的工具、载体和媒介。在全球化背景下,普世价值往往更易超越民族、文化、宗教、局域认知等,通过外语这座桥梁得以交流和沟通、发扬和传播,从而提升人类社会的福祉。

高等学校的根本任务是培养人才。为适应全球化和高等教育国际化的需要,外语院校和外语学科一项很重要的使命和责任,就是要践行"立足平凡、追求卓越"的教育理念,创新人才培养模式,着眼于培养全球化、高素质公民。这种人才,具有较高的公民素养,"不能仅仅是语言、翻译方面的专家,更要在此基础上成为对象国研究和区域研究的专家,成为外语精湛、专业突出、高素质的复合型、复语型的国际化人才"(教育部副部长郝平)。简而言之,全球化、高素质公民的内涵可以用"中国灵魂、世界胸怀、现代意识"十二个字来表述,它包含了人与自我、人与国家、人与世界三个命题。第一,大学生要追求自我完善,务求"格物、致知、诚意、正心",修身自持,赋予个体生命实际意义。第二,大学生要理性爱国,正确理解与认同传统文化,自觉参与现代中国的社会—文化转型进程。第三,大学生要用全人类而非单一国家民族的眼光关注诸如气候变化、核扩散、大规模传染病等国际性难题,不断提高跨文化交际能力,对外具有独立的品格和开放的心态。

在全球化语境下,外国语言文学需要遵循学科发展规律,顺应国家政策安排,不断加强自身建设,逐步提升学科的影响力和话语权。推进外国语言文学基础理论研究,密切追踪国外学术前沿,注意学习和借鉴,但不能满足于"跟随"和"阐释",要力争取得有突破性的、具有国际影响的原创性外文理论成果。充分发挥外语学科优势,整合相关学科资源,开展全球问题、国际区域和国别问题的长期跟踪研究,为国家外交战略服务。积极主动对接国家和地方战略需求,就外语教育教学和对外交往的重大理论和实践问题,鼓励个人自由探索,支持学科集体攻关,为党和政府提供高水平的决策咨询服务。比如,广东外语外贸大学在广东省政府的鼎力支持下组建的广东国际战略研究院,近年来就国际金融危机、中国—东盟自贸区成立、日本地震海啸等重大问题对广东的影响及对策,组织外语专家和相关学科学者进行专题研究，向有关方面提交了高质量的调研报告，对政府施政和企业决策产生了积极的影响。“走出去”，是繁荣发展我国哲学社会科学的重要环节。外语院校和外语学科可充分发挥自身独特优势，健全高端国际型人才培养体系，重点培育一批高水平、专业化的翻译团队，培养造就一批造诣高深的翻译名家，翻译并向海外推介一批中国文化经典和学术精品。要适应学科分化与综合的趋势，加强外语与经济、管理、法律、文化、军事、信息技术等学科的交叉和融合，在保持传统语言文学学科优势的基础上，努力催生出一批能与国际学术界直接对话、具备学术话语权的新型特色交叉学科。加强与港澳台外语界的交流与合作，积极参与国际学术活动和学术组织，积极参与和推动国际学术组织有关政策、规则、标准的研究和制定。

以“工程”、“项目”和“课题”等名义对高等学校发展实行管理和调控，是我国高等教育体制的重要特色。目前，少数外语院校进入国家“211 工程”建设高校行列，外国语言文学学科也拥有一批国家级重点学科、教育部人文社科重点研究基地、教育部特色专业建设点、国家精品课程、国家教学名师等，这些总体上构成了外语学科领域的学术制高点。2008 年，广东外语外贸大学“全球化背景下的外国语言文学研究”入选广东省“211 工程”三期重点学科建设项目，其系列专著凝聚了“语言·文学·文化”、现代技术与语言教学评估、跨文化交际与管理、翻译研究与实践等研究方向，来自政府的支持为广外外语学科的创新发展提供了新的机会和平台。出版“全球化背景下的外国语言文学研究丛书”，一来可作项目成果的初步展示，二来以此就教于同行专家学者。

慢工出细活，厚积才能薄发。全球化背景下外国语言文学学科的发展，与中国改革开放与现代化建设事业一样，依然任重而道远。

是为序。

徐真华[1]

2011 年 6 月

---

① 徐真华，广东外语外贸大学教授，博士生导师；广东省人民政府文史研究馆馆员，文史馆文学院名誉院长。

Contents

Preface

Lin Yutang and Translation as Reciprocal Cultural Transmission

Timothy Huson

Chu Dongwei's book, *Lin Yutang as Author-Translator*, is the first extensive work on Lin as a translator written in any language. This book carefully and skillfully locates the many facets of Lin as a translator and, as the title suggests, develops the ways in which Lin synthesized the role of author and translator, not only that he played each role in different works, but also that he played both roles in all of his works, using text translation in his own prose and being an original author when he translated. Dongwei traces historically Lin's development as a translator in a variety of senses, relating these senses of Lin as translator to other facets of Lin's life — his spiritual and political struggles, his career as a man in the world, and his dreams for China. By bringing Lin's translation work into the context of his engagement with his contemporaries and with major intellectual developments of the time, East and West, and locating this multifaceted figure in the context of contemporary translation theory debates, Dongwei has provided a most important starting point for future work on Lin — both for understanding Lin's thought and for continuing or renewing that tradition. For, as Dongwei once said in urging that the real heritage of Lin Yutang is not just to understand his ideas, but to continue his projects: We don't so much need to clarify Lin Yutang as we need more Lin Yutangs.

By broadening the concept of translator in the person of Lin Yutang, Dongwei's book also points us to a yet further sense of translation, one moving beyond the technical or narrowly linguistic side of the translation towards the rich cultural content. Here it is not only an issue of theory, but rather it invokes the author-translator as agent in the process of social change. Lin's works on Chinese culture not only incorporate direct translations and paraphrases of central ideas, but also, in that very process, they constitute a transmission of culture from China to the West, a transmission that, in that hermeneutic translation process Lin mastered, engaged the receiving culture as a key to appreciating what was truly of value in the culture of origin, thus making a unique contribution to both through the translation process. By no means does this entail that Lin evaluated China by a Western standard, as many Chinese have done and as many do today, but quite the opposite — Lin's gaze to the West enabled him to find the value in Chinese culture that would serve as the standard by which to evaluate and critique the West. It is this translation as an intercultural transmission, a sense of translation to which Dongwei's important work opens the door (and opened the door for me), that I'd like to explore here.

With the growing importance of China in today's increasingly international world, there is need of a solid intercultural understanding between China and the West. But much is currently lacking in that understanding, and particularly as regards the West's understanding of China. The fault, however, lies on both sides. A typical Western view assesses China on a Western model and sees China as inferior to the West, and the Chinese people as chaotic and not ready for democracy — but this stereotype of the Chinese people is reinforced by some Chinese who employ this typically Western stereotype. Motives on both sides can be found in terms of surplus value and profit for seeing the Chinese people as worthy only of serving others, and not ruling, for economic power-holders everywhere profit when any part of the working class is denied the chance to struggle for its well-being.

But it is not only the Chinese who suffer from this false depiction, for this stereotyped view of the Chinese people also deprives the West of a great benefit it could draw from a deeper understanding of Chinese culture. We must stand back and question the dogmatic Western ideology of historical development that depicts the Chinese as a people far behind the West in terms of their readiness to emerge from the political tutelage into freedom. Perhaps it is the other way around — perhaps Chinese culture harbors an element of political common sense, a deep grained sensitivity to the dignity of the human individual, that could awaken the West to its own forgotten and more human roots, roots covered over through the years by the exigencies of material capitalist culture.

Lin's cultural translation aims to bring to awareness this hidden sense of the true dignity of the individual hidden beneath the Western stereotype of Chinese culture as politically backward, as unprepared for freedom — and at the same time there is awakened in the Western reader the same higher form of human dignity buried in the Westerner behind the illusory Western concept of individualism based on group or class identification. The translation that brings the dignity of this higher individual to consciousness on both sides of the supposed cultural divide would constitute a genuine intercultural translation of culture, a cultural transmission that transmits something to the receiving culture that effects its self-awakening and in that transmission helps each culture to understand the other and in that process helps each to better understand itself.

It has often been said that one never knows oneself until one leaves home, that one never knows one's own culture until one has immersed oneself in another quite different one. Lin Yutang's practice of cultural transmission involves both sides of this intercultural process. His immersion in Western culture helped him understand what is truly of value in Chinese culture, and that enabled him to see what in Chinese culture was most worthy of transmission to the West, something at the very heart of Western culture, but hidden by the very success of Western culture in being mesmerized by material progress. Once one engages in translation as cultural transmission, it is already reciprocal, there are always two cultures involved, and for understanding one it is crucial to understand the other. Lin's influence from the West, though it has often been used as a critique against him, is in fact precisely what enabled him to understand what is genuinely of value in China. By contrast, others in China have yet to understand the deep sense of human dignity residing in Chinese culture that can now serve to awaken the core of humanity more deeply hidden in the technically more advanced Western world.

It is this broader and historically more important sense of a translator as cultural transmitter that is captured in Chu Dongwei's book on Lin Yutang the translator. The translator is no longer merely a technician or a mere transmitter of a message, but rather he or she is seen as an essential agent of cultural change, a transmitter of the very framework in which messages in the usual sense occur. In Lin Yutang as translator we thus see the convergence of two important themes: the growing urgency of reciprocal cultural transmission and intercultural understanding and, corresponding to that, a new conception of what translation itself essentially is. Dongwei's book is all the more relevant for the fact that the world of translation theory and the world of Sino-American intercultural understanding is today largely ignorant of Lin's work, both of his model of translation and the ever more important content of his translation, a content that, after all, is still vibrant and still captures in essence the core of the social problem, both of China and of the West. The potential of Lin's work on intercultural understanding has not yet been fully realized.

Let me delve into that content just a bit:

Lin, I would say, did what few today dare do or are able to do — to tell the truth about China to the rest of the world, a truth touching, in that deeper intercultural translational sense, the genuine identity of all cultures. In telling the truth of Chinese culture, the good and the bad, Lin also reveals the unacknowledged truth of Western culture — for, in revealing the truth of Chinese culture, Lin also betrayed the illusion of cultural difference. And, the current urgency of his thought is that it reveals the self-deception that marks so much of today's journalistic and academic parlor talk, for Lin's approach is anything but fashionable in this age dominated by the politically correct mantra of cultural difference. This veneer of cultural difference screens us from our ultimate individuality where we meet the other in the absolute one to one. At the heart of the Chinese culture Lin depicts we see humanity's ultimate sameness, one world, not many, and tolerance for the many expressions of that human entity in its cultural and individual variety. This awakened individual sees through the illusion of *discours* to a core of being quite independent of our various culturally conditioned perspectives, and from this awakened perspective emerges a deep compassion and understanding towards each individual instance within the one reality. This awakened consciousness at the heart of Chinese character, though it often slumbers, is the hidden potential of each individual to see through the vanity of cultural difference and life's humbugs, as Lin calls them (fame, wealth, and power), to what is *real*.

But lest we take too seriously this deeper self, lest we use this deeper self as a basis to scorn others caught up in the outer illusion, the other side of the human paradox brings us back to earth — the figure of that famous market recluse in Chinese literature. One can never really leave the world or outright reject the world, for that would be the deception that takes far too seriously what is thought to lie on the other side of the illusion — a substance or core of being that is only another illusion. When one must flee the world to achieve detachment, this can only mean that one is already too attached to one's own self, the illusion of a deeper substantial self. Opposed to this alternative self-deception, the flip side of attachment to the world, Lin offers as the trait of the Chinese sage a sort of middle way — an idea so famous in Chinese thought, and still residing somewhere in Chinese character — expressed so well with a famous metaphor adapted from Zhuangzi:

The Chinese philosopher is one who dreams with one eye open, who views life with love and sweet irony, who mixes his cynicism with a kindly tolerance, and who alternately wakes up from life's dream and then nods again, feeling more alive when he is dreaming than when he is awake, thereby investing his waking life with a dream-world quality. He sees with one eye closed and with one eye opened the futility of much that goes on around him and of his own endeavors, but barely retains enough sense of reality to determine to go through with it. He is seldom disillusioned because he has no illusions, and seldom disappointed because he never had extravagant hopes. In this way his spirit is emancipated.①

In the metaphor, life itself is seen as a dream, or a half-dream, and hence it loses its seriousness and its power over the individual. The cultural institutions that divide us constitute the world where the Chinese character plays, or pretends to play, but all the while, in the deep heart, knowing them to be but a dream, an illusion, fleeting and insubstantial. This moment of indifference enables the individual a measure of freedom from those institutions, from life's humbugs of wealth, power, and fame — he or she plays with them, but not to the point of letting them overcome the sense of humanity beneath the façade of cultural values and cultural difference.

With this insight into cultural illusion, Lin renders a critique of a conception of the individual, one dominant in the West, based on cultural particulars (an individual in the nation, in the social group, or in the party) and champions another individual, one on the other side of the illusion of cultural difference, an individual in the universe.② It is here, and not with cultural particulars, that Lin ultimately grounds his idea of *common sense*, along with the corresponding sense of fairness, that gave Lin

---

① Lin Yutang, *The Importance of Living*, New York: William Morrow (1996), p. 1.

② When Hegel, in his discussion of contradiction, says that "the father, outside of the relation to the son, is also something for itself; but thus he is not father, but rather a human in general." (*Georg Wilhelm Friedrich Hegel: Werke: 6: Wissenschaft der Logik II*, p. 77) The "in general" should here, in my opinion, move in the direction, not of a logical abstraction, but rather of a concrete moment of the individual that is both less particular (*überhaupt*, literally, above the head, above counting or enumerating) and more unique, since it bears no attributes that distinguish it from others, but also classify it with others — it's individuality is one of a kind, and for that reason identical to the highest universal.

hope in the vitality and resilience of Chinese culture, as well as in that of the West — for this *common sense*, though it maybe be covered over, can ultimately be found in all humans. The common sense of this individual provides a source of resistance to the illusory and self-deceiving concept of the individual based on identity with intermediate social categories — gender, sexual orientation, economic class, language community, clan, nation, party, organized religion — that has come to dominate in the cultural accretions in the West.

That Chinese spirit of wayward individualism that Lin depicted with the figure of the *scamp* can still be clearly discerned today, in spite of and indeed in resistance to the Western institutions that are trying to make inroads into Chinese life: the reduction of life to materialist economic factors, the division of society into embattled social classes, and the Western sort of individuals based on group identity — race, gender, party, and nation.

Lin does not take the Chinese scamp to be a uniquely Chinese figure — though China is where this figure is still most vibrant in the soul of the people. The scamp, the Chinese individual beyond cultural and individual identity (and difference), in fact forms a core of thought in Western culture and literature, as Lin demonstrates in his plentiful citations of writers like Thoreau, Whitman, and Emerson. So, when Lin turns to the Chinese scamp to assist the West, he is in fact appealing to the West's own repressed and hidden spirit, its hidden truth. And this is the true mark of translation as intercultural transmission — not so much a transferal from one culture to another as a reawakening of something inherent but dormant in receiving culture itself.

But, as intercultural, Lin's translation not only transmits something to the West, but also transmits something, reawakens something in a new form, within the Chinese tradition itself. Here Lin's work parallels in structure, if not content, Heidegger's idea of translation as *Überlieferung*, playing on the connection between transmission and tradition.① Lin is asking all of us, East and West, to reconsider just what China is, and what China can be. In doing that he upsets some of those in

① Heidegger writes of "the decisive characteristic ... that pervades all essential translations" ["translations that, in epochs when the moment has come, transfer works of poetry or thought"]: "that in such cases the translation is not only interpretation [*Auslegung*], but also transmission [*Überlieferung*]." (Martin Heidegger, *Der Satz vom Grund*, Stuttgart: Klett-Cotta (1957), p. 164.)

power, then and now, who are all too comfortable with the skewed social order that today is taken for China, misunderstood as China. Today, when so much of the debate in China concerns various claims to authentic Chinese culture, it is time to once again ask that question honestly, to squarely face both the good and the bad in Chinese culture, so that we may draw on what really is there of value in addressing the problems of the day. It is time once again to give voice to that true patriotism that Lin championed, that patriot who loves his / her country enough to care that she overcomes her problems, and has faith in her enough to believe that she will not be destroyed by truth, but by means of truth will find the solutions to the problems.

Again, we risk a misunderstanding when referring to Lin's patriotism, since, as Lin says, "one may wear the cloak of patriotism to tatters, and in these tatters be paraded through the city streets to death, in China or the rest of the world."① Where this line is found, in the preface to *My Country and My People*, Lin attacked those "little patriots" who whitewash China because they have lost faith in China's ability to address her problems openly. When Lin, in contrast, appeals to "the men of simple common sense," he is calling upon that nobler aspect of Chinese character that rises above identity with cultural categories and touches a core of humanity that the Chinese have best of all safeguarded. Genuine Chinese patriotism is beyond any sense of national chauvinism, since the concept of person it is grounded in is beyond cultural identity.

With Lin we should once again ask: What do we have to fear from truth? Does it reveal the self-deception of the blind patriotism that attempts to lower the individual to an identity with cultural institutions? And in this illusory identity, one must whitewash the faults of those institutions, hide the worst, and justify everything not hidden. In so doing, one loses one's true self, the deeper and more valuable meaning of that culture still present in every Chinese in the form of a core of human compassion and tolerance born out of an intuitive insight into the illusory reality of social conventions. Facing China's problem is at the same time a coming to terms with one's individual existence, for each Chinese must see, in his or her deep heart, the counterpart of this illusory social reality — the noble but disquieting fact that each of us is but a fleeting moment on the screen, a being to which no

① Lin Yutang, *My Country and My People*, London: William Heinemann (1936), p. xiv.

configuration of the stars will ever again give rise, a unique and once only invention of the universe. And that fate we share with every other being.

This sense of Chinese patriotism shines forth on every page of Lin's books — a pride in a culture in which there thrives a genuine compassion for others, one based on our flitting between two dreams in Zhuangzi's metaphor, and never quite knowing which is illusory and which is real, but attaining a stronger desire for life by ultimately comprehending them as one. If there is a superiority of Chinese culture for Lin, it is an ironical one, consisting precisely in the recognition that deep down we are all the same and that our national identity we will indeed live, but like the rest of life's illusions, we will skillfully dream it with one eye open, in that Chinese way — whether we are Chinese or foreigners — knowing that each is really something else. And it is here that Lin finds the hope for China, and for the world, a hope Lin wanted to convey to China and to the West through his translation, his intercultural transmission of Chinese culture.

Timothy Huson.
Hettick, Illinois,
April 25, 2011

Foreword

I had firmly believed that I was no worshipper of idols until I met Lin Yutang[①] in his English writings and translations. My belief wavered and I almost started to worship him. The great heroes with their extraordinary deeds and the great minds with their masterpieces have always impressed me but none of them has been so accessible to me as Mr. Lin, who has not only impressed me but also exerted a timely influence as a role model through his writings and translations.

Lin's writings failed to attract me at first sight. In 1994, I bought an anthology of Chinese essays at the roadside. His talk of bedbugs and smoking and the like sounded so trivial and insignificant. Almost a decade later I came across the same man again, this time in the English language. *My Country and My People* wowed me with its very first page. I had been learning and teaching English for well over two decades but had never read such an eloquent Chinese author in the English language. The ease, the confidence, the simplicity, the candor and the arguments of the author writing in a foreign language struck every heartstring of mine. He sounded so akin to me that I decided to be more like him as a Chinese teacher of English as a foreign language. I was eager to know more about him and to read more of his writings and translations and finally found myself writing a PhD dissertation on my favorite English-language author from a translation perspective.

My study of Lin Yutang as a translator follows a series of studies by Prof. Wang Yougui, author of three books on eight prominent Chinese translators: *Zhou Zuoren as Translator* (2001), *Translation East and West: Six Prominent Translators in China* (2004), and *Lu Xun as Translator* (2005). All the translators under Mr. Wang's investigation were also authors in the first half of the twentieth century and beyond. The two-fold identity of authorship and translatorship is the primary reason for his selection, for a translator who is meanwhile a writer with his own ideology and aesthetic taste " is self-conscious, autonomous and selective, very much different

---

① Also spelt as Lin Yüt'ang.

from the craftsman translator, who may have been highly skilled and capable of producing high quality translations without showing himself by making his own choices." (Wang, 2004. "Preface": 1. Translated from the Chinese.)

In the study of authors, we often find discussions of their translations and in the study of some literary translators we often find discussions of the translators' careers as authors. Due to the close affinity between the two forms of literature-making, it is all too easy to associate the one with the other. As Douglas Robinson says, "Translating IS writing. When I translate I sit at the computer and form sentences in my head and my fingers move across the keyboard and words appear on the screen. Something I do when I 'write' i.e., write 'original' things, or write postings to lantra [my note: an Internet forum]" (Robinson, 2001: 1–2). It is not a latest discovery. The association of translating with writing is an ancient tradition. The two trades are too close to have a border between them. The close affinity often results in an individual that does both jobs. Wang Yougui's research has brought such a species to the fore. This special species of translators in my view should be given a special label for the convenience of discussion. It should be fitting to call them **author-translators**, or in Chinese, *zuojiaxing fanyijia*.

A younger contemporary of Lu Xun and two years younger than Mao Zedong (1893–1976), Lin Yutang was active on the literary scene for over four decades in the middle of the twentieth century. As an author-translator he on the one hand falls into the general pattern of translating as part of self-expression but on the other hand is quite distinctively one of a kind. He not only wrote and translated for his countrymen but also reached the world audience as the first bestselling English language author from China.

Once unduly considered a reactionary figure in China, Lin Yutang now finds quite a few enthusiasts who are eager to reinstate him to literary fame. Some scholars suggest that his stature be next to Lu Xun's, others like him better than Lu Xun and there are still others who dismiss him as insignificant. In fact, as a deceased author, Lin probably does not care what fame or notoriety he receives. To me, he is a great charmer. That is sufficient to justify my digging of all available literature to shed light on his unique literary experience as an author-translator. Highly proficient in both Chinese and English, he is probably the first major Chinese author to write bestselling prose and fiction in English for a world audience. As a translator, he has produced volumes of Chinese and English translations in the arts and humanities.

From available library resources, I have identified over 70 books accredited to him and published in his lifetime, excluding the numerous anthologies unauthorized by himself. Twenty-nine of the books (including a bilingual dictionary) are translations and many of his non-fiction books are heavily loaded with translations (See Appendix I).

For the purpose of my study of Lin Yutang as an author-translator, I have developed an observation framework based on previous studies of author-translators by other researchers. We know such translators have some group characteristics. In an author-translator, the author function and the translator function inevitably acts on each other. In particular, the translator function may have a great deal to do with the self-representation of the author. Thus, the study of the author-translator is an integrated study of two perspectives: the author-translator as an author and the author-translator as a translator. Under these two perspectives, three dimensions must be considered:

1) translation competence (receptive competence and productive competence in languages-L1, L2, L3, etc.[①] — and transfer competence between languages), which opens up new possibilities or new channels of expression for her, making her different from the monolingual author.

2) poetics (her theory of literature and as part of it or as its extended application her theory of translation), which is her intended self-representation or a self-definition of her authorial identity, and which makes her translation meaningful culturally and aesthetically.

3) translation practice, partly through which the author constructs her authorial identity by manipulating her translations.

These three dimensions, together with the objective of understanding the author-translator's self-representation through translations, constitute a framework or a model for the study of an author-translator, and my study of Lin Yutang as a translator.

The methodology of this study may be called analytical-interpretive criticism, which is a combination of two critical approaches: analytical criticism and interpretative criticism. These two approaches, originally designed by art critics for the criticism of art works, are applied in my discussion of all major aspects of the

① L1 = first language, L2 = second language, L3 = third language, etc, if the languages can be simply numbered.

life, poetics and works of the author-translator. In some instances, analytical criticism is used and, in some other instances, interpretive criticism. The study on the whole follows a two-stage mythological framework of analytical-interpretive criticism but in an individual chapter I do not limit myself to only one of the two approaches.

The analytical approach is used to overcome the subjectivism in appreciative criticism. In appreciative criticism, researchers evaluate Lin Yutang's translations according to their personal taste. It is not sensible for me to assume a high aesthetic sensitivity and pass impressionistic judgments on a translator whose stature I at the present cannot reach. What I can do is to let meanings and structures emerge by the use of analytical criticism.

The method of my analysis is "thematizing." It is frequently used throughout the research — in my investigation of the translator's biographical details, of his translations (and where possible their source texts), of his discourse on translation in articles, letters, prefaces and other writings, and of his other texts that are relevant. In the study of Lin Yutang's translations for example, all his translations are seen as a unity. By considering as many works as possible and by turning them about I do my best to search for a structural pattern. Then I can identify a theme, which is the structural principle underlying the pattern. My description follows a bottom-up model, from the specific to the general. A theme is found and then themes are often found to work together to contribute to a greater theme.

When a phenomenon or theme is identified, I often feel the need to relate it to other phenomena or themes, or connect it to its context, personal or historical, or whatever, and try to see what possible significance there might be. In such instances of studying a phenomenon or theme in a context, I am using interpretive criticism. The analytical approach is meant to bring out the inherent meanings, but the interpretive approach is intended to make meanings. For example, when Lin Yutang's theory of translation is studied in relation to earlier and later translation theories, we have an understanding of his contribution to translation studies.

In the course of analyzing or interpreting, an important method is comparison and contrast. The types of comparison may include comparison of his translations with his writings, comparison of his translations or methods of translation with those of his contemporaries or a few translators before and after, and comparison of versions of his own translations.

More specifically, Chapter One is an analysis of the author-translator's biographical information. Chapter Two through an analysis of Lin Yutang's discourse on translation identifies the overriding theme of *xingling* or self-expression in his poetics of literature and translation and some sub-themes in his theory of translation, followed by an interpretation of his translation theory by connecting it to the history of translation studies. Chapter Three employs both the interpretive and the analytical approach. Lin Yutang's translation practice is seen as part of his system of expression. In the study of the general nature of his Chinese and English translations and his supra-textual strategies, I have used the method of thematizing. Chapter Four reconstructs Lin Yutang's translation strategies through analyses of excerpts from his translations. Then, in an interpretive attempt, the strategies are matched against the translation continuum. The leading method for this chapter is textual analysis. This involves identification of textual features through close reading of translated texts in juxtaposition with their originals. His translations are often studied in comparison with his other versions or versions by other translators. Chapter Five offers an interpretation of Lin Yutang's translations in a personal and historical context based on findings of previous chapters. The interpretation is two-fold. First, the identified themes, when allied, are mutually explanatory. Second, themes may be related to their historical context so that the author-translator's significance may be brought out.

This seems to be an ambitious project. Some professors who are used to "small topics" may be outraged by this gigantic project and they may understandably raise doubts. Driven by Lin Yutang's spell over me and undaunted by the difficulty of the task, now I am proud to say that I have seriously worked on it and that my work has not only enlightened me on Lin Yutang as an author-translator but also on translation. With so many translations to his credit Lin Yutang is a translation textbook.

At the outset of the research project, I had the following in mind:

This comprehensive research of a major modern Chinese author-translator is intended to contribute to the developing academic area of translator studies.

It may have implications for translator education. A thorough description of Lin Yutang the translator outlines one example of translator development and one translator's way of translating.

It is also wished to contribute to the study of Lin Yutang. As translation is an important part of the Lin Yutang we know, the understanding of him is incomplete without the translation perspective.

As China is trying to get its proper share of the international book market today and actively pushing forward the China Book International Program, the commercial success of Lin Yutang as an author-translator on the international book market may have positive implications for the program. Hopefully, this study can bring out some of them.

I have also had a secret hope that upon closing the book my reader will realize that this in-depth study of a major Chinese author-translator is in fact also a textbook of translation, theory and practice combined.

I hope that I have not disappointed myself. Please kindly allow me to candidly report my findings after conversing with the man's texts and contexts just for your reference.

Finally, I would like to express my thanks for Prof. Wang Yougui, who directed my PhD thesis *Lin Yutang: Authoring the Self and Manipulating Translation* (2007), which is the basis of this book, and continued to provide valuable advice after my graduation, Prof. Feng Zhilin, Prof. Zhu Hui, Prof. Liu Jichun, Prof. Cao Shanke and Prof. Ping Hong for their constructive advice. I am deeply indebted to Dr. Timothy Huson, who has read every word of my manuscript and filled the pages with comments and suggestions. A special "thank you" shall go to Prof. Kelly Clark of Calvin College, who during his busy visit to Oxford kindly read the manuscript and wrote an encouraging letter with very good suggestions for publication. I am also indebted to Prof. Xu Zhenhua, who has shown a genuine appreciation of my work and is generous enough to lend his helping hand.

Chu Dongwei
August, 2010

CHAPTER One

Self-Making and the Accidental Translator

1 The Search for Self

In the case of Lin Yutang, translatorship is just one of his many identity traits, for the world has known him as a philosopher, writer, educator, inventor, critic, scholar and translator, among other labels. Translating is part of his self-making and the translator is but an occasional branching-out, a by-product of self-development. It is the spirit, the illuminating personality of Lin Yutang that stands him in good stead before his translations, while many other translators no less skilled in words remain almost anonymous behind their translations. To understand how Lin Yutang became a translator requires us to go back in time to visit his origins.

This is an inspirational story of an individual's search for self. The search starts with curiosity. We are born ignorant and then we are curious about the world that harbors our selves, body and soul. Curiosity is a natural reaction to ignorance, but not everyone consciously and constantly keeps up their struggle to get out of the dark and see the light. In the process of identity seeking, different identity traits emerge, modifying and asserting themselves, seeking expression and aspiring for recognition. An admirable quality in Lin Yutang is that all through his life he was a seeker of knowledge and truth, forever hungry.

Words have their contexts and so do individuals. To understand Lin Yutang's self-development we need to go back in time to see his circumstances. The hard times his family and the nation were going through certainly had a role to play. As a basic unit of society the family plays a role of primary importance in the individuation and socialization of an adolescent. The legacy Lin Yutang received from his family was more spiritual than material. If we are looking for any proof that his father and grandfather once lived a leisurely life something like what he describes in *My Country and My People* (1935a) and *The Importance of Living* (1937), we will be disappointed. Life was rather hard for Lin Yutang's grandparents and parents. Not to be defeated by fate, Lin Zhicheng, Lin Yutang's father, struggled against the odds of life. In order to make a living, in his early years, the diligent and intelligent young man sold sugar candies and fried crisp beans on the streets. He used to carry bamboo shoots with his shoulder pole to sell in Changchow (Zhangzhou), which is over twenty kilometers away from home. He also sold rice to prisoners. At the age of 24, Lin Zhicheng entered a theological seminary and later became a primary school teacher and Presbyterian pastor. From the present-day point of view, life was not easy for Lin Yutang's father but the later famous Yutang was more reminiscent of his spiritual legacy from the father. He remembered the pastor as "a self-made man" and "an incorrigible optimist, keen, imaginative and humorous." (Lin, 1975: 12, 13) Among the Presbyterian pastors, his father "was known as an ultra-progressive, known to have sent his children to Shanghai for English education, at a time when very few boys from Amoy[①] had heard of St. John's." (ibid.)

Yutang's second elder sister had a similar intellectual bent to his. She wanted a good education for herself badly, but family resources could not support her luxurious ambition. On the morning before her wedding, she took out her pocket money, which was forty cents, and said to her favorite brother into whom she put her hopes, "Holok[②], you are going to college. Don't waste your opportunity. Be a good man, a useful man and a famous man. That is your sister's wish for you." (Lin, 1975: 19) Holok understood that what she said was also part of his father's enthusiasm for college education. He felt the full force of these simple words, which stuck in his mind for the rest of his life.

Guided by the self-improving spirit of an adventurist-opportunist rather than

① Xiamen in *pinyin*.

② Lin Yutang's childhood name.

face-to-face instructions from learned scholars, he was to be continuously shaped by what he saw and what he read, Eastern and Western. He and his family were expecting something to happen sometime in the future. They knew not what, but they continued hoping and working for it.

The family planted in the adolescent Holok the seeds of optimism, humor, diligence, a Christian faith and a desire to go beyond their horizons. The seeds grew, flowered, and fruited into the adult philosopher, writer, educator, inventor, critic, scholar, and translator.

The key to the family dream to better their circumstances was education. The whole issue became an obsession with language. Born in a non-typical Chinese family and son of a local church pastor, Lin Yutang was lucky to have a somewhat educated father who was eager to teach the kids. The pastor was learned enough to tutor his sons and daughters in Chinese poetry, the classics, and couplet-making. This gave the childhood Yutang the early acquaintance with the Chinese language and activated his thinking about life and society. At the age of eight, he had the desire for authorship and wrote a "textbook" which imitated the style of the *Sanzijing*, a Chinese primer read in groups of three characters. One page went as follows:

> 人自高/终必败/持战甲/靠弓矢/而不知/他人强/他人力/千百倍(One who is too proud/Eventually will fall;/Relying on armor/And bows and arrows,/He does not know/That the others' power/And the others' strength/Are a hundred times greater.)
>
> (Lin, 1975: 16)

The pastor father had an intense admiration for Western civilization. Through the father's Christian connections and the education provided by the church, Lin Yutang came in contact with the West at an early age.

According to *Memoirs of an Octogenarian*, a few Westerners exerted a direct influence on him:

Dr. Warnshuis, a foreign missionary, struck Yutang as a man of broad vision. It was he that brought the Lins under the influence of Western learning. The Christian Society of Shanghai, under Young J. Allen (misspelt as "Grant Allen" in *Memoir*, error due to old age), published a weekly sheet, the *Christian Intelligence*. Dr. Warnshuis sent the family the weekly and many books. Pastor Lin and the missionary struck up a very close relationship. Through the *Christian Intelligence* and the books translated into Chinese by Young J. Allen in collaboration with his Chinese assistant, the Lins developed a strong desire for Western learning. The father even admired the Victorian glory in England. It was from the *Christian Intelligence* that the pastor heard about St. Johns and started to dream of the University of Oxford and the University of Berlin. The father was earning 20 Chinese silver dollars a month, later increased to 24 dollars, but that did not prevent him from sending one of his sons to one of the places of learning. He sold his inherited house in order to send his second son to St. John's. The second son graduated and taught at the same college and was able to support Holok through college together with his father who had borrowed 100 dollars from a former pupil. Another Westerner to influence Holok was Mrs. Pitcher, wife of the American principal of a church-run secondary school. This was a sweet English lady, whose soft voice and intonation was music to the child. The choral soprano singing of Sa-loh of the missionary ladies had made a great impression on his Chinese ears. He was fascinated by Western music. St. John's had a few good professors who came to China as missionaries, like Prof. Barton McNair and Remer. The President, Dr. F. L. Hawks Pott, was a methodical man, in whose library Yutang saw a volume by T. H. Bradley.

Again according to the *Memoirs* and Lin Yutang's autobiographical sketch①, the scientific achievement of the West impressed the curious boy. In his childhood he saw the movements of the steam-engine of a steamer. He stood fascinated, speechless. Later in school, he saw a diagram of the piston and fully understood. From that time on, his interest was always in science, and he wanted to be a teacher of physics. If asked what profession he would like to enter, his answer was one of the three: (1) to be a teacher of English, (2) to be a teacher of physics, and (3) to open a shop for "arguing" in which he would challenge from either side of the controversy (Lin, 1975: 24). This early propensity for science resulted in his later invention of an advanced Chinese type-writer. The same propensity also partly accounted for his choice of linguistics as an academic specialty instead of literature at St. Johns, for he thought linguistics was a scientific discipline requiring an analytical mind. The

① Translated into Chinese as *Linyutang Zizhuan* (《林语堂自传》). Originally published overseas, the English version is not available.

first two of the three career options were evidently the results of Western influence. The idea of being a translator did not occur to him in his early years. What is important is not whether he ever wanted to be a translator but what finally made him a translator. He had developed at a very early stage an awareness of manipulating his own fate. It is his effort to make meaning out of life that motivated him to do anything he deemed fit for the purpose. Translation happened to be his convenient tool. And he was no worshipper of tools. Trying to be a master of his own fate, he happened to be a master of languages and one of translation.

II The Buildup of a Translator's Potential in Self-Making

As we come to the translator part of his career, we need to know what makes up the translator. This involves on the one hand, the translator's potential and, on the other, the actualization of the potential.

In educational institutions it is believed that translating skills can be developed through training. While they may have a certain level of success in translator training, we have to admit that there are other possibilities. Not every successful translator has been a graduate of a training institution. Some people become translators through conscious self-training. Some become immediate translators (maybe good ones) when they are called on or feel the need to do some translation. In Lin Yutang's case, his translator's potential was but a natural development in the process of seeking knowledge, truth, and meaning in life. His approach to making meaning out of life was largely linguistic. His study of languages broke the barrier between him and the world. When the barrier was down, knowledge revealed itself to him. Therefore he became "good," "useful" and "famous" as his sister had wished. The linguistic approach — his unusual devotion to language study, and extensive reading of English and Chinese books — gave him expert knowledge of the two languages. The translator's potential was built up in the course of time whether he had intended to or not.

What is a translator's potential? It is the competence of an individual in languages that permits him to do translations. It is translator competence before actualization. Wolfram Wilss (1976) outlines three aspects of translator competence: first, receptive competence in a source language; second, productive competence in a target language; and third, transfer competence between the two languages. No one can deny the truth of the commonsensical statement. In fact, in 1933, much earlier than Wilss, Lin Yutang himself made a similar statement in his famous essay *On Translation*, in which he declares, "The art of translating depends on three things: first, a thorough understanding of the language and content of the source text; second, the translator's good command of the native language to enable him to write clear and fluent Chinese; and third, training in translation to give him a proper understanding of the standards of good translation and translation procedures. There cannot be anything else to regulate the translator as English grammar cannot regulate English writers." (Lin, 1994b: 305) This in effect is saying: if one has the necessary credentials he can translate; if not he cannot. In making the remark Lin Yutang is talking about translating from English as a foreign language into Chinese as the native language, but he believes that the three things can be applied in a more general way. In fact, he makes references to translating from Chinese to English. For example, when he criticizes word-for-word translation, he jokingly puts 趣味横生 (extremely interesting) into *the interest flows horizontally* besides jeering at English-to-Chinese translations like 我目的苹果 (the fruit of apple of my eye) for *the apple of my eye* (a favorite person) and 将其心拿出 (take out his heart from his body) for *took the heart out of him* (frightened him) (ibid: 308). Lin Yutang's statement and that of Wilss are of the same nature, but the former has a more specific reference.

If reformulated in more general or theoretical terms, the three requirements for the translator in Lin Yutang's *On Translation* can be:

- a thorough understanding of the language and content of the source text;
- the translator's good command of the target language to enable him to write clearly and fluently in that language;
- a proper understanding of the standards of good translation and good translation procedures.

However, both in Lin Yutang's prerequisites for the translator and in

Wilss's formulation of the translator's competence, we must note that "language" is a fairly broad category. Knowledge of a language includes knowledge of the language itself and what it carries: knowledge of the world. The two are closely bound. Therefore, in what is to follow, reference to linguistic development often includes the knowledge that is acquired through each language that Lin Yutang commands.

Lin Yutang had gradually developed the three kinds of competence required of a translator before he actually undertook any sizeable translation projects, especially the first two. His linguistic profile (Table 1) developed over time was to qualify him for an advantageous two-way translator between Chinese and English①.

Table 1 Lin Yutang's Linguistic Profile

Language	Productive Competence	Receptive Competence
Chinese	Strong	Strong
English	Strong	Strong
German	Not known	Not known
French	Not known	Not known

Lin once lived in France and Germany, but we have little documentation of his proficiency in French and German. Anyway, his translations are found almost invariably in Chinese or English.

1 Development of Receptive and Productive Competence in English as a Foreign Language

With his masterly use of English, Lin Yutang was able to speak subtly and directly to the Western world. He also produced volumes of English translations

① I have gathered such information from *Memoirs of an Octogenarian* (1972) by Lin Yutang himself, *Biography of Lin Yutang* (《林语堂传》) by Taiyi Lin (1981), the Lin Yutang House website (www. linyutang. org. tw), and various library and online bookstore resources such as alibris. com and abebooks. com.

from the Chinese. His success with the English language may be testified by the obituary in the *Times* upon his death:

Dr Lin Yutang, the Chinese scholar, writer and journalist, has died in Hongkong at the age of 80. A prolific writer, he used his extensive knowledge of Eastern and Western culture to make classical Chinese philosophy accessible to the West in translation, as well as producing a number of best-selling novels....

Lin Yutang's reputation was that of a man almost as much at home in the English language and in western civilization as he was in the culture of his own country. His ability to write for a large audience while maintaining scholarly standards came with *My Country and My People* in 1936. In this widely read and much reprinted book he gave the best modern account of the essence of China; ironic, nostalgic, at times whimsical, he stressed those aspects of the people most likely to appeal to a western reader in the 1930s. The spirit of compromise, a natural pacifism and in particular Dr Lin's exposition of the nature of Chinese humanism as the essential creed of the educated man in China, was welcome to an age given to agnostics. Coming as it did after a century in which the virtues of China seen by the European enlightenment had been dismissed or questioned Lin Yutang's book was able to resuscitate the old respect.

At that time, however, Lin was already disappointed by the new China of Chiang Kai-shek. His first book, *China's Own Critics* (1932), written in collaboration with Dr Hu Shih, attempted to ventilate unofficial opinions in the West. By 1936 he admitted frankly that the "optimism and cheerful idealism of 1926 have given place to cynicism and disillusionment." He saw little hope for a new China that would overcome the corruption and futility that abounded. In 1936 he left China for New York with his family, where he remained for several years. His works gained in popularity. *The Importance of Living* (1937) went through 40 editions in the United States and was translated into 15 languages.

With the war, however, feeling for China under the Japanese assault found an even larger audience ready to read such a readable author. *Moment in Peking* (1940) was a novel set in China against the background of the first three decades of this century which followed the fortunes of a wealthy family in Peking. Two years later *A Leaf in the Storm* took the setting of China at war to illustrate the fortunes, beliefs and habits of characters struggling with the conflict of a China rapidly changing in face of western ideas.

Collections of essays and several more novels followed. Lin's popularity to some extent imposed upon him a style and an outlook that could easily become hackneyed. The detached Taoist — ironic, nostalgic, yet deriving strength from a rich cultural tradition — found a place in *The Pleasures of a Nonconformist* ... .

Other works maintained his scholarly interests as in a study of the poet Su Tung-po *The Gay Genius*, essays on the Chinese theory of art, and *Lady Wu*, a colorful account of the T'ang dynasty Empress. ... ①

Lin Yutang himself is immensely proud of his achievements in English and his English-learning experience. In both his autobiographical sketch and *Memoirs of an Octogenarian* he makes a detailed account of his learning the language. The following English-learning story is from these two autobiographies.

He started to learn English in his childhood partly as his father's wish for the kids to go out into the world. The father, a church pastor, encouraged the kids to speak whatever little English they had picked up — *pen*, *pencil*, *paper*, etc. — although he knew nothing of the language. His enthusiasm to send his sons to St. John's mainly came from the fact that it was then the best English language school in the country. To learn from the West, the English language was a stepping-stone, a crucial means to an important end. Luckily, in 1911 Lin Yutang was able to attend St. John's preparatory school in Shanghai at the age of 17.

At St. John's, the gifted boy studied with a vengeance. With great excitement, he took to English "like duck to water" (Lin, 1975: 28). By dint of hard work, the pastor's son more or less perfected his English in the one-and-a-half years in the preparatory school so that he was elected to the editorial board of the English language *Echo* in the freshman year. The secret as he said was the *Concise Oxford Dictionary*.

His enthusiasm for English turned the *Oxford Dictionary* into interesting reading matter and he was fascinated and somewhat addicted to the *Concise Oxford Dictionary* and the *Pocket Oxford Dictionary*. He was full of thanks for the Fowler brothers, who had compiled the two versions of the dictionary. In 1930, he recommended the dictionary to his Chinese readers:

> I have never heard that anyone has taken to a dictionary as interesting reading or a summer pastime, not to say anyone getting addicted to a dictionary, but I do have a feeling of addiction to the *Concise Oxford Dictionary* and the *Pocket Oxford Dictionary*. Ever since my acquaintance with the *Oxford Dictionary* twenty years ago, I have been hugely fond of it. In the first ten years I was in love with the *Concise Oxford Dictionary*. Later the *Pocket Oxford Dictionary* appeared and took its place. In the past ten years, wherever I went I brought with me the *Pocket Oxford Dictionary*, which is a handy travel companion,

① "Dr Lin Yutang; Chinese scholar and novelist." (Obituaries) *The Times* Mar 29, 1976; pg. 16; Issue 59665; Start column: F 792 words. Elec. Coll.: CS271154813.

> and which as its name suggests can be put into a pocket. It is good travel reading and it occupies no more space than two pairs of stockings.
>
> (Lin, 1994c: 185. Translated from the Chinese.)

The advantage of these dictionaries over other dictionaries is that instead of giving a parade of definitions they "showed how a word is tumbled about in a sentence so that the phrase rather than the definition gave the background, vivid and unmistakable, but gives the word the peculiar tone and timbre." (Lin, 1975: 27)

He recalled in his old age how he had used the dictionary:

> I did not let go an English word or phrase until I knew how it was used. Thus "precarious" (hold, grasp) could never be confused with "dangerous." In this way, I formed an image of a precarious grasp of something unsteady or might be slipping①, which could never be forgotten. Best of all, it contained the cream of the English language. That was how I learned the many choice phrases of the English language. I carried it with me wherever I was traveling.
>
> (Lin, 1975: 27 –28)

As long as any occasion permits, he mentions his love of the *Pocket Oxford Dictionary*. He says in *The Importance of Living* when he talks about the art of writing:

> A writer always has an instinctive interest in words as such. Every word has a life and a personality, usually not recorded by a dictionary, except one like the *Concise or Pocket Oxford Dictionary*.
>
> A good dictionary is always readable, like the *P. O. D.*
>
> (Lin, 1998b: 393)

Nonetheless, this dictionary alone did not bring his success in learning English. He had a keen interest in English books. St. John's had a library of five thousand books. He read them all and found the library too small. Some of the books were browsed through, others carefully studied. He was particularly fond of Chamberlain's *Foundations of the Nineteenth Century*, which greatly impressed Mr. Barton, his history professor. He also closely read Darwin on evolution, Haeckel's *Riddle of the Universe*, Ward's *Sociology*, Spencer's *Ethics*, and

① The grammatical mistake is in Lin's original.

Westermarck on marriage, among other things.

In 1913, his talent for English writing was first shown in a campus writing competition in which he emerged as the first prize winner, his work being a love story based on a *huaguxi* opera①.

He was thinking in English when he was at the typewriter and became a Chinese native when he was with a writing brush. Thanks to his competence and confidence, he could brush aside criticism from his fellow Chinese writers who did not understand why his "poor English" could have enjoyed tremendous success overseas. From time to time, he wrote about the learning or teaching of English② besides compiling the Kaiming English textbooks in 1930 and *Readings in Modern Journalistic Prose* in 1931, all of which were very popular in China and made it financially possible for him to be a freelance author and translator.

In the course of learning, studying, and teaching English Lin Yutang developed a systematic view of how to learn a foreign language. In his later writings on the learning and teaching of English, we can learn about his approach to foreign language learning, which is best stated in *English-Learning Methodology*, in which he outlines five guidelines in learning English:

(1) English has life. It is currently in use. Therefore, the learner of the language shall see this clearly and learn current English.

(2) Listening, speaking, reading, and writing are all important. English is a living language currently in use. Therefore, all the four skills are important. Language cannot exist and function independent of the writers and speakers who would like to express themselves and the listeners and readers who want to reach the speakers and writers. Language varies with the position and mood of the speaker, listener, writer, or reader.

---

① See "Lin Yutang Timeline"(林语堂年表) in Zitong (Ed.). *Seventy Years of Comments on Lin Yutang*. Beijing: China Huaqiao Press: 441. [子通编. 2003.《林语堂评说七十年》. 北京:中国华侨出版社:441.]

② "On the Teaching of English in Taiwan"(论台湾的英语教学), "How to Learn English Well — The First Lecture on English Teaching"(怎样把英文学好——英文教学讲话之一)(*Wu Suo Bu Tan He Ji*, 1974);"A Dictionary That Has Benefited Me"(我所得益的一部英文字典)、"English-Learning Methodology"(英文学习法)(*Da Huang Ji*, 1934).

(3) It is important to speak the language. For one thing, speaking is the easiest exercise, for another, grammar is a matter of habit-forming.
(4) Learning (or teaching) English in English and the translation method may each have their different uses. The former is good for direct concept formation in the foreign language. The latter is helpful if the sentence rather than the word is taken as the unit of translation.
(5) Imitation and repetition are the only correct ways to success in learning English. Imitation shall be on sentence basis and it shall be followed with repeated practice until a natural outflow is produced.

(Lin, 1994c: 189 –221)

Following these guidelines, he highlights seven major points:

(1) The size of vocabulary is of primary importance, as can be seen by everybody.
(2) It is important to use words that sound natural. Chinese writers tend to be over-elegant by choosing high-sounding words following the Chinese tradition of writing, while really good English carries with it the smell of soil.
(3) Common words are worth the while. The learner shall start with common phrases and it will not be difficult to put abstract words in between. It is better to read novels by Stevenson, Dickens, and Bennett, and the familiar essays by Chesterton, Shaw, Heywood Broun, and Hillaire Belloc, than to read Macaulay's academic writings.
(4) Modern prose shall be preferred over earlier writings. Language changes. Modern writings contain modern culture and modern phrases.
(5) The vocabulary one uses can be categorized into passive vocabulary (hearing vocabulary and reading vocabulary), and active vocabulary (speaking vocabulary and writing vocabulary). When one is acquainted with a word long enough, it passes into the active vocabulary.
(6) Therefore, intensive reading to English learning is like chewing to digestion. This is to get the right pronunciation, feel the language, learn the words in sentences and to know the usage of the word.
(7) On the foundations laid by intensive reading, it is beneficial to read extensively, and it is necessary to stop from time to time learning a certain word, phrase or sentence, "According to my experience, in this period, I still did not easily let go of a word. After two years of extensive reading, I formed my reading ability, which came to serve my writing pretty well."

(ibid.: 194 –203)

Lin Yutang believes in the learning of grammar but he believes that grammar should be learned in examples. A grammar offers a system of examples. It is not easy to encounter examples of a same nature in reading although reading helps build knowledge of grammar. The learning of grammar should not be the learning of the jargon of the grammarians like "demonstrative," "descriptive," "quantitative," "numeral" and "distributive," etc. To learn grammar is to learn the precise use of language in a systematic way and it shall be not separated from reading. To learn grammar well, three things must be done: close observation, systematic study, and practice to form habits. Phonetics is a must-know for the English language teacher but not for the average student of English.

Lin Yutang may have a genius for language, but his acquisition of English is more through thoughtful learning and practice. It is not only hard work. It is hard thinking as well.

He started to contribute to the English language journal *China Critic* in July, 1930 and quickly established a reputation as an outstanding English-language writer.

2 Development of Receptive and Productive Competence in Chinese as the Mother Tongue

His rapid progress in English came at the cost of entirely neglecting his Chinese during college years. It is a problem of opportunity cost. People get one opportunity at the cost of other opportunities. In learning English as a foreign language or learning anything, concentration is good. But Lin Yutang thought that his cost was too great and when he realized he had only had a "half-baked knowledge of Chinese" he decided to make remedies. Now that he was at home with English, he had plenty of free time to pick up the learning of Chinese. By the standard of the average boys of his generation his Chinese was not bad at all when he entered college, because by then he had already developed a taste for the Song Dynasty writer Su Tungp'o (Su Dongpo) and was starting to read the *Shiji* (*Book of History*) by Sima Qian①, an impossible achievement for most present-day Chinese students.

His primary education came from his father. The pastor taught his own

① In *Memoirs of an Octogenarian*, he says that prior to his entry to St. Johns he had read Yuan Liao-fan's *Short Outline of Chinese History* (袁了凡《刚鉴易知录》).

children and a few adolescents from the Christian believers. Pastor Lin taught these children *Sishu* (*The Four Books*), *Shijing* (*The Book of Poetry*), *Shenglüqimeng* (*A Beginner's Book of Prosody and Rhymes*), and *Youxueqionglin* (*Gems for the Young Learner*). The pastor also encouraged his pupils to read translations by Lin Shu, such as the Holmes stories, the *Arabian Nights*, *Pygmalion* as well as works by Walter Scott, Charles Dickens and Maupassant.

However, Lin Yutang's early education in Chinese was regrettably incomplete. Real proficiency in a language has a cultural dimension in it. Language and culture are bound. Nobody really understands a language unless he or she knows the culture, and culture is not only in books. There is culture in the classics and culture in popular life. He spoke Chinese and read Chinese, but he was too far away from the real Chinese people, especially the atheist majority, or in Christian terminology, the pagans. He had some distance from Chinese culture and that distance was not geographical.

At the missionary school in Amoy[①], he was not allowed to read Chinese language newspapers, nor to attend traditional Chinese operas or even to hear folklore by blind minstrel singers. The missionary school provided him with free education but also took away his freedom to be immersed in Chinese culture. The later successful author had ambivalent feelings about his missionary school education and expressed it in his autobiography. On the one hand, he owed the church for the opportunity to "go out into the world," and on the other hand he resented it for trying to take his roots away from him (Lin, 1994: 13).

When he graduated from St. John's in 1916, he accepted a teaching post at Tsinghua College in Beijing. There he found himself surrounded by Chinese history and realized what his Christian education had deprived him of. He was extremely ashamed of himself and decided to make up for what he had lost. Before the age of 20, he had known that Joshua's trumpet blew down the walls of Jericho but did not know the Chinese folk story of Meng Jiang, whose tears for her lost husband at the Great Wall caused a section of the wall to collapse and expose his dead body. He had long known that Jehovah stopped the sun so that Joshua could kill all the Canaanites before he learned the Chinese tale of Hou Yi

---

① This refers to the *xunyuan shuyuan* in Xiamen, which was known as Amoy in English (厦门寻源书院).

shooting down nine out of ten suns and his wife flying to the moon to become the moon goddess. There was also the tale of Nüwa mending the sky with 365 of 366① stones and the remaining one became the story of the *Hongloumeng* (*Dream of the Red Chamber*). It was not until he was in his thirties that he learned these well-known stories here and there in the books.

With an equal vengeance as with English he seriously tackled the Chinese problem. He learned the Pekingese colloquial by reading the *Hongloumeng*, the unmatched masterpiece of the colloquial dialect up to his time. Many other Tsinghua teachers knew little about Chinese literature but Lin Yutang was more strict with himself. His pride forbidding himself to ask anybody what the best commentary on Tu Fu's poetry was, he found the Liulits'ang (Liulichang), where there were old secondhand bookshops in a row. From conversations with the shop owners, he found out many gaps in his knowledge that should be well known to Chinese scholars. In time he learned to talk about books and early editions. Tsinghua had then the most modern and best-equipped library in China and it was headed by Yuan Tung-li, one of China's foremost librarians and a well-read scholar. It had rows upon rows of the complete works of the leading Western writers as well as fine editions of ancient Chinese books. Durham S. F. Chen, Lin's former student at Tsinghua described him as "so much at ease in such surroundings" (1974). Later, when Lin was working for a Ph. D. degree at Leipzig in Germany, he was still learning Chinese. During that period, he was lost in Chinese philology in *Hanxueshichengji* and in *Huangqingjingjie*, particularly in its sequel *Jingjiedubian* edited by Governor Yüan Yüan of the later Manchu period, and was at home with the exegetical works of the different writers, with giants like Wang Niensun and son, Tuan Yü-ts'ai, and Ku Yen-wu (Lin, 1975: 54). He was turning from a Chinese language learner into a Chinese language researcher.

Let there be no myth about this celebrity. True, he was endowed with genius but his later success can be largely attributed to his diligence. The Confucian work ethic — the spirit of hard work — has been acknowledged even by his critics. Many of his important writings and translations have been

---

① The numbers are wrong due to Lin's incorrect memory. According to the *Hongloumeng*, Nüwa prepared 36,501 huge stones and only used 36,500 to mend the sky.

marked with a light-hearted tone but the author is a serious man. His ability to write in both Chinese and English has had a process of development.

His earliest writings in Chinese were in 1918. His Chinese then was good enough for writing publishable articles on linguistics①. In 1923, he published a few more academic articles.

Interestingly, he has never given a systematic account of the learning of Chinese. In studying his Chinese learning process we find that it shares some similarities with his English learning process: both processes involve a conscious effort at language learning; the inseparability of language and literature is duly recognized; the use of dictionaries is emphasized; a high level of language productivity is aimed at in the learning of both languages; there is the genuine enjoyment of reading at his own choice; reading is done for knowledge and enlightenment.

After all, Chinese is his mother tongue and it was learned in a much more natural environment in spite of his English-only college education. By "almost totally neglecting the Chinese language," he probably means that he virtually read little literature in Chinese while attending college. In Chinese, *guoyu* (Chinese language) and *guowen* (Chinese literature) are basically the same thing, or they are closely bound.

With what he had learned from his father and early school education, with the native speaking environment, in his learning of Chinese he imaginably did not meet with the same difficulty as he had with English. He almost never cared to talk about the learning of Chinese vocabulary and grammar. When the later scholar Lin Yutang talked about Chinese, his concerns were mainly reading and writing, or academic research.

In Lin's learning experience, he developed his idea of reading as represented by two lectures, "The Art of Reading"②, given at St. Johns and

---

① "On the Chinese Index System and the Western System of Writing"（论汉字索引制及西洋文字）, "About the Chinese Index System"（汉字索引制说明）, "The Compilation of a Dictionary of Classified Idioms"（分类成语辞书编纂）.

② "The Art of Reading"（读书的艺术）. Lin, Yutang. 1934. *Da Huang Ji*. Shanghai: Shenghuo Bookstore, 1934.

Guanghua College, and "On Reading"[①], given at Fudan University and Daxia University. His idea of reading in the two lectures consists of the following points:

(1) The educational establishment only encourages students to "read" for degrees or diplomas; the purpose of reading should be to get enlightenment, knowledge and nourishment of the soul.
(2) The reader should have his freedom to read at his own choice; interest helps overcome problems the way children reading the *Hongloumeng* (*Dream of the Red Chamber*) and the *Shuihu* (*Outlaws of the Marshes*) do not need to consult the dictionary.
(3) Reading can help one get rid of vulgarity and make his language appealing.
(4) Reading should never be forced on the reader; some books are to be read, some not; some books are only to be read in certain places or on certain occasions.
(5) The reader should choose what he likes as reading matter and get its flavor.
(6) The reader can find a writer with similiar temperament and be guided by him in the reading process.
(7) Good Chinese is acquired through the reading of novels like the *Sanguo Yanyi* (*The Three Kingdoms*) and the *Shuihu* (*Outlaws of the Marshes*), not through the scores of pages in the school textbook.
(8) The reader should have his own independent judgment and courage to express his judgment.

(Lin, 1994c: 159 –166)

"Reading" in this context is not exactly the same word as in "English Learning Methodology." In the other context, it is more of a tool of language acquisition. It seems that expectations are higher in the native language while he might have felt the same for reading English at the highest level.

He shares his writing experience and insight with his readers in the flirtatious *Six Tricks of Writing*[②].

He believes that the guiding principle of a piece of writing shall be *xiaochang* (clarity and fluency). To achieve clarity and fluency there are six tricks. The writer should:

---

① "On Reading" (论读书). Lin, Yutang. 1934. *Da Huang Ji*. Shanghai: Shenghuo Bookstore, 1934.

② "Six Tricks of Writing" (作文六诀). in Lin, Yutang. 1934b. *Xing Su Ji*. Shanghai: Shidai.

(1) express himself in his writing and should not be elusive about what he wants to say.
(2) affect his readers emotionally — he should tell his readers something they do not know and convince the reader by showing knowledge of the special jargon of the subject.
(3) respect his readers by avoiding clichés and commonsense knowledge such as "Education is the human process of imparting knowledge" and "As far as I know, marriage is the union of a man and a woman".
(4) write when he is in a happy mood and stop for a cigarette when necessary.
(5) write as the heart dictates, not in the way of an academic paper.
(6) stop when he is tired.

(Lin, 1994e: 63 -72)

Flirtatious as the tone is, this puts in a nutshell Lin Yutang's idea of writing.

In September, 1932, he founded, together with others, the *Analects Fortnightly*, whose mission was to propagate humor in literature and whose motto, put into English literally, was "Two feet in two cultures and one heart on world literature." The magazine provided the convenient stage for the actor. It turned out to be a success and Lin's name as a Chinese language writer was further promoted.

3 Development of Transfer Competence

Lin Yutang's transfer competence between English and Chinese first comes from his parallel proficiency in the two languages. This alone makes him exceptional as a translator, for most translators find themselves comfortable only when translating from a foreign language into their mother tongue. Lin Yutang translates both ways. A translator's linguistic proficiency — receptive proficiency in one language and productive proficiency in another — is where his transfer competence is grounded and may be considered part of his transfer competence. Lin Yutang is almost a perfect bilingual of Chinese and English (his knowledge of other languages is not our concern here), with similar receptive and productive competence in both languages. In learning a foreign language, one cannot completely forget the mother tongue even if he tries to. Consciously or unconsciously, the two languages are mapped, compared and contrasted. It is unimaginable to find a bilingual who does not have the slightest idea of differences and similarities between the foreign language and the mother tongue, or between the second language and the first.

Another source of Lin's transfer competence is the transfer knowledge gained from reading translations. Reading involves active use of the mind. Particularly it involves judgment and reflection. It is a critical process. One may enjoy or dislike a translation. There may be preference of one translation over another. The likes and dislikes are not without reason. One's taste has an empirical foundation. Behind the taste is perception of the translation, perception of what has been done by the translator so that a certain feeling is generated. Lin's reading of translations was extensive: Chinese translations of Western classics, including the works translated by Yan Fu and Lin Shu; Chinese translations of Buddhist sutras from Sanskrit; Fitzgerald's English translations of *The Rubaiyat* by the Persian poet Omar Khayyam; English translations of Chinese classics by Arthur Waley, James Legge, Ku Hung-ming, and Helen Waddell. He was also a reader of Buddhist sutras in English translation. These are certainly not all the translations he read over time, given his extensive interest as an avid reader. Such readings should have been sufficient to give him some idea of what translations are like and should be like.

A third source of his transfer competence is his conscious study of the issue of translation. In the beginning, through his reading of translations and original writings, he might have developed some ideas about translation unconsciously, but as time moved on, he grew more and more conscious of the issue of translating. He began to pay more and more attention to remarks on translation by famous Chinese and Western scholars. He was aware of Yan Fu and Benedetto Croce on translation and had his own judgment of translations by Ku Hung-ming, Yan Fu, Lin Shu (Lin Qin-nan), Fitzgerald, James Legge, Helen Waddell, among others. As he saw more problems in translation or increasingly felt the importance of translation, his conscious study became active study when he read translations against their originals and did comparative reading of translations. His conscious study of the issue of translation consists of study of translations and reading about translation. He developed his own position in the controversy of literal versus free translation and was able to make critical reviews of the translations of his predecessors and contemporaries.

His transfer competence was also built through trial-and-error hands-on experience. From time to time he was tempted to make translations of his own.

Over time, his translations grew to a vast body of literature. He translated and reflected. In his translations, different strategies were followed as the text type or purpose changed. He was able to make self-corrections. In *Six Chapters of a Floating Life* alone he revised the manuscript over ten times. As his translations grew in volume, he became so competent in translation (especially from Chinese to English) that he practically translated all entries in the *Chinese-English Dictionary of Modern Usage*, his crowning work (Chen, 1974).

Interestingly, although he is a self-taught translator, he believes in translation training. It is understandable that some knowledge of translation can be transferred from individual to individual. Some training may provide kind of a shortcut for a would-be translator as some issues may be clarified and some errors may be avoided.

III Moonlighting as a Translator

Lin Yutang translated sporadically. This makes it difficult to give a linear description of his side occupation as a freelance literary translator. Suspending the temporal discontinuity in this line of his career, in broader terms we can still see a few developmental stages: the commencement, years of experiment and years of excellence.

1 Taking off as an Impressive Translator at the Age of 30

Confucius said, "At fifteen I set my heart upon learning. At thirty, I had planted my feet firm upon the ground. At forty, I no longer suffered from perplexities. At fifty, I knew what were the biddings of Heaven. At sixty, I heard them with docile ear. At seventy, I could follow the dictates of my own heart; for what I desired no longer overstepped the boundaries of right." (Confucius, 1997: 12) It might have been a coincidence that in 1924, the year Lin Yutang started seriously to translate, he was exactly 30 and ever after he was standing firm as a translator. The age of 30 marked the commencement of his translating career. However, this does not mean that a translator starts at thirty! The quote from Confucius is merely to show an interesting coincidence which is worthy of note.

Once the basic receptive competence and productive competence were there and once Lin Yutang started translating it was quite an impressive beginning. And as a translator, he was soaring to great heights. Some translators of his generation took to translation as an experimental literary exercise, but in Lin's case, a greater part of his literary education had been completed much earlier.

At the age of 30 (1924), he published three articles, which marked his impressive entry into the enterprise of translating: "Call for Translation of an Essay and for Humour," "Miscellaneous Remarks on Humour,"① and "A Proposal for the Standardization of Names in Translation."②

The earliest known translation he made was of one word, which earned him the reputation of *dashi*, a master. The word is *youmo*, a Chinese transliteration of the English word *humor*, and the word mistakenly and unmistakably stuck with him ever since. He has been known as *youmo dashi*, master humorist, or master of humor.

The reason for his transplanting the English word is told in "Call for Translation of an Essay and for Humour" (1924): In spite of the tradition of humor in China, in Chinese literature humour has not been used and appreciated the way it deserves to be. There is a clear-cut line between business and joking. Business has been too serious and light talk tends to be too nasty. The Chinese writer either writes seriously about morality and government (a thousand-year-old fault that has given rise to *Maoxü*, *Hanxü* and *Shenpeishishuo*, and Liu Yin the moralist in *Zuozhuan*), or writes about the bizarre and obscene (another ancient Chinese tradition which has generated innumerous masterpieces like *Zashi Mixin*, *Feiyan Waizhuan* and *Hanwudi Neizhuan*). On the other hand, in reading William James on psychology and Friedrich Schiller on

---

① "Miscellaneous Remarks on Humour" (幽默杂话). *Chenbao Supplement* (晨报副刊), June 9, 1924.

② "A Proposal for the Standardization of Names in Translation" (关于译名统一的提议). Written on March 21, 1924.

humanism, even a sixty-year old, who is no longer as indulgent of sensuality as the young, can derive the pleasure of reading, for their works contain irrelevant jokes that are of a different kind, which can be called "humor." In order to make life less boring, he maintains that writers of academic books and newspaper editorials should include a jovial element. In the Chinese tradition, he points out, it is fine to crack a few jokes under the pseudonym of Lu Xun, but categorically unfitting to do so in the name of Zhou Shuren, the real name of the scholar.

Before writing this he had read an English essay in *The Far Eastern Times*①, an English language newspaper. It was about a horse in an open-air stable and illustrated with five photos. Some interesting comments were made by the author. Lin Yutang thought such a jovial style could never be found in a Chinese newspaper and decided to recruit translations as a "test.", whatever "test" means.

In this case, the size of the translation was extremely small and yet the influence was tremendous. It was much more than a mere translation of a single word. It was the beginning of an ambitious cultural venture. The translation of the word was based on a good understanding of the difference between Western and Chinese cultures. It represented his attitude toward life and reflected his idea of good literature.

"Call for Translation of an Essay and for Humour" was quickly followed by another article, "Miscellaneous Remarks on Humour," which states that the word *youmo* is first a mere transliteration which may well be replaced by some other Chinese characters but hints at something "quiet and silent." These two articles on humour were just the beginning of a large campaign. The use of *youmo* was controversial② and yet the word got around despite challenges it met. *Youmo* became Lin's obsession. He continuously wrote about humor, defended his translation and advocated his position. He even started a journal called the

① 《东方时报》(1923—1928).

② See "A Discussion of 'Youmo'" (关于"幽默"的讨论), "A Discussion of 'youmo' and 'yumiao'" ("幽默"与"语妙"之讨论), and "In Reply to Qingya's Discussion of the Chinese Translation of 'Humor'" (答青崖论"幽默"译名). *Analects Fortnightly*. No. 3. Oct. 16, 1932.

Analects Fortnightly, which was dedicated to the promotion of *youmo* and its vehicle the familiar-style essay (*xiaopinwen*)①, gathering around him a pack of writers with a similar interest. The literary clique has been known as the Analects School. In fact, the fortnightly and the idea of *youmo* became so popular that Lu Xun, leader of the leftist writers, obsessed with a broader agenda of cultural and social revolution, sarcastically remarked, "Boom! The whole world started to be humorous."② On Lu Xun's side, the criticism is not unfounded:

> As long as it is not used to solve national problems and guide warfare, I see no harm in *youmo* (So, by then Lu Xun had accepted the translation) between friends. Even a revolutionary sometimes needs to take a stroll. Neo-Confucianists cannot avoid having children as evidence of their less serious moments. The familiar essay may establish a permanent presence in Chinese literature, but it is a little bit inadequate just to focus on "familiarity."
>
> (Lu Xun. 1998: 374 -275. Translated from the Chinese.)

In *On Humor*③, he makes a systematic study of the theory and practice of Western and Chinese humor, citing Aristotle, Plato, Kant, Hobbes, George Meredith, Will Rogers, Stephen Leacock, C. K. Chesterton, Lloyd George, Bernard Shaw etc. on the one hand, and *The Book of Poetry*, Laotse, Chuangtse, Confucius, Tao Yuanming, Han Yu, Li Yu, Yuan Zhonglang, *Outlaws of the Marshes*, *The Scholars*, etc. on the other.

2 Nine Years of Experiment: 31-39

From 1925 to 1933, Lin Yutang's presence as a translator was increasingly felt and at the end of this period his theory of translation took shape thanks to his

---

① The journal was founded on September 16, 1932.

② Lu Xun. 1998. "Thinking Once Before Acting" (一思而行). First published in the *Ziyoutan* column of the *Shenbao* newspaper (《申报 · 自由谈》), May 17, 1934. In Wang, Dehou (Ed.). *The Complete Edition of Lu Xun's Works (1): Essays*. Hangzhou: *zhejiang wenyi*: 374 -375. [王得后编. 1998.《鲁迅作品全编:杂文卷(下册)》. 浙江文艺出版社: 374—275.]

③ First published in Nos. 33, 34, 35 of *Analects Fortnightly* (《论语半月刊》), 1934.

experience and research. In terms of translation quality, we can hardly say that his translations done in 1933 are definitely better than those done in 1925, 1926 and 1927, but his hands-on experience, his reflection and his research certainly did give him more ideas about translation as the years went by. He was more and more disciplined in his translations.

His earliest translations were sporadic and experimental. As a translator he started with small pieces of literature. In 1925, he published his first translation of a complete text — *Sylvesterabend*, a poem. *Sylvesterabend* is the German word for the Austrian New Year Eve. It was published in the *Yusi* magazine as the translator's celebration of the Chinese New Year Eve. Since he did not clearly cite the source of the song and he knew German, we do not know whether the translation was from German or English. In 1926, also in the *Yusi* magazine, he published his translation of five quatrains of Edward Fitzgerald's English translation (1859) of *Rubaiyat* of the celebrated ancient Persian poet Omar Khayyam. A complete Chinese translation of Fitzgerald's translation was later done by the Chinese poet Guo Moruo①. Accused of infidelity, he defended himself while unwillingly acknowledging the criticism②.

From March to September, 1927, under the influence of Eugene Chen, he served briefly as a secretary in the Ministry of Foreign Affairs of the Nationalist government in Hankow. For a foreign ministry secretary whose English and Chinese were as good as his, translating would have been an important part of his business. He was editor of the English version of the literary supplement of the *Central Daily News*③, making or handling translations should have been part of his routine. In the English paper, he published his English translations of some of Ping-ing's letters from the front of the Northern Expedition against the warlords. Hsieh Ping-ing, then a girl cadet at the Wuchang Military Academy and admirer of Dr. Lin and Sun Fu-yuan (editor of the Chinese edition of the supplement), frequented their office. She sent Sun

① Kayyam, Omar. 1930. *Rubaiyat*. Trans. Guo Moruo. *Chuangzaoshe* [(波斯)莪默·伽亚谟撰. 1930. 鲁拜集. 郭沫若译. 创造社, 1930.]

② "In Reply to a Critique of the Translation of Omar Kayyam" (答《对于译莪默诗底商榷》) published in *Yusi* (68), March 1, 1926.

③ 《中央日报》

letters from the war front. Both men liked the letters as good real-time war reports. To the girl's flattery, Sun published them in the Chinese edition and Lin translated them and published them in the English edition. The diary of Ping-ing the girl soldier is the earliest known sizeable English translation published by Lin. The letters from the girl soldier aroused great popular interest in China. Lin Yutang first translated one of the letters and published it in the English edition of *Central Daily News*. It was equally liked by English-language readers and an American columnist even bothered to write him a letter requesting more of the kind①. This must have reinforced his confidence. He translated the rest of the letters and finally put them in a collection under the title of *Letters of a Chinese Amazon and War-Time Essays* (1930).

At that time, Dr. Lin and S. F. Durham Chen, his former pupil at Tsinghua conceived the idea of translating Dr. Sun Yat-sen's complete works into English and Chen actually made a rough draft of some paragraphs and showed it to Dr. Lin, who thought well of his effort and encouraged him to go on. Unfortunately their stay in Hankow was cut short and they had to go their separate ways. The "pet project" they had fondly contemplated was abandoned for ever②.

In September, 1927, seeing the split of the revolutionary camp and the bloody suppression of the Communists by the Kuomintang, Lin Yutang was disillusioned with politics and moved to Shanghai, where he became for a time English-language chief editor of Academia Sinica under the respectable Mr. Ts'ai Yüan-p'ei (Cai Yuanpei). The year 1928 saw very little translation published but that does not mean he did not translate. He was going to harvest a great deal in the following two years. The only known translation published in that year was found as fragments in "Thomas Hardy on Life, Death and God," his article in the *Yusi* magazine③.

With more time on hand for translating and writing, in 1929 and 1930,

---

① See "Preface to *Congjun Riji*" (《从军日记》序).

② Chen, Durham S. F. "Dr. Chen as I Know Him: Some Random Recollections." *Huagang Xuebao* (华岗学报). No. 9.

③ "Thomas Hardy on Life, Death, and God." (哈第论死生与上帝). *Yusi*, No. 11, Vol. 4, March 12, 1928.

Lin Yutang turned out to be a prolific Chinese translator of wide-ranging current topics. Nikolai Ognyov's *The Diary of a Communist Schoolboy* was translated into English by Alexander Werth in 1928. Lin Yutang, in collaboration with Mr. Zhang Yousong, quickly created a Chinese version in the following year. Almost simultaneously, two rival publishers, Guanghua and Beixin, came up with Chinese editions of the same book. When he published his translation of *The Chinese Puzzle* by Ransome, a sympathizer of the Chinese Nationalist revolution and a critic of British policy in China, the original book was only two years old. Translation of Mrs. Russell's feminist *Hypatia, or Woman and Knowledge* (Russell, 1925) was published in 1929 but deplorably it received little attention from readers. On March 3, 1929, he completed his translation of *Pygmalion* by Bernard Shaw[①]. By that time, Shaw had already been well known in China but his works were not yet much translated. He thought that Shaw's unusual works contained wisdom that would do good to the Chinese people, who had been too familiar with a roguish philosophy of life of "Don't know life, how know death?[②]" He particularly admired Shaw's pungent criticism of middle-class mentality in this work and Shaw's masterful use of humor. Also in 1929, he published his translation of a critical biography of Henrik Ibsen and his love letters. In the same year, he completed his translations from the English of excerpts in literary and art criticism. The collection was published the following year as *Xinde Wenping*, or *The New Criticism* (Lin, 1930), which comprises part of J. E. Spingarn's *Creative Criticism: Essays on the Unity of Genius and Taste* (Spingarn, 1917), selections from Benedetto Croce's *Aesthetic as Science of Expression and General Linguistic*, J. E. Spingarn's "Seven Arts and Seven Fallacies" (back-translation from the Chinese title), an excerpt from Oscar Wilde: *Intentions* ("The Critic as an Artist"), "French Criticism" by E. Dowden, and Van Wyck Brooks's "The Critic and Young America."

From 1931 to 1933 not much translation was done. He was more

① Chinese translations by other translators were made half a decade later, one by Yang Xianyi (杨宪益) in 1982, another by Ge Chuangui (葛传槼) in 1986. By 1949, Lin's version of *Pygmalion* had seen four reprints. It was also reprinted in the *Complete Masterpieces of Lin Yutang* (林语堂名著全集) in 1994.

② His preferred pidgin translation of the Confucian maxim.

concerned with directly expressing his own ideas. He was determined to make *his* voice heard. In this period he published a number of self-translations. "Zarathustra and the Jester" can be regarded as one of his earliest self-translations. The essay, appearing first in "The Little Critic" column of the *China Critic*, was republished in *The Little Critic: Essays, Satires and Sketches on China* (*First Series: 1930 -1932*), which was published in 1935 by the Commercial Press in Shanghai. The Chinese original appeared in the *Yusi* magazine, No. 33, Volume 4, 1928. Such a practice of self-translation continued for many years to come. In most cases, it is difficult to decide whether the Chinese or the English is the original writing. Here are some of his self-translations or his writings on the same topic in both Chinese and English. It is relatively easier to identify the dates of publication than the time of writing or translation. We need to bear in mind that the earlier date of publication does not necessarily mean that a particular text is the "original." Since both the English text and the Chinese text are by the same author, we may as well consider them as twin texts, which include

"*Satianshi yu Dongfangshuo*," the *Yusi* magazine (IV), No. 33, 1928.

"Zarathustra and the Jester," *The Little Critic: Essays, Satires and Sketches on China* (*First Series: 1930 -1932*), 1935.

"*Satianshi Yulu* (3)," the *Yusi* magazine (IV) No. 15, 1928.

"A Pageant of Costumes," *The Little Critic, Essays, Satires and Sketches on China* (*First Series: 1930 -1932*). Shanghai: The Commercial Press, 1935.

"My Last Rebellion Against Lady Nicotine," *The Little Critic, Essays, Satires and Sketches on China* (*First Series: 1930 -1932*). The Commercial Press, 1935.

"*Wo de Jieyan.*" *Xing Su Ji*, 1934.

"*Rang Niang'ermen Gan Yixia ba!*" *Shenbao*, August, 1933.

"The Little Critic: Should Women Rule the World?" *The China Critic, VI* (August 17, 1933).

"*Xiaobona*", *Analects Fortnightly* No. 12, March, 1933.

"The Little Critic: A Talk with Bernard Shaw," *The China Critic, VI* (February 23, 1933), 205 -206.

Up to 1933, through experience and reflection, he developed a systematic view of translation and translating. In "On Translation," which was written to preface Wu Shutian's *On Translation* (1937), he ripened as a translator and translation thinker. In this article, he emphasizes the importance of the competence of the translator in the success of translation jobs and claims that "there are no set ways for translating (Lin, 1994e: 305)." He gives a detailed account of his three standards of good translation: fidelity, fluency, and beauty. His *fidelity* is more precise than that of Yan Fu's and advocates a method of sentence-for-sentence translation instead of word-for-word translation, dismissing the traditional dichotomy of literal versus free translation. By *fluency* he means a piece of translation should be like a piece of writing in its composition except that the ideas are already provided in the source text. The composition of the translation should be on sentence-by-sentence basis. "The translator shall extract the precise meaning of a sentence in the source text and then express the sentence meaning in Chinese grammar① (ibid: 317)." The translation shall follow the conventions of the Chinese language. His standard of *beauty* applies to "works of art". On the one hand, he does not think works of art can be translated, and on the other, if they have to be translated, he agrees with Benedetto Croce that translation is production, not reproduction. In the production, equal attention should be paid to both the style and the content of the source text. Although he admits that the three standards are equivalents to Yan Fu's standards of *xin* (fidelity), *da* (fluency) and *ya* (elegance), the elaboration is entirely his. By then, Lin Yutang had known what he had been exactly doing as a translator. This is coincidental with the Confucian "At forty I no longer suffered from perplexities."

3 Thirty-Nine Years of Excellence: 40-78

As a translator, Lin Yutang's knowledge and experience were accumulative. For the rest of his life, he worked with unabated enthusiasm and diligence. To crown his translator's career, he compiled a Chinese dictionary and translated all its entries into English (Chen, 1974).

In the mid-1930s his Chinese translations were mainly full-length books with occasional essays from the English such as "The Declaration of

① Lin was particularly referring to English to Chinese translation. Same below with "Chinese language."

Independence" in colloquial Chinese[①] and "On Ku Hung-ming" by the famous Danish critic George Brandes[②]. These books include *Keeping Mentally Fit — A Guide to Everyday Psychology* by Joseph Jastrow, *The Autobiography of a Super Tramp* by W. H. Davies (translated in 1935)[③]. A little bit quaint and awkward by today's standard of Chinese, these books are still much read in the Chinese speaking territories.

His English translations of essays and stories by his contemporaries or earlier writers include "On My Library"[④], "Unconscious Chinese Humour," "A Cock-Fight in Old China," "A Chinese Aesop," "The Humor[⑤] of Mencius," "The Humor of Liehtse," "A Chinese Galli-Curei," "The Donkey That Paid Its Debt," "The Epigrams of Chang Ch'ao[⑥]," "A Chinese Ventriloquist," "T' ang P' ip' a," "'Taiping' Christianity," and "Chinese Dog-Stories"[⑦].

A masterpiece was born in 1935. *Six Chapters of a Floating Life*, his translation of Shen Fu's autobiographical novelette *Fu Sheng Liu Ji* was published in the *T'ien Hsia Monthly* by five installments, the first being his preface. The complete translation was published in 1939 by the Shanghai-based Hsi-feng She (Sifeng She). It was published again later in *The Wisdom of China and India* (1948). Two excerpts of the story were later reproduced as "In Memory of a Woman" in *The Importance of Understanding* (1960). One reader found it such an excellent work that the story alone made the fat volume containing it worth buying. "Lin Yutang's translation of *Six Chapters of a Floating Life* is available in the Modern Library Giant, *The Wisdom of China and India* (perhaps the best book bargain in America, as this story is certainly Lin Yutang's best work),"

---

① *Shi Yi Ji (1)*, 1934.

② *Shi Yi Ji (2)*, 1934.

③ The Translator's Note" was dated July, 1935. The first edition was published in March, 1941 by *Shuofeng Shudian* in Shanghai.

④ It is common for Lin's short translations to be published more than once, usually the first time in a newspaper or magazine and then in one or more collections.

⑤ The word *humor* is spelt as *humour* in *A Nun of Taishan (a novelette) and Other Translations* (1936)

⑥ Entitled "Quiet Dream Shadows" in *The Importance of Understanding* (1960).

⑦ "圣师录·王言." Entitled "Some Dog Stories" in *The Importance of Understanding*, 1960.

thus spoke the great American poet, essayist and social critic Kenneth Rexroth (1905 – 1982) in a 1958 book review entitled *The Chinese Classic Novel in Translation: The Art of Magnanimity*. ①

Some of his earlier English translations and self-translations were incorporated in his two bestsellers, *My Country and My People* and his most successful book *The Importance of Living*. The former contains a few translated poems and passages such as the story of Chienniang, "A Young Nun's Worldly Desires (The Mortal Thoughts of a Nun)," poems of Li Po (Li Bai), Tu Fu (Du Fu), Hsin Ch'ichi (Xin Qiji) and other Chinese poets, excerpts from Li Liweng, Cheng Panch'ao (Zheng Banqiao), and Chang Tai (Zhang Dai). The latter contains in a larger proportion the gems of his English translations such as "The Half-and-Half Song" by Li Mi-an, "Ah, Homeward Bound I Go!" by T'ao Yüanming (Tao Yuanming), Chin's (Jin Shengtan's) "Thirty-Three Happy Moments," select passages from *Reminiscences under the Lamp-Light* under the title of "Ch'iufu" and from *Six Chapters of a Floating Life*, Cheng Panch'iao's letter to his younger brother, the "Vase Flowers" of Yüan Chunglang (Yuan Zhonglang), "The Epigrams of Chang Ch'ao (Zhang Chao)," Chin's dissertation on the true art of travel, "The Travels of Mingliaotse," "The Familiar Style" by Lin himself, etc. When readers and reviewers speak of the two books, they usually concentrate on the author's witty statements and delightful style of writing. But suppose we take those translations from the two books, especially the latter, the statements would be somewhat dry. These translations are an integral part of the masterpieces.

As time went on, he gradually moved from short pieces to complete books, complete in the sense that fragments of his translations gradually came together and took shape as books, not in the sense that he translated complete books from one language to the other, which he only occasionally did. The media that carried his translations used to be newspapers and magazines but gradually shifted to books in impressive volumes. This is the case both of his English and of his Chinese translations. Standing alone, an individual piece of

---

① This 1958 book review was reprinted in *Bird in the Bush* (New Directions, 1959). Copyright 1958. Electronic version available at Kenneth Rexroth Archive website: http://www.bopsecrets.org/rexroth/chinesenovels.htm.

translation may not have had much influence but together in a collection they make an impact.

1938 saw the publication of *The Wisdom of Confucius* by Random House in New York. Much of the book was to be included later in a large volume *The Wisdom of China and India* in 1942 and a reproduction of "The Wisdom of China" section as a separate book in 1949. *The Wisdom of Confucius* provides a pleasurable reading experience for English readers. According to a book review by Chan (1940), Oriental Institute, University of Hawaii, "What might be a dry subject is presented as full of human interest and literary beauty. The translation is superlative for its enchanting style and the shades of meaning brought out from the Chinese texts. Dr. Lin's rendering has both truth and beauty." This is not a rendering of a Chinese book into English. It is the creation of a book in English based on Chinese materials, given Lin's skills as a translator and his good taste and judgment as an editor. It consists of selective translations of Confucian classics and the translation of a biography of Confucius by the great Chinese historian Si Maqian. The first selection from the Confucian classics, *Chung Yung*, or *The Doctrine of the Mean* is basically a Ku Hung-ming translation, upon which Lin Yutang has made some improvements. In this book, he devotes a section of the "Introduction" to the explanation of his translation method which he calls *paraphrase*. Though the Lin Yutang way of selection may be debated, the book is interesting and the translations are well done. Lin is true to the original in both letter and spirit.

This is the first of Lin Yutang's four "Chinese wisdom" books. The other three are: *The Wisdom of China and India* (1942), *The Wisdom of Laotse* (1948), and *The Wisdom of China* (1949). These four books are basically one. The second of them, *The Wisdom of China and India* (1942), contains the essence of all the four books. It is an anthology of English translations of Chinese and Indian texts and in the "Wisdom of China," and much of the translation is by Lin Yutang himself. Apart from *The Wisdom of Laotse*① and *The Wisdom of China*, other partial reproductions of the book include "The Epigrams

---

① In *The Wisdom of Laotse*, Lin Yutang translated more chapters of Chuangtse and blended his translation of *Chuangtse* with the *The Book of Tao*, using the former to explain the latter, a practice which he claimed to be original.

of Lusin, translation and comment by Lin Yutang" in *Asia*, XLII (December, 1942), *Tales and Parables of Old China, Translated by Lin Yutang*①, and *Chuangtse: Translated by Lin Yutang* (1957). Lin Yutang thematizes English translations by himself and some other translators under six headings: Chinese Mysticism (*Laotse, the Book of Tao; Chuangtse, Mystic and Humorist*), Chinese Democracy (*The Book of History, Documents of Chinese Democracy; Mencius, the Democratic Philosopher, Motse, the Religious Teacher*), The Middle Way (*The Aphorisms of Confucius, The Golden Mean of Tsesze*), Chinese Poetry ("Some Great Ancient Lyrics," "Ch'ü Yüan," "Li Po," "The Tale of Meng Chiang," "The Mortal Thoughts of a Nun"), Sketches of Chinese Life ("Chinese Tales," *Six Chapters of a Floating Life*), and Chinese Wit and Wisdom ("Parables of Ancient Philosophers," "Family Letters of a Chinese Poet," "The Epigrams of Lusin," "One Hundred Proverbs"). This anthology displays Lin Yutang's erudition as well as his taste and skill as a master translator. After publication, the book was extensively reviewed in the press and its popularity is borne out by the following book news in 1943:

> Immediate public response to the publication of Lin Yutang's magnificent anthology, The Wisdom of China and India, has prompted Random House to advance plans for two succeeding volumes in this series. "The Wisdom of Greece," first planned for late 1944, will be published in November, 1943, if the new production schedule can be met. "The Wisdom of Israel" has been moved up from the 1945 list to spring, 1944. Random House will announce the names of the editors of the two new volumes, along with partial tables of contents, in a special brochure, now in preparation.
>
> (*Syracuse Herald-American*, Sunday, February 7, 1943, Page 18)

After the publication of *My Country and My People* in 1935, Lin Yutang decided to translate wholesale a number of Chinese works he liked such as *A Nun of Taishan*, vignettes from the Ming and Qing dynasties, epigrams of Ch'ang Ch'ao, and the family letters of Zheng Banqiao (Cheng Panch'iao) and Zeng Guofan, etc. Because of the success of *My Country and My People*, on the advice of Mr. Walsh, his publisher, Lin delayed his translation projects and wrote *The Importance of Living*, which contains a sizeable portion of translations.

---

① *Tales and Parables of Old China.* Translated by Lin Yutang. San Francisco: The Book Club of California, 1943. The text is reproduced from *The Wisdom of China and India.*

Over the years, he did translations whenever he could. The following years saw an intermittent, selective and somewhat systematic translation of Taoist and Confucian classics, and a vast body of poems, essays and stories from antiquity down to his day. The longer translations appeared in stand-alone editions and the shorter ones were first published here and there in a book or a journal and often combined later to make a large volume. Among smaller volumes of essays/stories and the stand-alone editions of some longer works were *Ancient Chinese Vignettes Translated by the Have-Not-Done Studio* (1940) and *The Travels of Mingliaotse.* (1940), *Miss Tu* (1950, also in *Widow, Nun and Courtesan*), *Widow, Nun and Courtesan: Three Novelettes from the Chinese Translated and Adapted by Lin Yutang* (1951), *Widow Chuan: Retold by Lin Yutang, Based on Chuan Jia Chun by Lao Hsiang* (1952), and *Famous Chinese Short Stories: Retold by Lin Yutang* (1952).

His translations of a more philosophical nature have entered the 500-page-plus "China" part of *The Wisdom of China and India* (1942), and the pieces about the Chinese way of life are found in *The Importance of Understanding: Translations from the Chinese* (1960), which is another 500-page anthology of 107 pieces of writing on human nature, love and death, the seasons, nature, human adjustments, women, the home and daily living, art and literature, "after tea and wine," ancient wit, "fools to this world," wisdom, Zen (a selection from the *Lankavatra Sutra* translated by Professor Suzuki and Dwight Goddard in *A Buddhist Bible* and a selection from the *Surangama Sutra* translated by Wai-tao in *A Buddhist Bible*), and some epigrams and proverbs are also included. Significant overlapping exists between the two books. For example, authors often appear again in the latter book, such as Chuangtse, Shen Fu, and Chang Chao. One of his favorite translations, "The Mortal Thoughts of a Nun" is also reproduced. The selection from the *Lankavatra Sutra* and the selection from the *Surangama Sutra* by English translators from Sanskrit are also put into the book. The anthology contains the rich materials on which his ideas in *The Importance of Living* are formed. As its title suggests, the book is intended to bring about more understanding between the races. That purpose has been very well served. Today it is still read and enjoyed, as a contemporary reader Jon T. Windsor from California comments in an Internet posting:

> A book of Lin Yutang's that I almost overlooked, *The Importance of Understanding* is a

> collection of the sayings of several Chinese writers, from prominent poets to complete unknowns, all organized under various subjects. The book is a great reference and is highly quotable; but it also provides a universal theme of Chinese thought that I find invaluable. The texts I enjoyed the most were the dialogs between poets and philosophers. ①

The Chinese Theory of Art: Translations from the Masters of Chinese Art in 1967 is a well-quoted source for the study of Chinese art. This anthology consists of writings on art by 23 Chinese masters of art from Confucius in the sixth century B. C. to Shen Ts'ung-Ch'ien in the eighteenth century A. D.

Not only was Lin Yutang interested in translating between Chinese and English, he was also interested in the compilation of a bilingual dictionary for future translators. The crowning work of his life, his *Chinese-English Dictionary of Modern Usage* (1972), represents the translator and scholar at his best. The dictionary is remarkable in more ways than one. First, it has an instant Chinese index system based on his work as a linguist. Second, there is also an index of English vocabulary to accommodate reverse use. Third, it focuses on the usage of words in different contexts. Most importantly, Lin Yutang has proof-read every Chinese entry and provided the English translation.

The success of Lin Yutang as an author and translator is the result of his conscious self-making. He does not attribute his achievements to flashes of genius. Rather, he believes in diligence. During an interview, he spoke on work, "I believe in regularity and concentration. I do not believe in inspiration for authors. Those who wait for inspiration will probably never come by it. Somewhere in the human body there is a mysterious clockwork — the body likes to be regular — and we accomplish most by leading a regular life." ② Such is Lin Yutang, the self-made man, author, and translator.

---

① From: http://www.judysbook.com/members/jonthysell/posts/2006/4/334979 April 13, 2006 3: 12 PM PST

② "Philosopher Says 'To Forget To Loaf At All Makes No Sense'" by Spencer Moosa, Mansfield, O., News Journal Sunday, June 4, 1967, Page Twenty-Two—A.

CHAPTER

Two

Song of the Self: the *Xingling*[①] Poetics of Literature and Translation

When we observe an author-translator, it is better to see him first as an author before we see him as a translator. We shall realize that an author-translator is guided by his poetics of literature more than anything else. In this chapter Lin Yutang's poetics of translation is considered in the light of his poetics of literature.

Expressing the Self: an Advocate of *Xingling* Literature

1 Two Aspects of Self-Expression

In Lin Yutang's Chinese discourse on literature, the keyword is *xingling* (spelt as *hsing-ling* by himself), and in his English discussion of literature, it becomes "self-expression" (1998b: 390). His poetics of literature can be

① 性灵. Spelt by Lin himself as *hsing-ling*. Its meaning varies in different contexts: self-expression, individuality, sensibility or sensitivity. The modern *pinyin* form *xingling* is adopted for this book.

summarized by his own words in "On Literature"[①] as "Literature is the expression of a person's *xingling*" (Lin, 1994e: 148). He thus defines *xingling:* "*Xingling* is the self" (ibid: 147). Therefore, his poetics of literature is: Literature is the expression of the self. The following excerpt from "On Literature" best represents the gist of this poetics:

> A piece of writing is the expression of the *xingling* of an individual. *Xingling* is something that the writer alone knows. Neither his parents nor his bedmate knows it. Yet in it lies the very life of literature. Therefore, the believer in *xingling* is a disbeliever in the ancients, because it is neither necessary nor possible to learn from the ancients. The believer in *xingling* is also a disbeliever in rules and laws, because once acquainted with the pulse of literature, one creates as the heart dictates, never to be confined by any set of rules or laws.
>
> (Lin, 1994e: 148. My translation.)

He believes that all writings that contain insights from personal experience and told in earnest can be passed on "because humans share feelings, and something told in honesty by one can touch others." (Lin, 1994e: 149) The word *xingling*, he says, "is not only the lifeline of prose in recent history, but also a cure for hollowness, shallowness, uniformity, and dumbness, the common ills with writers of the day" (Lin, 1994e: 152). The word, he believes, is to start a new tradition of modern prose whose "technique" is to "form a personal tone by combining argument and sentiment, which come out of liberated sensitivity and meditated enlightenment, instead of books on rhetoric and writing" (Lin, 1994e: 152).

Therefore, for Lin Yutang, expression is two-fold, involving both matter and manner, or content and form. The matter is individuality and the manner is a style that transcends any stereotyped format. A writer should speak up his own mind and show his own feelings. Consequently, he uses a liberated style. The style is made to suit the content instead of the other way around.

---

① First published in two installments in *Analects Fortnightly*, respectively on April 16, and Nov. 1., 1933.

2 Individuality as the Content of Expression

Lin Yutang's "self-expression" is, first of all, expression of the author's own individuality:

> ... In modern [Western] literature, the author speaks for himself. He does not speak for the sages nor for God. Therefore, in his *Confessions*, the first of modern literature, Rousseau speaks about his own business and speaks up his own mind. By disclosing his sex life and other privacies only to shock readers in a society which has been dominated by classicism, he has raised the storm of romantic literature ...
>
> (Lin, 1994f: 146. Translated from the Chinese.)

With such a belief, he writes about anything for which he has something to say, gossiping about any "trivial" subjects such as bedbugs, pidgin English, Bertrand Russell's divorce, the beggars of London, buying birds, eating, drinking, cigarette-smoking, shaking hands, dressing, gardening and tea-drinking, or delivering discourses on weightier topics such as the spirit of the Chinese people, freedom of speech, the wisdom of the philosophers, and world peace. Similarly, he translates anything that suits his temperament. His poetics of literature also governs his translations. In the "Preface" to *The Importance of Understanding*, he says that he feels no obligation to translate any author except those he likes, even if he does not approve them.

Behind his *xingling* poetics is a humanistic philosophy of life, which is not all about grand things. Wang Zhaosheng[①], a researcher on Lin Yutang, lists four aspects of his philosophy of life: (1) attention to the physical comforts such as dressing, food, travel and sex; (2) emphasis on reasonableness; (3) the happiness of the individual's self as the end of living; (4) ignorance of issues larger than the life of the individual (Wang, 2003). The end of living to Lin Yutang is living itself.

To go with the familiar subjects is Lin Yutang's emphasis on common

---

① Whose publications include: Wang, Zhaosheng (1998). *The Cultural Vision of Lin Yutang*. Beijing: China Social Sciences Press [王兆胜(1998).《林语堂的文化情怀》.北京:中国社会科学出版社] and Wang Zhaosheng (2002). *Random Remarks on Lin Yutang*. Beijing: China Radio International Press. [王兆胜(2002).《闲话林语堂》.北京:中国国际广播出版社]

sense, which he defines as "the plainest and simplest yet sound and reasonable sense required for a problem or situation" (Lin, 1994e: 214). Having common sense to Lin means being close to human nature. With common sense, one can dismiss his own follies with a hearty laugh. Therefore, humor is the cure for human problems. There is humor in words and humor in deeds. According to him, the Chinese are great humorists: "They have a farcical view of life, and a way of withering theories with a laugh. They laugh at everything from the constitution to library and museum regulations." (Lin, 1936: 156) Chinese humor in his view consists more in deeds than in words. Therefore he calls it "unconscious Chinese humor." He explains things in terms of common sense, and a lack of common sense to him is funny enough:

> Recently a "goodwill tax" has been instituted in Szechuen. It is in fact one of those surtaxes which are already over thirty times the regular farm tax. The origin of the name "goodwill" requires, however, a little elucidation. There has been, I suppose, a good deal of bad will between the unpaid soldiers and the people, because the former are always helping themselves from the people. This tax is designed therefore to help pay the soldiers, making it theoretically unnecessary for the soldiers further to help themselves, and therefore it has the tendency of increasing the goodwill of the people towards the soldiers, provided, of course, the soldiers are really going to get the money.
>
> (Lin, 1936: 156)

The whole business is not at all funny. The institution of the "goodwill tax" is outrageous. In this case, it is an irony to say the Chinese are "humorous." Using commonsense knowledge, Lin Yutang exposes the absurdity of the surtax. This is typical of the Lin Yutang humor: it may not be humorous at all but it is viewed as humorous.

In this vein, humor is everywhere. Confucius is a "humorous" guy, and so are Mencius, Liehtse, Su Dongpo (also spelt as Su Tungp'o, Su Tungpo or Su Tung-p'o by Lin), and Feng Yühsiang. In "On the Humor of Confucius" (Lin, 1994h), Lin Yutang cites some anecdotes of Confucius to prove that the sage is a humorous man. Faced with starvation, his disciples started to complain. Confucius stayed calm and continued to sing and play music. "This gang of us, what a sorry shape we are in! Neither like cows nor tigers. Why do we sink so low?" On another occasion, Confucius and his disciples got lost on the way. Someone found him at the east gate of the town and later described him as a "homeless dog." When this was reported to Confucius, he said, "I don't know what else I was like. A homeless dog? Kind of." In the case of Confucius, what Lin Yutang wants to stress is the humanity of the man, not the saintliness of the sage.

To Lin, "humor is an attitude, and a philosophy of life" (1994h: 285). It is humanity itself.

> ... Only one who has the proper philosophy of life and an understanding of the nature of things and who can speak with good sense can produce humor. The culture, life, literature, and philosophy of any nation need to be nurtured in humor, without which culture grows hypocritical, life fraudulent, thinking sterile, literature withered, and the human soul bogged.
>
> (Lin, 1994h: 285. Translated from the Chinese.)

Besides being a doctrine of the *Analects Fortnightly*, humor is an important part of what he has translated. For example, *A Nun of Taishan (a Novelette) and Other Translations* is full of "humorous" pieces.

3 The Familiar Style as the Form of Expression

Second, "self-expression" means the individual author's own style of expression.

A believer in self-expression is certainly a disbeliever in rules. He will do away with all techniques of writing. In "There Are No Rules for Composition"①, he says:

> The *baguwen* [Note: stiff, formatted writing for civil examinations in Imperial China] has rules but a [good] composition doesn't. A rule-governed composition becomes a *baguwen*. Chinese students are fond of studying the literary rules of the Tongcheng School of old, and love to read the modern subject of rhetoric. Students of literature would like to have a course called "Introduction to Literature." Such stuff is virtually equal to nonsense. Western professors are also in the habit of compiling "College Writing" textbooks, telling the reader that "there must be unity in each paragraph," or "there is a development among the paragraphs," as if the readers were morons. The fact is, the style of a composition lies in the inside rather than the outside.

① "文章无法"

> The idea governs the style. The words are just spontaneous outflows of the author's spirit. One is doomed to fail who strives to learn the techniques of writing rather than cultivating his sensibility of the self.
>
> (Lin, 1994e: 184. Translated from the Chinese.)

As literature should be from the heart and soul of the author and is ungoverned by any rules, Lin's translation theory also displays a distrust of rules for the translator.

The best vehicle of Lin's self-expression is *xiaopinwen* (the familiar essay), the style of his magazine *This Human World*. He speaks for the familiar essay in a number of his own essays published in the magazine: "The Legacy of the Familiar Essay"①, "More on the Legacy of the Familiar Essay"②, "On the Familiar Style"③, "University and the Familiar Style"④.

According to Lin (2004: 219), the so-called *xiaopinwen* may also be called "the familiar style, the lyrical style, the expressive style, the leisure style, the gossip style, or the intimate style." Essays expressing feelings are often emotionally involved and do not make a point of literary techniques. They follow the natural bent of the author's thought.

From the time span of his writings on the familiar style we can know he is quite consistent in his promotion of such a style of writing. In 1937, he translated one of his earlier writings on the subject into English and published it in *The Importance of Living* and in 1960 published it again in *The Importance of Understanding* under the title of "The Familiar Style," in which he says,

> A writer in the familiar style speaks in an unbuttoned mood. He completely exposes his weakness, and is therefore disarming.
>
> The relationship between writer and reader should not be one between an austere schoolmaster and his pupils, but one between friends. Only in this way can warmth be generated.
>
> He who is afraid to use an "I" in his writing will never make a good writer.
>
> I love a liar more than a speaker of truth, and an indiscreet liar more than a discreet

---

① "小品文之遗绪"

② "再谈小品文之遗绪"

③ "论小品文笔调"

④ "大学与小品文笔调"

one. His indiscretions are a sign of his love for his readers.

I trust an indiscreet fool and suspect a lawyer.

The indiscreet fool is a nation's best diplomat. He wins people's hearts.

(Lin, 1960: 326)

Such a preference for expression of individuality in the familiar style has led to Lin's translation of writers of such a tradition.

4 Theoretical Basis: Croce (1866-1952) and Spingarn (1899-1911)

However, Lin Yutang is not an originator of the ideals he has advocated. Such ideals come from a Western current of expressionism in literature and a Chinese artistic tradition, which he calls "the *xingling* school" or "The School of Self-Expression" (1998b: 390). He is an accepter, interpreter, and integrator of both Western and Chinese expression theories of art.

In a number of writings on literature, art, and translation, Lin Yutang unambiguously gives the sources of his expression theory: the expressionistic criticism of Spingarn, the expressivism of Benedetto Croce, and Chinese theories of expression in the nation's literary and artistic tradition.

In 1919 –1920, Lin Yutang studied comparative literature at Harvard. One of his teachers was Irving Babbitt, who "raised a storm in literary criticism" and "was for maintaining a critical standard, as against the school of J. E. Spingarn." (Lin, 1975: 42) Babbitt's influence on the Chinese was far-reaching. Mei Guangdi, Wu Mi, and Liang Shiqiu carried his ideas to China. Despite his admiration of the character and prodigious learning of Babbitt, Lin Yutang became an exponent of the opposite school. He admits in *Memoirs of an Octogenarian* that he refused to accept Babbitt's criteria and once took up the cudgels for Spingarn and eventually was in complete agreement with Croce with regard to the genesis of all criticism as "expression." He was against the Chinese idea of style, which reduced all good writing to a series of "laws" of composition and sentence structures (Lin, 1975: 43).

As early as 1934, Hu Feng pointed out from Lin's 1930 essay "The Destruction of Old Grammar and the Construction of New Grammar"① the

① "旧文法之推翻与新文法之建造"

central philosophy in his work: the aesthetics of the Italian philosopher Benedetto Croce (Hu, 1935). In the essay, Lin Yutang thus speaks of the aesthetics of Croce:

> ... He regards all fine arts as expression and the ability to express as the standard of all fine arts. This fundamental idea does away with all discipline imposed on the expression of individuality. It contradicts traditional ideas and produces a great impact in many fields. It overthrows all the sham of writing techniques, negates the existence of rhetoric, threatens to shed off the confinement of meter and rhythm of poetry and, ethically, gets rid of all moral hypocrisy, a total denial of morality.
>
> (Lin, 1994c, p. 223. Translated from the Chinese.)

To support his understanding of Croce, he translated from English 24 sections from Croce's seminal work *Aesthetic as Science of Expression and General Linguistic.* Among the selections are Croce's comments on translation.

With equal enthusiasm Lin Yutang also embraced the creative criticism of J. E. Spingarn (1899 –1911), who was an American believer in the aesthetics of Croce and applied Croce's theory in literary criticism. Following Croce's line of thinking, Spingarn advocated the same concept of literature as an art of expression. According to Spingarn (1917), advocates of the New Criticism, or Creative Criticism, had done away with "all the old Rules," "the genres," "the comic, the tragic, the sublime and an army of vague abstractions of their kind," "the theory of style with metaphor, simile, and all the paraphernalia of Graeco-Roman rhetoric," "all moral judgement of literature," "the confusion between the drama and the theatre which had permeated dramatic criticism for over half a century," "technique as separate from art," "the history and criticism of poetic themes," "the race, the time, the environment of a poet's work as an element in criticism," "the 'evolution' of literature," and "the old rupture between genius and taste" (pp. 24 –43). Thus, the New Criticism of Spingarn abolished all laws and rules. As part of his promotion of the literary ideals of Spingarn, Lin Yutang translated Spingarn's "The New Criticism" into Chinese and indicated his affinity with such criticism in his preface to the translation. Such criticism according to Lin acknowledges the individuality of each individual work. His belief in Crocean expressionism is unequivocal:

> The expressionists can shed all shackles and overthrow all archetypes because they think that literature (and all works of fine arts) cannot be without the individuality of

> which the work is a natural, unstoppable expression. Now that the individuality is diverse, there cannot be eternal abstract archetypes. The *qinqiang* opera would be lousy if it were judged by the standards of the *kunqu* opera. It is stupid to compare Beethoven's symphonies with the dance music of African barbarians. ①
>
> (Lin, 1994c: 194. Translated from the Chinese.)

5 Theoretical Basis: the Chinese Tradition of *Xingling*

Lin finds similar ideas in the writings of Chinese artists and art critics. For example, in the preface to *The New Criticism*, a collection of his translations, he quotes from Yüan Mei (1716 –1796), who says, "Poetry is from the nature of the individual and has nothing to do with [the ancient models of] the Tang and Song dynasties. If one meticulously and constantly models themselves on the ancients, what they get is a lost country instead of freedom of the spirit, and the value of poetry is lost." (Lin, 1994d: 194. Translated from the Chinese.)

The same idea of expression of the spirit of the individual is found in the works of Zhang Xuecheng of the Qing Dynasty who wrote an article entitled *wenli*, or "The Nature of Composition," which is quoted by Lin Yutang:

> Here are two examples. Someone away from home becomes homesick at the sight of the moon. Is there a necessary connection between the moon and home? A traveler to a remote country becomes nostalgic upon hearing the pattering of the rain. Is there a necessary connection between the rain and nostalgia? The homesick person under the moon. The nostalgic person in the rain. Don't they make the most beautiful writing? But, if such feelings at such moments are kept as secrets or as patterns to be passed on to the students who are told that the moon and the rain must be appreciated in such sad moods, good friends meeting again after a long lapse of time won't believe in the connection, nor will the newlyweds. Therefore, in the learning of writing, what can be taught is some rules of thumb, and what cannot be taught is the use of the heart and the mind ...
>
> (Lin, 1994d: 194. Translated from the Chinese.)

A believer of Croce and Spingarn of the West, Lin finds a kindred spirit in the Kung-an School of poetry, which in his English translations he calls the

---

① "Introduction to *The New Criticism*" (《新的文评》序言), first published in *Yusi*, Vol. 5, No. 30.

School of Expression, or the School of Self-Expression. Yüan Chung-lang (1607 –), with his two brothers, was the founder of the Kung-an School of poetry. The school emphasized *xingling* and dismissed imitation of the ancients in artistic creation. In Yüan's theory of art, there are no formulas for prose, poetry, or paintings. Yüan's emphasis of the expression of individuality in a work of art and his idea of art may be represented by his "On Painting," translated into "Be Yourself" by Lin Yutang. In this essay, Yüan says that "a good artist derives from nature, not from any one person," and therefore a good student "learns the spirit instead of the doctrines," that "a good master takes for his master not someone in the past, but the whole glorious creation" (Lin, 1967: 136). One should try to learn the spirit instead of the mere patterns and stroke techniques of masters of art.

Lin Yutang's "no formulas for translating" and his translation method based on the sentence as a unit and the psychology of writing can also be traced to the writings of other Chinese artists whom he calls "expressionist" and "revolutionary." For example, there is very much in common between the following discourse on art and Lin Yutang's theory of translation:

> In the primeval past there was no method. The primeval chaos was not differentiated. When the primeval chaos was differentiated, method (law) was born. How was this method born? It was born of one-stroke. This one-stroke is that out of which all phenomena are born, applied by the gods and to be applied by man. People of the world do not know this. Therefore this one-stroke (*i-hua*) method is established by me. The establishment of this one-stroke method creates a method out of no-method, and a method which covers all methods.
>
> All painting comes from the understanding mind. If, then, the artist fails to understand the inner law and catch the outward gestures of the delicate complexities of hills and streams and human figures, or the nature of birds and animals and vegetation, or the dimensions of ponds and pavilions and towers, it is because he has not grasped the underlying principle of the one-stroke ...
>
> (Lin, 1967: 150 –151)

Here, the similarity between the "one-stroke method" of painting and Lin Yutang's "one-sentence method" of translating is impressive.

6 A Lonely Song of Self-Expression

To understand Lin Yutang's theory of self-expression we need to put it in a historical perspective. It may be viewed as one of the developments of modern Chinese literature, which started around the May Fourth Movement of 1919, a political movement in nature. At the turn of the century, as the feudal empire was coming to pieces and had been reduced to a semi-feudal, semi-colonial state of being, the nation's intellectuals tried to revitalize the old literature by introducing literary innovations from whatever sources they might discover. A revolution had to take place in the nation's literary tradition, yet the destination was unclear. Many of the nation's leading intellectuals looked to the West for a reinvigoration of the national spirit. The May Fourth Movement brought the spirit of democracy and science to China. Progressive intellectuals devoted themselves to the propagation of new ideas. A literary revolution was part of the cultural revolution to bring about fundamental changes in Chinese thinking and outlook. Chen Duxiu pointed out in 1915 that China's literature and art were then "still in the ages of classicism and romanticism" and that henceforth "the trends should be towards realism."① He called for an emphasis on the truthful recording of facts and events. In 1917, Chen Duxiu came up with a formal proposal for a literary revolution in the February edition of the *New Youth Magazine*②. In January, 1917 Hu Shi published a systematic proposal for a literary reform, emphasizing a reform of the means of literary expression. Later, he summarized his ideas into "a vernacular literature and a literary vernacular." Chen Duxiu, described by Tang Tao as "the true holder of 'the banner of the literary revolution'" and "prime representative of the radical democratic intellectuals", proposed three major principles in his call for reaction against feudal literature in his "On the Literary Revolution":

(1) Get rid of the ornate, adulatory aristocratic literature; create a simple, honest and expressive national literature.

(2) Get rid of the stale, ostentatious literature in the style of classics; create a fresh, sincere and realistic literature.

---

① *Youth Magazine* (《青年杂志》), Vol. 1, No. 4, December 1915.

② 《新青年杂志》

(3) Get rid of the obscure and difficult literature of hermit style; create a lucid and popular literature. (Tang, 1993: 4)

Belonging to a younger generation, Lin Yutang evidently was caught in the intellectual current that was gaining momentum. He looked not only to the West but also to the ancient. Matching Lin's theory with the principles of Chen Duxiu, we can conclude that Lin Yutang basically was an adherent of the idea of new literature except for some minor differences. He detested "ornate, adulatory aristocratic literature" and preferred "simple, honest and expressive literature" except that he was more concerned with individual expression rather than national expression. He renounced the "stale, ostentatious" style of the *baguwen* in favor of the familiar style of writing except that he did not renounce all classics. He preferred a "lucid and popular" familiar essay except that he called for a unity of the vernacular and the classic language in the construction of a new literature.

Lin Yutang adhered to his theory of self-expression from the 1920s and the 1930s all the way to the end of his life. And, after all, there is nothing wrong with expression of the self. The creative mind of the Chinese had been inhibited too long in history. On the positive side, it contributed to the healthy development of the nation's culture. Even today, the idea of self-expression is still important for the development of Chinese literature.

However, Lin's theory of self-expression has its limitations. First, the concept of individuality or self is too abstract. It seems to be independent of any objective conditions, as Hu Feng points out in "On Lin Yutang." An interest in anything under the sun is "individuality," including an interest in bedbugs, smoking, and lying in bed. Confucianism was the target of the literary revolutionists for the inhibition of individuality and sometimes Lin Yutang's own target of criticism for the same reason, but Lin Yutang from time to time arbitrarily describes Confucius as a great humanist and humorist. Second, although the idea of self-expression is good, there were more important agendas in the first half of the twentieth century than mere individual self-expression. National self-expression was more urgent because of the country's semi-feudal and semi-colonial status, which accounted for a flourishing of a proletarian literature for a good part of the century. Partly due to the limitations of such a self-expression theory, Lin Yutang has remained unfortunately a marginal figure in the history of modern Chinese literature, virtually unaccounted for in histories of Chinese literature such as Tang Tao's *History of Modern Chinese Literature*. One of his essays, "A Single Flower on a Lone Cliff" thus describes his persistence in self-expression and the accompanying loneliness and solitude:

> As I was walking along a mountain path, a red flower on a lone cliff caught my eye with its singular brilliance. It seemed to be smiling at me and my fellow travelers. On a closer look, the plant was seen to take roots in a small crevice in the rock! I marveled. Everything in the universe has a beginning and an end, but in the course of life they never fail to give full play to their nature. A flower opens. Such is the nature of the flower. Following nature is the Tao. The flower in bloom does not care if anyone notices it. A flower opens anyway, be it in the hustle and bustle of the city, among the wild plants in the mountains, or even on the top of a deserted cliff. The orchid has a natural fragrance, which is emitted whether or not a butterfly is passing. Such is the nature of the flower and it simply cannot be helped. If anyone treats the flower against its nature so that it does not open, they simply kill it. Even the tyrant's servant whose mouth has to keep shut would like to bellow at the sky once he could get away for a while to a place with no people. Qu Yuan, the great patriot, before ending his life in the Miluo River, wrote his plaintive swan song in desperation. Laotse wrote his five-thousand character *Dao De Jing* before he went beyond the Han'gu Pass and disappeared into nowhere. Was he really coerced into writing by the general at the Pass? Certainly not. The ancients wrote as their hearts felt. If they found their dissertations on government a total waste of their talent they would turn to fiction writing as an outlet of their energies. In their times, there was no such thing as royalties nor could they accrue any literary fame. Instead, their lives might be endangered. However, they would not be happy unless they spoke their minds. In the history of Chinese literature, it is such stories by anonymous authorship that are worthy of passing down from generation to generation, not the well-polished and well remunerated epitaphs. These stories are each like a single flower on a lone cliff. Thus, it is human nature that drives humans to talk, to write, to draw, to paint, and to express themselves in any other form. As the Chinese saying goes, "the cat calls in spring to mate and spring calls on the cat to mate," but the old monk never dares to call. He is confined by a civilization that is human. As a matter of fact, he does not call for sex. He steals it. With an understanding of this, it is easier to see that it is not so possible to gag a person to keep his mouth shut. As long as the plant has life, in time its flower is to open, even on a lone and bare cliff.
>
> (Lin, 1994a: 150 –151. Translated from the Chinese.)①

① The translation was first published in a latest book of mine *A Revolution: Learn to Learn English*, Hubei Education Press, 2007. pp. 145 –147.

The "single flower on a lone cliff," an image of pathetic beauty, is a kind of self-portrait of Lin Yutang.

II *Xingling* in Translation

The typical approach to studying Lin's theory of translation is to go to his thesis "On Translation," which so far has defied many interpreters. For one thing, it seems to include everything that concerned the translator at the time it was written. For another, it does not follow a fully logical organization. Despite its inner systematicity, it remains very much a fragmentary account of the subject of translation. It is by no means easy to sort it out into better logic. Different researchers always have different findings or conclusions. For instance, one researcher says that "beauty" is the end of Lin's translations, because she notices that the last of the three principles Lin Yutang holds for translation is "beauty." Without distinguishing between beauty and aesthetics, she calls Lin's translation "formal aesthetic translation", which I suppose many people like me do not understand. Chen Rongdong rightly states that Lin's translation theory covers three aspects of translational aesthetics: the aesthetic subject (the translator), the aesthetic object (the original) and the aesthetic product (translations) though Lin Yutang himself does not use those terms (Chen, 1997). Zhou Shibao analyzes the text and finds that Lin Yutang is the first Chinese theorist to study translation from the perspectives of linguistics and psychology (Zhou, 2004). On its own, "On Translation" defies interpretation but viewed in the light of Lin Yutang's *xingling* theory of literature, it gives the interpreter an easier time. When links between this thesis and other texts (of his own or of other theorists) are followed, it is not difficult to see that Lin Yutang is framing his translation theory in terms of the expressionist aesthetics of *xingling*. The major concepts and propositions of his translation theory generally agree with his theory of self-expression, which is born of Western and Chinese expression theories of art. The following is a rough comparison:

Table 2 Lin on Translation and Expressionists on Art

Lin Yutang in "On Translation"	Expressionists on Art
Translation is an art.	Literature, painting, sculpture, music and dance are forms of art. (Croce, *Aesthetic as Science of Expression and General Linguistic*)
Translation is impossible.	Each work of art is an individual expression and therefore translation is impossible. (Croce, *Aesthetic as Science of Expression and General Linguistic*)
"the relative possibility of translation"	"expressions share resemblances" (Croce, *Aesthetic as Science of Expression and General Linguistic*)
"There are no formulas for translating (Translation is intuition)."	There are no formulas for writing (Art is intuition). (Croce, *Aesthetic as Science of Expression and General Linguistic*, Spingarn, *Creative Criticism*, Zhang Xuecheng, "The Nature of Composition")
"the total concept"	"the indivisibility of a work of art" (Croce, *Aesthetic as Science of Expression and General Linguistic*)
"translating by the sentence"	The "one-stroke method" of painting (Shi Tao)
"I never translate anything except those I like."	Art is expression of the self. (Croce, *Aesthetic as Science of Expression and General Linguistic*)
"inner form" and "outer form" in translation	Inner form and outer form in art (Shi Tao)

Thus Lin's theory of translation can be called the *xingling* theory of translation.

1 The Artistic Nature of Translation: Translatability vs. Untranslatability

As can be seen from the above table, Croce's aesthetic as the science of expression is the underlying theoretical framework of Lin Yutang's theory of translation in its explanation of such issues as translatability, artistic genius, translation procedures and translation criticism. As Lin's poetics has touched on the role of literature, he does not care to reiterate the role of translation. His translation theory is mostly dedicated to the study of procedural issues of the art, i.e., translation proper.

Chinese translators prior to Lin Yutang were complaining about the enormity of their difficulties but did not quite understand the cause of the difficulties. Yan Fu never prescribed the so-called "three principles of translation." He dared not venture to do so. In fact, he called them "the three difficulties of translation." Because of the relative accuracy of his description of the translator's predicament and the great influence of his serious work as a translator, the three words (*xin*, *da*, and *ya*) have been sanctified by mainstream Chinese translators and theorists and only occasionally challenged by scholars like Chen Xiying. Yet, Yan Fu did not say, and it cannot be known whether he knew, what is behind the enormous difficulties. Then came Lin Yutang, who was one of the earliest if not the first theorist in the country to define the limits of translation in terms of impossibility versus possibility, or in today's academic terminology, untranslatability versus translatability.

From an aesthetic perspective, Lin Yutang focuses on the impossibility to translate *yishuwen*, or "artistic texts", his way to refer to literature, particularly poetry. Quoting Croce, he says, "All genuine works of art are impossible to translate," and "as the purest works of art among all literature, and made of the essence of a language, poetry is the least possible to translate." (Lin, 1994b: 318) In Crocean aesthetics, any expression is an independent expression and stands on its own and modes of expression do not exist, and a philosophical classification of expressions is not possible:

> Single expressive facts are so many individuals, of which the one cannot be compared with the other, save generically, in so far as each is expression. To use the language of the schools, expression is a species which cannot in its turn perform the functions of genus. Impressions, that is to say contents, vary; every content differs from every other content, because nothing in life repeats itself; and the continuous variation of contents follows the irreducible variety of expressive facts, the aesthetic syntheses of the impressions.
>
> (Croce, 1909: 110 –111)

Therefore, it is impossible to make translations:

> A corollary of this is the impossibility of translations, in so far as they pretend to effect the transference of one expression into another, like a liquid poured from a vase of a certain shape into a vase of another shape. We can elaborate logically what we have already elaborated in aesthetic form only; but we cannot reduce that which has already possessed its aesthetic form to another form also aesthetic. In truth, every translation either diminishes and spoils; or it creates a new expression, by putting the former back into the crucible and mixing it with other impressions belonging to the pretended translator. In the former case, the expression always remains one, that of the original, the translation being more or less deficient, that is to say, not properly expression: in the other case, there would certainly be two expressions, but with two different contents. "Ugly faithful ones or faithless beauties" is a proverb that well expresses the dilemma with which every translator is faced. In aesthetic translations, such as those which are word for word or interlinear, or paraphrastic translations, are to be looked upon as simple commentaries on the original.
>
> (ibid.: 111 –112)

Lin does not really neglect the untranslatable elements in other types of literature. In real life, it is hard to separate what is "art" and what is not "art" in a text. A non-artistic text such as a news story, a speech transcript, commercial literature or even a technical document may contain elements that are "artistic." Metaphors, puns and other word-plays abound. Besides, there are nuances of the meaning of words which do not have exact equivalents in the target language. He does not directly address this issue, but in his proverbial casual style of writing, this seeming negligence is compensated for in his discussion of the *fidelity* principle. In his definition of *fidelity*, he states, "absolute fidelity is impossible":

> Words can be beautiful in sound, in signification, in communion of the spirit, in tone, in style and in form. The translator either gets the meaning (*yi*) at the cost of the spirit (*shen*), or gets the spirit at the cost of the form (*ti*). It is not possible at all to render at once the meaning, the spirit, the tone, the style and the sound. Every word is unique. A word can find a close synonym in another language but there are no equivalents that are exactly identical.
>
> (Lin, 1994b: 315. My translation.)

However, there is something that the translator can do, according to Croce's *Aesthetic as Science of Expression and General Linguistic*. Translations as works of art and as likenesses are relatively possible because expressions (works of art) share resemblances, and

> It is in these resemblances that lies the relative possibility of translations. This does not consist of the reproduction of the same original expressions (which it would be vain to attempt), but in the measure that expressions are given, more or less nearly resembling those. The translation that passes for good is an approximation which has original value as a work of art and can stand by itself.
>
> (Croce, 1909: 119 – 120; See Lin's translation: Lin, 1994d: 230.)

In Lin Yutang's discussion of "artistic texts," he embraces the idea that translation is not reproduction but production and adds that "translators of art shall treat translation itself as a fine art." (Lin, 1994b: 320)

Although Lin Yutang is not the originator of the concepts of translatability and untranslatability, his quotes and selected translation of Croce's discourse on the subject shows his sensibility as a translator and translation theorist. The problem is that in the aesthetics of Croce translation is doomed in untranslatability. Aesthetics or the philosophy of art alone does not disclose all the truth about translation, which is not a prototypical art form. Ten years after Lin Yutang wrote "On Translation," the subject came to the attention of Mr. He Lin (1902 – 1992), philosopher and translator, who, through a logical analysis of translation, pushed translatability to the fore. In his 1940 article "On Translation," Professor He points out that the relationship between message (*yi*) and media (*yan*), and between thought (*dao*) and literature (*wen*) is that between noumenon (*ti*) and phenomenon (*yong*), and between one (*yi*) and many (*duo*). He Lin's argument in rough translation goes like this:

> The signifier expresses the signified and literature is the vehicle of thought. In such a relationship, noumenon and phenomenon are at one. Therefore, the truth of the message and the profundity of thought can be checked against the embodying language. One who truly knows something or understands the message from others cannot fail to express himself in appropriate language. The task of the translator is to express what he knows or what he understands in appropriate language. Therefore translation is possible. Only works that rely on wordplays and are particular to a certain community cannot be translated. Nor are they worthy of translation. As to poetry, poems that carry shared meanings, feelings or truth can be translated, but the beauty of sound, rhythm and form cannot be translated and where possible can only be translated with a reinvented beautiful form on condition that the meaning and feeling of the poem be grasped.

In contrast, it can be said that Lin Yutang's aesthetic theory like many other theories of translation has its weaknesses. Translation after all is always open to discussion.

2 Artistic Genius in Translating

In the eyes of Lin Yutang, the art of translating involves a special artistic genius but that genius is born with the translator. There is a passageway between the layman and the expert translator. For beginners of translation, a certain training is beneficial.

Translation Is Intuition. Lin Yutang's understanding of the nature of translation as art is the keynote of his entire discourse on translation. It leads to identification of translation with the fine arts. In its important aspects, translation is like any other fine art. The leading argument in his 1933 article "On Translation" is "There are no formulas for translating". This same statement may also be translated into English as "There is no set way for translating," "There are no laws for translating" or "There are no rules for translation." In his view, translation is primarily a psychological process, and a satisfactory translation solution shall be based on an understanding of the linguistic and psychological facts of writing. Knowledge of the nature of word meaning is the basis of accepting or rejecting word-for-word translation. Understanding of the psychological processes of writing is the basis of the translator's strategy in translating[①]. Thus, he denounces any techniques for translation. Now that there are no formulas, who decides how to translate? None but the translator. The thesis — "There are no formulas for translating" — is exactly Crocean in nature. If there are no formulas, then each translation is an individual product (expression). The success or failure of a translation depends on the translator's artistic genius and experience, or in other words, artistic intuition, one of the two forms of human knowledge in Croce's aesthetics, which states: "Human

① In fact, the psychological processes of writing constitute his constantly explored theme in quite a number of essays which appear in his collections: the *Xing Su Ji* (1934), *Pi Jing Ji* (1936), *Da Huang Ji* (1934), *Shi Yi Ji* (1934) in two volumes, and *Wu Suo Bu Tan He Ji* (1974).

knowledge has two forms: it is either intuitive knowledge or logical knowledge; knowledge obtained through the imagination or knowledge obtained through the intellect; knowledge of the individual or knowledge of the universal; of individual things or of the relations between them: it is, in fact, productive either of images or of concepts." (Croce, 1909: 1) As art is intuitive knowledge, it is guided by no rules and bound by no discipline of any kind.

Intuition Can Be Cultivated. Believing that translation is "an art" and that the success of translation depends on the translator's genius, Lin Yutang does not think that genius only belongs to a few elite translators. He would rather believe that translators can be trained. In "On Translation," he makes a point of training for a successful translator. As has been quoted earlier, "The art of translation requires, first, a thorough understanding of the language and content of the source text, second, the translator's good command of the native language to enable him to write clear and fluent Chinese, and third, training in translation to give him a proper understanding of the standards of good translation and translation procedures. There cannot be anything else to regulate the translator as English grammar cannot regulate English writers." (Lin. 1994b: 305) Lin makes a point that experience and training in translation are needed for a non-genius to become a genius, providing a passageway from the former to the latter. Again, this is an instance of applying Croce's theory to translation. According to Croce's Aesthetic as Science of Expression and Generial Linguistic, differences between a genius and a non-genius are merely quantitative. There is the identification of nature between great artists and the common people. There is a passageway from non-genius to genius. Thus, theoretically the cultivation of translator's genius is feasible. Lin's vision is borne out by the flourishing translator training programs all across the world today.

3 The Transfer of Content

An artistic expression needs to have its matter or expressive content. Translation as an expressive activity involves the transfer of matter from one language to another. In terms of matter or content, the translator faces two tasks: what to transfer and how to transfer, because for the translator who is supposed to be an artist, translation shall be understood to be a means to an end and then the means itself shall be shaped toward an effective realization of the end.

In "On Translation," virtually nothing is said on the first task. This does not mean that Lin Yutang does not care about what to translate. The concern is already in his *xingling* theory of literature which demands that content echo feelings. The original expression must have the sympathies of the translator. When the spiritual communion is reached with the original author, the translator understands what the author was trying to say, and given freedom in expression shall speak the way the author would say it in the target language if he were thinking and writing in that language. To Lin Yutang identification with the original author is of primary importance, as evidenced by the following selection from the "Preface" to *The Importance of Understanding*:

> ... But I am also a translator, and felt no obligation to translate any author except those I liked, if not approved. Translation is a very subtle thing; unless you are emotionally in contact with the original author, you cannot do a good job of it. In translating an author, you practically engage to speak for him in a new language, and you cannot do so unless you are speaking for an old friend, so to speak. And your friend, knowing how strange his own expressions must often sound in a foreign language, gives you some freedom in expression, provided that he can trust that you truly understand what he was trying to say, and that it would be the way he would say it in English if he were thinking and writing in English.
>
> (Lin Yutang, 1960: 19)

Thus, theoretically, translation to Lin Yutang is part of his expression.

After the first task is done comes the second task: how to transfer the content, the professional part of the artist's job. This, first of all, involves an understanding of fidelity.

But the word *fidelity* is too ethical and its meaning is not fixed. Traditionally, translators may agree on fidelity as a goal but they disagree on the means to achieve it. Some translators think that every word should be preserved in order to be faithful. The result of their translation is what Dryden (1992, pp. 13 –17) terms "metaphrase": turning an author word by word, and line by line, from one language into another. Some translators would consider meaning or sense more important than the words themselves. Such an attitude toward fidelity leads to what is termed by Dryden "paraphrase," or translation with latitude, where the author is kept in view by the translator, so as never to be lost, but his words are not so strictly followed as his sense, which is allowed to be amplified but not altered. Other translators regard fidelity as the production of the spirit of the original and consequently they use a method which Dryden calls "imitation," where the translator assumes the liberty not only to vary from the words and sense but to discard both as he sees occasion and, taking only some general hints from the original, to run division on the groundwork as he pleases.

In "On Translation," Lin does speak of four degrees of translational fidelity he has observed from the works of his contemporary translators, using the terminology of the day: literal translation (*zhiyi*), word-for-word translation (*siyi*), free translation (*yiyi*), and licentious translation (*huyi*). "Word-for-word" is the worst-case scenario of being literal and "license" the worst of being free. In his view, literalists tend to be enslaved by their worship of the words of the source text if they go too far, and liberalists, when they go too far, are likely to justify any liberty to achieve fluency, elegance, and a likeness of the ancient Chinese ideology in the target text at the cost of the source text. Nobody can surpass Yan Fu and Lin Shu in their license. In his view, the very terminology is inadequate, for one can hardly distinguish between literal and word-for-word translation, between liberal and licentious translation. "Liberal" and "literal" not only fail to account for the procedures of translation but also are likely to give rise to confusion and misunderstanding. Lin Yutang's solution to this confusion is to drop the technical issue and shift the attention to inner laws governing translation.

He sees fidelity in a trinity of fidelity, fluency, and beauty. The three principles of translation represent three responsibilities: that toward the original author, that toward the reader, and that toward art. Here, fidelity becomes three-fold. It is no longer fidelity to the original author. It is also fidelity to the translation reader and to art (or the translator himself as an artist).

Therefore, we have this sophisticated definition of fidelity interlocked with fluency and beauty, a summary of his explanations scattered in "On Translation":

Fidelity needs to be understood in four ways: (1) *Fidelity* does not mean translating word for word. The translator has to understand but has no responsibility to translate every word in the source text. His fidelity shall go to the meaning of the words combined instead of the individual words. (2) The translator in addition to transferring meaning of the source text shall transfer its spirit. A translation shall faithfully preserve the tone and implied meaning of its original. The "tone" is the emotional coloring of a word, or its implicative power. Language is not only used to represent images and meaning but also to communicate feelings. It is not only to get the meaning across but also to get the reader emotionally engaged. (3) Absolute fidelity is impossible. Translational fidelity is relative. Word-for-word translators want 100% fidelity, which can only be found in a utopia. The best translator can arrive at a fidelity somewhere between 70% to 90%. The sounds, the meaning, the tone, the genius, the style, and the form of the words are respectively beautiful in their own right. The translator either gets the meaning and neglects the spirit or has the spirit but loses what contains it. By no means can he translate all of these simultaneously. (4) Fidelity does not mean that awkward language is acceptable in the target text. As the translator has a responsibility for the original author, he also has a responsibility for the readers. His translation has to be fluent.

4 The Creation of Form

As has been noted, in Lin Yutang's explanation of the *fidelity* principle, he particularly points out that *fidelity* does not mean awkwardness in the target language. Since he favors the familiar style of writing, he has an outspoken preference for a form of translation readily accessible to the translation reader. A translation must be as readable as an original writing in the target language (though Lin himself has not always succeeded in doing this). In the creation of the acceptable form, fluency is the guiding principle.

In Lin's view, fluency in translation is identical to fluency in writing:

> Both translating and writing follow basically the same psychological processes. In writing, the sentence is the basic unit and in translating the sentence must also be the basic unit so that the translation can be fluent. Writing is analytic rather than synthetic. One has a general idea (total concept) first and then breaks it down to different parts. It is not the other way round. A fluent translation gives priority to sentence meaning instead of word meaning.
>
> (Lin, 1994b: 317)

Thus the Crocean intuition of artistic expression is applied in translation.

Here we see that Lin Yutang advocates the subordination of form to content. A form is good only if it serves to convey the content well.

Lin thinks that the issue of form particularly stands out in *yishuwen*, or "artistic texts" (Lin, 1994b: 318 – 319). Poetry, for example, so much depends on the author's play with the source language that content and form are often inseparable. When beauty lies exclusively in the use of the source language, translation is impossible. When an "artistic text" has to be translated, the translator needs to first get an idea of the demeanor and style of the original author and then produce an imitation of the work.

In the same way as Shi Tao talks about the outer and inner principles of painting, Lin Yutang calls the translator's attention to "outer form" and "inner form" in literature (Lin, 1994b: 320). The outer form refers to the length and complexity of the sentences and types of poetry. The inner form reflects the author's character and personality traits. Knowledge of the outer form may be acquired by trial and error, but knowledge of the inner form can only be acquired through accumulated literary experience instead of instruction by the teacher or the textbook.

The form should be beautiful. Lin Yutang's concern with the beauty of literary language has continued all through his creative and translating career. He not only emphasizes beauty but also proposes ways to achieve it. In "On Elegance and Rigor"①, he points out that the English language is elegant and rigorous because it has an indigenous Anglo-Saxon origin, which gives it vigor, and an aristocratic French origin, which gives it elegance. He maintains that, if the Chinese language is to achieve elegance and vigor, it has to embrace two sources, the vernacular and classical Chinese literature. In his view, the three translation principles proposed by Yan Fu can actually represent the trend of the development of the Chinese language. In "On the Unity of the Vernacular and the Classical Language"② he proposes two principles for achieving beauty in literary Chinese: (1) The vernacular shall be the basis for literary language and classical Chinese idioms can be used when necessary; (2) Classical idioms can

---

① "On Elegance and Rigor" (释雅健) in *Wu Suo Bu Tan He Ji* (1974).

② "On the Unity of the Vernacular and the Classical Language" (论言文一致) in *Wu Suo Bu Tan He Ji*, 1974.

be used on some occasions but shall not be used on others, depending on whether an idiom is appropriate and can best serve the writer's intention.

5 The Harmony of Content and Form

The trinity of *fidelity*, *fluency*, *and beauty* must not be understood separately. Lin's reference to beauty and aesthetics does not mean that he advocates and makes "beautiful translations." We do not lack evidence that he sometimes makes "ugly translations." Rather, his aesthetics actually means giving an appropriate form to matter. Translational aesthetics to him means harmony of content and form.

Transcending the Dichotomy of Literalism vs. Liberalism

Literalism and liberalism are no more than two translation strategies that can be adopted by any translator at one time or at different times based on the translator's comprehensive assessment of a specific task. The two strategies may serve the same end. Liberalists may have the same reverence toward the original as the literalists do. For example, in biblical translation, liberalists may be as devoted to the spirit of the original as translators who produce more "accurate" versions of the New Testament. Either strategy can be employed to preserve the holiness of the original. The liberal approach brings what is in the original close to the reader and the literal approach brings the reader to what is in the original. We know that both approaches shorten the distance between the reader and the content of the original. However, the technical issue has often been problematized by people taking extreme views, especially in religious or ideological contexts. The theoretical battle between the two strategies interpreted in extreme terms has never ceased, often veiled in new terminologies. The contending parties often do not admit that however different the views they have they often do things the same way, nor do they admit that, under the guidance of the same theory, different translators always translate the same thing differently. In fact, the difference between the two strategies or approaches is but a matter of degree. In the 1920s and 1930s, the two types of translators in China were heatedly engaged in debates among themselves over literalism and liberalism or their political counterparts, Europeanization and domestication. It was in this historical context that Lin Yutang came up with a depoliticized theory of self-expression, trying to put an end to the dispute by a professional analysis of the issue. Contention over literalism or liberalism to him was not worth the while as they were such vague terms (See Lin's definition of *fidelity* in this Chapter). His solution was to discard and transcend the dichotomy①.

"Total Concept" and "Translating by the Sentence"

Lin Yutang's approach is not to concentrate on the word or the sense of the word. In his discussion of *fidelity* and *fluency* in "On Translation," he moves up to a higher level, the meaning derived from the combination of all the words in a sentence. Here, he introduces the concept of "total concept" and translation to him is about the reproduction of the total concept through an analytical method. In accordance with his analysis of the psychological processes of text formation, he dismisses the word-for-word strategy and proposes a sentence-based strategy. In his view, word-for-word translators are wrong in that they believe that the meaning of a sentence is the mathematical sum total of the meanings of isolated individual words. He sees the meaning of a word as elusive and changing in different contexts and a sentence has its structure organized by a total sentence meaning. The meanings of words are interconnected and combine to make a new meaning, a total meaning, which he calls *zongyiyi*, which he equates with the German word *gesamtvorstellung*② (Lin, 1994b: 310) in one place and with the English expression *total concept* (Lin, 1994b: 316) in another. This total meaning is based on the flexible use and organization of individual words. While translating, the translator shall first of all accurately extract the meaning of the whole sentence and then convey that meaning

---

① However, despite his dislike of the two terms, he has been unable to eradicate them in his discussions of translation.

② The word should be spelt as *Gesamtvorstellung*. It is said that nouns begin with capital letters in German and this in general should be preserved. In addition, I have no idea whether the word is used accurately by Lin Yutang. Timothy Huson (an American scholar who knows German) says that the German word must be translated into *total representation*, *complete representation*, etc.

according to the grammatical convention of the target language. Therefore, we have a sentence-based translation process that may be graphically represented below:

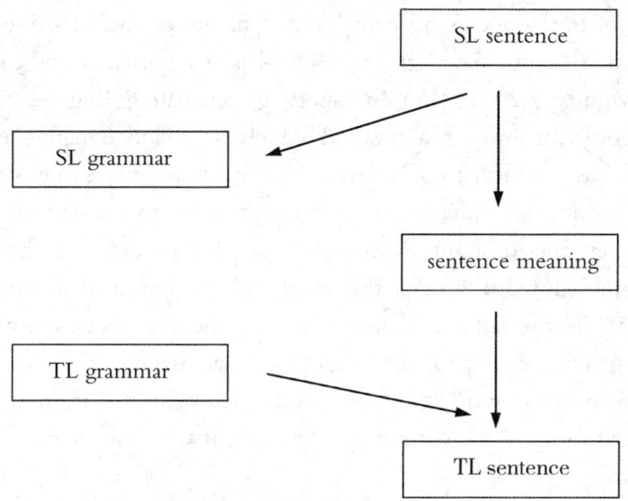

Figure 1 A Graphic Demonstration of Lin Yutang's Sentence Translation
SL = source language; TL = target language

Thus, translation techniques do not exist. In order to reproduce the total concept, any method may be adopted, and the contention between *yiyi* (liberal or free translation, sense translation) and *zhiyi* (direct or literal translation) is dissolved.

Such an insight makes Lin Yutang's theory quite progressive in the history of translation. This sentence-based strategy marks a move-away from the tangle of literalist-liberalist contention and offers a comprehensive solution for the translator, permitting him to use any methods at his convenience. It is a significant methodological progress in translation studies. Unfortunately, the Lin Yutang approach is not so much propagated as the much later American approaches such as Eugene Nida's dynamic (functional) equivalence and Catford's translation shifts (1965). In China, Lin's theory has been undervalued, as pointed out by Chen Rongdong (1997), and in today's craze for Western theories of translation, it continues to be ignored by the leading translation researchers of the country. In the West, in contradistinction to his popular translations, his progressive translation theory is virtually unknown, as borne out by Jeremy Munday's comment on Nida: "The key role played by Nida is to point the road away from strict word-for-word equivalence. His introduction of the concepts of formal and dynamic equivalence were crucial in introducing a receptor-based (or reader-based) orientation to translation theory." (Munday, 2001: 42) In the 1960s and later, Eugene Nida wrote a number of books promoting a method which he called dynamic equivalence, later rephrased as functional equivalence①. Nida distinguishes between dynamic equivalence and formal equivalence as two approaches to translation. The former seeks to convey the thought expressed in a source text (at the expense of literalness, original word order, the source text's grammatical voice, etc., if necessary), while the latter attempts to render the text word-for-word (at the expense of natural expression in the target language, if necessary). One emphasizes readability and the other literal fidelity to the source text. Nida's approach is the former. This is but an old method with a new name, as pointed out by Marlowe. ②

Behind Catford's well-known concept of *translation shifts* is something similar to Lin Yutang's "total concept," which permits the translator to make changes across different linguistic levels and categories. Catford (1965) painstakingly explains the various shifts that may occur in linguistic transfer, but no matter how hard he tries, his linguistic or "scientific" approach is very sophisticated and cannot take into account of all *shifts* that may occur. Lin Yutang's theory is directed to the "inner form" while Catford addresses the "outer form." Therefore, Lin Yutang's discussion is more profound.

---

① Nida's books include *Message and Mission: The Communication of the Christian Faith* (New York: Harper and Brothers, 1960); *Toward a Science of Translating, with Special Reference to Principles and Procedures Involved in Bible Translating* (Leiden: Brill, 1964); *The Theory and Practice of Translation* (Leiden: Brill, 1969); *From One Language to Another: Functional Equivalence in Bible Translation* (co-authored with Jan de Waard, Nashville: Thomas Nelson, 1986).

② Marlowe, M. (2004). Against the Theory of "Dynamic Equivalence" (Revised, April 2004). Bible Research, Internet Resources for Students of Scripture. http://www.bible-researcher.com/dynamic-equivalence.html

Thus compared with the two later theories, Lin Yutang's aesthetic theory of translation has an obvious advantage in the theoretical high ground it holds and its practicality.

However, Lin Yutang focuses his discussion of the "total concept" only on the sentence level. The focus on the sentence is a matter of procedural convenience. It makes the three principles of translation more workable. In comparison with what has been called Yan Fu's theory, Lin Yutang has moved a step forward in his theoretical sophistication.

Although it is not explicitly stated, the idea of "total concept" may also apply to units lower or higher than the sentence. Many of the examples he cites are not sentences, e.g., "parson's nose" (席上清炖鸡或烧鸭之臀部), "street Arab" (街上无依之儿童或其他乡顽不受教育者), "a young man in a hurry" (热心改革社会的青年), etc. It may equally hold well if applied to the textual level. Such application is found in his discussion of poetry translation, but in that case, "total concept" becomes *yijing* (*essence*, *spirit* or *total feeling*).

What Lin Yutang means by *juyi*, or translating by the sentence is in effect: (1) For fidelity, in approaching the source text, the sentence is a much more meaningful unit of understanding than the word; (2) For fluency, in producing the target text, the sentence is a much more plausible unit of expression than the word.

Some people translate *juyi* into sentence-for-sentence translation. This is the result of taking Lin Yutang literally. Translations do not consist of perfect sentence-to-sentence correspondences. Lin Yutang's own translations are not made up of perfect sentence-to-sentence correspondences as you may see later in this book. One kind of deviations from sentence-to-sentence correspondence has been pointed out by Yang Liu: translation of words into sentences (Yang, 2004, 2005).

In reality, the boundaries between sentences are not always clear. Colons, question marks and exclamation marks may serve as superficial boundaries. Very often there is a very close logical connection between sentences which may be treated as one, and there are also sentences which involve sophisticated relationships so that they may be broken apart while the sentence meaning is intact.

Furthermore, as words shall be viewed in contexts, so shall sentences. The meaning of a sentence is not always decided by the organization of the individual words. The sentence acquires meaning from its context too. Sometimes, the context is not linguistic even. A *New York Times* article is entitled: "To All the Girls I've Rejected" (March 23, 2006). The average reader quickly associates it with the popular song "To All the Girls I Have Loved Before." It is the author's intention to establish such a link in order to be funny and attract the eyeball. When such a title appears in the education column with the picture of a letter from the college admissions officer, the meaning of the sentence takes a drastic change. Another title: "Way Upstairs, Downstairs," published in the *New York Times Magazine* (April 16, 2006) acquires meaning through the name of the column "The Way We Live Now" and the content of the article, which is the increasing gap between the rich and the poor. In this second article, the meaning of a sentence often has a great deal to do with a sentence or sentences before and/or after. For example:

> *I've seen the prices on the menus. I've also seen the pay stubs of the cooks. I've stood in the mansions, let in by the maids, and listened to the string quartets, whose players I've met in the coat aisle at Goodwill.*

Without context, we will never know the prices are high in the first sentence, the pay is low in the second. The three sentences combine to make a new meaning: The rich are very rich and the poor are very poor. In this case, the three sentences can be treated as one unit and put into one Chinese sentence or as many Chinese sentences as the translator feels right.

Lin Yutang is certainly not blind to the limitation of the sentence-based strategy of translation, for he is aware that there are no formulas for translating. In the elaboration of his theory, he does not go any further than what he feels is practical, necessary and adequate.

Identification with "Paraphrase" in The Wisdom of Confucius

It is interesting to note that Lin Yutang never talks in the English language about translation the way he does in the Chinese language. In Chinese he has dedicated articles to the issue of translating and framed his view of translation in accordance with the popularly known three concepts of *xin* (fidelity), *da* (fluency) and *ya* (elegance, beauty) by Yan Fu, an early Chinese translator of Charles Darwin and Adam Smith. In his Chinese discourse on translation, he proposes a translation method called *juyi* (sentence translation, sentence-based translation, or translation by the sentence). Neither the principles nor the method of "sentence translation" occurs in his English discourse on translation.

As a matter of fact, despite his impressive volumes of English translations and despite his many remarks on translation in Chinese, in English he is rather silent on the topic. After all, among the English readers, he does not see as many learners of translation as he has seen in China. He has never written in English anything like "On Translation." His English discourse on translation mainly appears as passing remarks in his English writings or in prefaces and introductions to his books.

In the "Introduction" to *The Wisdom of Confucius*, he declares that his method of translation in the book is *paraphrase* and believes that in this case it is "the best and most satisfying method" (Lin, 1938: 48). His method of paraphrase is based on meaning or thought. After the translator has grasped the meaning of the sentence, he is faced with two jobs. He has to choose one out of a number of synonyms and failure to get at the exact word would completely fail to render the meaning of the remark clear to the reader. Therefore, he has to translate the same *teh* (*de*) into different words in different contexts: *virtue*, *character*, *temper*, *soul*, etc. In the second place, the translator cannot avoid putting the thought in the more precise concepts of a modern language. Thus, "Language expressive only" in the ancient Chinese text has to be translated by the modern translator into something like "Expressiveness is the only principle of language," or "Expressiveness is the sole *concern*, or *aim*, or *principle*, of rhetoric." (ibid: 48 -52)

It is evident that the so-called method of *paraphrase* is exactly in keeping with the "total concept" and the method of "sentence translation".

On another occasion, in *The Wisdom of China and India*, Lin Yutang does not use the word *paraphrase* but says something to the same effect by emphasizing the need for "certain stupidity," i.e., not to be "brilliant" by trying to reproduce everything in the original and placing "undue and incorrect stress on individual words in regard to their etymology." It is important to seek the exact word for the preservation of the style, but the exact word is a suitable word in the target-language context, not necessarily an equivalent to a word in the original. He says,

> ... Laotse's style is epigrammatic and his language is terse and vigorous, and I have tried to preserve its terse, epigrammatic quality and its sentence rhythm, but I have not tried to reproduce the rhyme in its many passages. Translation is an art of seeking the exact word, and when the exact word is found, circumlocutions can be avoided, and the style preserved. Translation also requires a certain stupidity, and the best translation is the stupid one which does not go out of its way for "brilliant interpretations." Laotse's advice to "be aware of the male but keep to the female" has been my principle. For only the stupid man has fidelity. Many translators betray that undue and incorrect stress on individual words in regard to their etymology as beginners in a foreign language place undue stress on individual syllables, the one rising from lack of familiarity, the other from lack of fluency ...
>
> (Lin, 1942: 582)

Both Lin Yutang's sentence-based strategy and his method of "paraphrase" focus on meaning. His translation theory is meaning-oriented whether it is stated in Chinese or English. Thus whether Lin Yutang speaks in English or Chinese his basic idea of translation is the same however different the verbiages are. In order not to confuse the reader, he shifts between two universes of discourse when addressing different readerships. The same theory wears two different cloaks.

Total Concept and Imitation in Poetry Translation and the Indivisibility of a Work of Art

Lin Yutang's idea of poetry translation is represented by "*On the Translation of Poetry*" (Lin, 1994h: 317 –334). The two fundamental elements of a poem either English or Chinese are (1) concise diction and (2) *yijing* (sentiment or total feeling, a variant of "total concept"). In the case of translating from Chinese to English, the translator shall be able to understand the Chinese poem and write excellent English; in translating the other way round, the translator shall be able to have a perfect understanding of the English and write excellent Chinese. Apart from linguistic proficiency, a leisurely mood is required for the translation of poetry. Rhyming is optional. It is better not to rhyme. It is more important to use the right word to preserve the rhythm and flavor of the original poem. Too much attention to rhyming may distort the poem itself. The *yijing* should always be the priority. To translate *yijing* involves adept diction. So, in his view, to translate a poem, one needs to have a general idea of the poem (*yijing*) and then reproduce the general idea rather than the rhymes, except in this case the general idea is the "rhythm and flavor." So, poetry is just a particular field of translation, to which the "total concept" also applies.

In his Chinese discourse, the "total concept" in poetry is represented as *yijing*, but in his English discourse, it becomes *essence* or *spirit*. In his evaluation of Hellen Wadell's poetry translation from the Chinese, he emphasizes creation of the essence or spirit of the original in the translation:

> I have tried here to give a few representative samples, by two translators who know Chinese thoroughly and one who does not. Of all translations of Chinese poetry, I think Helen Waddell's is the best, (Lyrics from the Chinese, Holt-Lin's original note). She based her translations on James Legge's translation and his notes, and her translations are far from literal. Her method is to catch the essence or spirit of a poem and weave it into an exquisite creation with whatever material from the poem she needs for that particular purpose. And she is completely successful. One cannot help being impressed by the fact that the fleeting thought, the sudden heart cry of a second of some peasant woman some three thousand years ago in China can be recaptured for us in the English language by one who does not know her language ...
>
> (Lin, 1942: 868)

Here is one of Helen Waddell's "translations" which he admires and includes in *The Wisdom of China and India*:

*780 B. C. Jacques Bonhomme*① *complains of the useless stars.*
I see on high the Milky Way,
But here's a rougher road.
The sacred Oxen shining stand;
They do not draw our load.
The Sieve is sparkling in the South,
But good and ill come through.
The ladle opens wide its mouth,
And pours out naught for you.
At dawn the Weaving Sisters sleep,
At dusk they rise again;
But though their Shining Shuttle flies,
They weave no robe for men.

(Lin, 1942: 877 –878)

---

① Jacques Bonhomme, a name given to a French peasant as tamely submissive to taxation.

Waddell's "translation" is based on the following serious scholarly work of James Legge:

There is the Milky Way in heaven,
Which looks down on us in light;
And the three stars together are the Weaving Sisters,
Passing in a day through seven stages (of the sky).
Although they go through their seven stages,
They complete no bright work for us.
Brilliant shine the Draught Oxen,
But they do not serve to draw our carts.
In the east there is Lucifer;
In the west there is Hesperus;
Long and curved
Is the Rabbit Net of the sky;
— But they only occupy their places.
In the south is the Sieve,
But it is of no use to sift.
In the north is the Ladle,
But it lades out no liquor.
In the south is the Sieve,
Idly showing its mouth.
In the north is the Ladle,
Raising its handle in the west.

(Excerpt from James Legge's translation of ODE 9. THE TÂ TUNG) (*The Shih King*, 2001, pp. 51 – 52)

The Chinese Original of the *Tâ Tung*:

有饛簋飧,有捄棘匕。
周道如砥,其直如矢。
君子所履,小人所视。
睠言顾之,潸焉出涕。
小东大东,杼柚其空。
纠纠葛屦,可以履霜。
佻佻公子,行彼周行。
既往既来,使我心疚。
有冽氿泉,无浸获薪。
契契寤叹,哀我惮人。
薪是获薪,尚可载也。

哀我惮人，亦可息也。
东人之子，职劳不来。
西人之子，粲粲衣服。
舟人之子，熊罴是裘。
私人之子，百僚是试。
或以其酒，不以其浆。
鞙鞙佩璲，不以其长。
维天有汉，监亦有光。
跂彼织女，终日七襄。
虽则七襄，不成报章。
睆彼牵牛，不以服箱。
东有启明，西有长庚。
有捄天毕，载施之行。
维南有箕，不可以簸扬。
维北有斗，不可以挹酒浆。
维南有箕，载翕其舌。
维北有斗，西柄之揭。①

（《诗经·小雅》大东）（Chen, 2002: 305 –307）

James Legge gives the whole of this piece, because he thinks that it is an interesting instance of Sabian views. In this poem, the writer, despairing of help from men appeals to heaven. Legge gives the poem an introduction and plenty of notes, which for the sake of space I have removed. Helen Waddell, not knowing Chinese, extracts the spirit of the poem and writes her own poem, which is consequently a new one. Waddell's use of "Jacques Bonhomme" culturally displaces the poem.

This recreation of *essence* or *spirit* by Helen Waddell is Lin's meaning-centered translation in the extreme. Here "concise diction" definitely means the finding of exact words to recreate the idea and feeling the translator has extracted from the original instead of finding exact words to match the original wording. As long as the essence or spirit can be transferred, the translator is entitled to disregard all formal restrictions that might come from the original.

Here Lin Yutang in the emphasis on the spirit goes a little bit too far in the promotion of Waddell's "translation." With the reduced length and the removal

① Only the underlined part is "translated" by Waddell.

of so much specific material in the new poem, do we really have the same meaning and feeling? Even if there is no deviation in meaning and feeling, can a part replace the whole and a summary or abstract replace the text proper? Is there any difference between this kind of devotion to art and Lin Shu's approach which is dismissed by Lin Yutang as licentious? Lin himself rarely goes this far in his translation of poems. Basically he takes the sentence as a unit allowing for occasional radical changes in the organization of sentences, and freedom takes place at the local level. Here are two of his poetry translations:

Two Shingshiangtse Poems by Su Tung-p'o

1

清夜无尘	O the clear moon's speckles, silvery
月色如银	night!
酒斟时须满十分	When filling thy cup be sure to fill it quite!
浮名浮利	Strive not for frothy fame or bubble
虚苦劳神	wealth!
叹隙中驹	A passing dream —
石中火	A flashing flint —
梦中身	A shadow's flight!

2

虽抱文章	O what is knowledge, fine and
开口谁亲	superfine?
且陶陶乐取天真	To innocent and simple joys resign!
几时归去	To be myself and in contentment face
作个闲人	A valley of clouds —
对一张琴	A sweet-toned *chin* —
一壶酒	A jug of wine!
一溪云	

(Lin, 1994h: 321 -322)

A plausible explanation is that Lin Yutang is trying to give readers a clear idea of how "total concept" works.

Lin Yutang's "total concept" in translation echoes Croce's idea of the unity and indivisibility of a work of art either at the sentence level or at the textual level. A sentence or a text shall be treated as a meaningful whole. An individual word does not count in translation. Word-for-word translation is absolutely wrong. When the text is viewed as a whole, sentence-for-sentence translation is wrong. What matters is the matter (meaning). The matter shall be extracted and given an appropriate new form in the target language. Croce's aesthetics affirms unity of expression. Thus speaks Croce on the indivisibility of a work of art:

> The fact that we divide a work of art into parts, as a poem into scenes, episodes, similes, sentences, or a picture into single figures and objects, background, foreground, etc., may seem to be an objection to this affirmation. But such division annihilates the work, as dividing the organism into heart, brain, nerves, muscles and so on, turns the living being into a corpse. It is true that there exist organisms in which the division gives place to more living things, but in such a case, and if we transfer the analogy to the aesthetic fact, we must conclude for a multiplicity of germs of life, that is to say, for a speedy re-elaboration of the single parts into new single expressions.
>
> (Croce, 1909: 33 –34)

Yan Fu's Principles Redefined Aesthetically: Translation Is a Spiritual Activity

Lin Yutang does not start his theoretical speculation from scratch, he tries to think in concepts so that the issue may be better framed, but unlike the jargon-loving scholars of today, he builds his theory on existing concepts which he thinks somewhat justified. For him, the important thing is not to coin new terminology. Rather, it is how to define some valuable existing concepts. Therefore, despite his criticism of Yan Fu's translations, he accepts his popular concepts — *fidelity*, *fluency*, *and elegance* — for the discussion of translation problems, gives each his own definition and makes them the pivotal concepts of his aesthetic theory of translation. The substitution of *beauty* for Yan's *elegance* is catalytic: it changes the nature of Yan's concepts altogether.

His definition of *fidelity* unambiguously clarifies the translator's responsibility for the original author. His *fluency* is the responsibility for the target language reader. His *beauty* is a responsibility for art. Thus the three concepts bind three relationships. When the superfluous *elegance* becomes *beauty*, an optional obligation toward the translation reader becomes a compulsory responsibility for art, which is equal to an obligation toward the translator himself as an artist. Thus, translation becomes the translator's self-expression and we have an aesthetic theory of translation supported by three pivotal concepts:

Translation is a unity of three principles: *fidelity*, *fluency*, *and beauty*, each defined as follows:

fidelity: devotion to content extractable from the source language text fluency: creation of appropriate target language form

beauty: spiritual activity of the translator as an artist, which creates appropriate target language form for content extracted from the original text

In this trinity, we have a balanced relationship between three parties: the author, the reader, and the translator. In the light of such a theoretical framework, all author-centered theories, reader-centered theories, and translator-centered theories, modern or of old, are nothing more than departmental specifications.

6 "Individuality" of Words and Unreliability of Dictionaries

"Every word has its individuality," says Lin Yutang (Lin. 1994b: 315). As a linguist, he understands the variation of word meaning in contexts. In his early years, he relied heavily on the *Concise Oxford Dictionary* and the *Pocket Oxford Dictionary* in learning English, but when it came to translating he showed less enthusiasm for dictionaries. In his view, dictionaries are not reliable. If one's command of English is not good enough, he shall not translate by the help of a dictionary. This is because the meaning of a word changes in different contexts. On the other hand, dictionaries are not entirely useless because the translator may take to the dictionary for an accurate understanding of a word if he is not quite sure about that word. For this purpose, a good dictionary shall provide, in addition to the definition of a word, its exhaustive usage illustrated by examples including idioms. With such a good dictionary, the translator no longer needs to consult anybody else but himself. Lin Yutang's recommendation is of course his favorites. He loves them because they provide exhaustive usage of each word. He applauds the *Pocket Oxford Dictionary* in an article entitled "A Dictionary That Has Benefited Me"①, later in his bestselling book *My Country and My People*, as well as his autobiographical sketch and *Memoirs of an Octogenarian*. Such an idea of the role of dictionaries in translating is consistent with his belief in translator competence.

① "A Dictionary That Has Benefited Me" (我所得益的一部字典) in Lin, Yutang. 1934. *Da Huang Ji*. Shanghai: Shenghuo Books, 1934.

In 1925, *Xiandai Pinglun* (*The Modern Review*) published an article by Dr. Hu Shi, which criticized Wang Tongzhao's translation errors caused by a failure to understand English words like *card* and *lie* and which began with a doggerel by Dr. Hu Shi:

Good Advice
Spare some of your money,
Sell two more acres of your land,
Do remember to buy a dictionary good,
Take her where you are,
Consult her often and your face is saved.

(Lin, 1994i: 3. Translated from the Chinese.)

Lin Yutang did not agree. He was all for the use of a good dictionary in the learning of a foreign language but he distrusted its use in translation, for in his opinion, a translator's competence rather than the dictionary is the crucial factor. He published in the *Yusi* magazine "Good Advice for the Literary Guru," in which he called on readers not to listen to Dr. Hu Shi:

In the dim light of evening,
In the dead of the night,
The modern literary guru,
Who has read an English grammar
Consults the English dictionary.
Yet the original is not to be understood.
Two more dollars, he'd like to spare,
Two more acres of land, he'd like to sell.
One dictionary he buys, bigger and fatter.
But the problem is not solved.
The combinations are weird though he tries very hard.
How can a word be so promiscuous!
"to lie to someone," "to lie in bed" as the word *lie* can be used,
"to play cards," "to give somebody your card as the word *card* can occur,
To know which *lie* and which *card* these letters are
For the famous man of letters, is a little bit too hard!
Is there a way?
Is there a solution?
Here is my advice:
First, not to translate.

Second, not to publish.
Trust not what Dr. Hu said,
Take care of your reputation,
And of yourself take care!

(ibid: 4. Translated from the Chinese.)

We do not see any contradiction between the two doggerels. It is a matter of tilting emphasis. In fact, the two doggerels supplement each other. Putting the two men's comments side by side, we get a fuller view of the issue:

(1) One should use a good dictionary in translating.

(2) A good dictionary is not enough if the translator's English (as a foreign language and source language) is not good enough, because the word is apt to change its meaning in its varying context.

(3) A good dictionary is helpful to the translator in that it helps the translator to be sure about a certain word by providing usage illustrated with examples in addition to definitions.

From today's point of view, Lin's view of the use of dictionaries in translation was not fully developed. He was only obsessed with the monolingual dictionary and did not mention the role of bilingual dictionaries, which are directly relevant to translating and have proven to be very useful. Over a long period of time, especially since the turn of the Ming and Qing dynasties, foreign missionaries, translators, lexicographers and the Chinese government had been doing a lot in the compilation of bilingual dictionaries. The years from 1911 to 1937 saw a boom of English-Chinese dictionaries: 212 in total. This was a period in which Chinese society was undergoing a drastic change and the dictionary boom accompanied a translation surge.

As a competent bilingual writer, when translating, Lin Yutang was less reliant on dictionaries than most of his contemporaries. Naturally he could afford to ignore or neglect the existence of and the need for good bilingual dictionaries. A little biased as his view was, his idea of a good dictionary was exactly what the then Chinese lexicographers were pursuing. Thus speaks a researcher in lexicography:

> In the compilation of English-Chinese dictionaries, that period saw a trend of moving away from the decoding type to the encoding type. This trend marked the maturation of English-Chinese lexicography in China. The decoding type of dictionaries

involved input in English learning and were intended for the English learner to understand English texts. Such dictionaries offer basic information of a word such as definitions and parts of speech. The encoding type took care of linguistic output of the English learner. In addition to definitions and parts of speech, they provide word usage and guidance for verbal and written communication.

(Hu, 2005: 40)

7 Intervention of the Scientific Mind in an Art Theory: Toward Relative Standardization in the Translation of "Names"①

So far, I have focused my discussion on Lin Yutang the artist. It must be pointed out that the man has not only an artistic mind but also a scientific mind②. The artistic mind seeks unbounded expression in writing and the scientific mind looks for models or regularities. The two minds meet in his translation theory. The former believes in no rules or techniques, but the latter endeavors to clarify concepts and establish a procedural pattern or a methodology of translation. His scientific mind is particularly manifest in his attempt to look for cross-lingual phonetic patterns and standardize the translation of names (from English to Chinese).

Names, common nouns and proper nouns alike, pose a major challenge to Chinese translators, who have been theorizing about the problem since over a thousand years ago. Xuan Zang's brief elaboration of "five cases of transliteration"③ for the translation of Buddhist sutras is commonly regarded as the earliest theoretical statement of the issue. In the early years of the twentieth

---

① In the early years of the twentieth century, when Chinese scholars discussed *yiming* (译名, the translation of names) they were referring to both proper nouns and common nouns.

② His scientific mind led to his interest in linguistics and the invention of the Mingkuai Chinese typewriter, the most advanced when it was invented.

③ "Five cases of transliteration" (五不翻): 1. transliteration of the esoteric; 2. transliteration of polysemous words; 3. transliteration of words for things that have no counterparts in China; 4. preservation of conventionalized transliterations; 5. transliteration for the sake of respect and awe.

century, as translation began to be done on an unprecedented scale, the problem stood out. It came to the attention of scholars such as Hu Yilu, Rong Tinggong, Zhang Shizhao, and Zhu Ziqing①. Hu's article was seminal. It triggered serious discussions of the general approaches to and procedures of the translation of names. The article, entitled "On the Translation of Names", makes a systematic study of the translation of nouns. In Hu's view, "names" (nouns) in general should be translated according to meaning. He lists 20 cases where the meaning approach should be followed. However, he also advocates transliteration for cases where translation is not possible: such as names for persons and places, names for some animals and plants, some scientific and philosophical concepts, mystic religious terms, and concepts particular to the experience of a certain people. The scholarly discussions resulted in the gradual standardization of names in fields such as medicine and chemistry but in general translated names in Lin Yutang's view were still in a chaos. A relative order was needed. In 1924, Lin Yutang set out to address the problem in "A Proposal for the Standardization of Names in Translation," which does not cover all the aspects of name translation as the misleading title suggests. His discussion only focuses on a standardized way of transliteration. The very concept of standardization of translated names is his contribution to Chinese scholarship on translation. Besides, his idea of establishing conventionalized phonetic matches for transliteration is brilliant and in fact is what has been done in China.

Complete standardization is mission impossible, he admits, but it is necessary to have some principles to be less chaotic. Not endeavoring to make a systematic account, his discussion focuses on how to make standardized phonetic transcriptions, or transliterations. "There is no perfect solution to transliterate

---

① Hu Yilu: "On the Translation of Names"(论译名). Rong Tinggong: "Letter on Translation of Names"(致甲寅记者论译名). Zhang, Shizhao: "Answer to Rong Tinggong's Letter on the Translation of Names"(答容挺公论译名书). See *Articles on Translation* (1894 – 1948) edited by the Editorial Board of *Translation Newsletter* of the China Translators Association. Beijing: Foreign Language Teaching and Research Press. [中国翻译工作者协会《翻译. 通讯》编辑部编.《翻译研究论文集(1894—1948)》. 北京:外语教学与研究出版社.]

Western phonetics[①] into Chinese." (Lin, 1994: 322) He admires the Buddhist sutra translators in Chinese history, who meticulously marked the sounds of proper names in smaller Chinese characters. The ideal translation, he argues, is one that enables people to trace the name to its original so that one thinks of *Appollo* at seeing the Chinese characters 阿波罗. In China today, this issue of traceability has been solved in a number of ways, among them: (1) conventionalized characters are used for certain sounds; (2) the Chinese translation is followed by the foreign language original in brackets; (3) the direct borrowing of a name or an acronym in English as today's readers are more English-literate, especially in the case of less familiar names, fresh names or as expediencies. One key problem Lin Yutang wants to solve is the translation of consonant clusters (cri-, bri-, etc.) in European languages, as the Chinese language does not have such clusters. He proposes to conventionalize a set of twenty to thirty Chinese characters out of over forty thousand to represent the consonants that are not immediately followed by vowels. The same logic should also be applied to the translation of sounds that have no equivalence in Chinese. Thus, at seeing a particular Chinese character in a proper name, people conveniently recall its original sound value. The following are some of the 30 pairs he proposes to conventionalize:

Table 3 Proposed Matches Between Foreign Sounds and Chinese Characters in Transliteration

Proposed matches		Examples	Today's translation norm in the mainland of China
1	克 =k	as *k* in English *Peck*	克林顿(Clinton)/克莱尔(Claire)/星巴克(StarBucks)/约克(York), but 纽约(New York), 赛珍珠 (Pearl S. Buck)!
2	倔 =g	as *g* in English *Hogg*	霍格(Hogg)
3	拍 =p	As *p* in English *Dunlop*	邓洛普(Dunlop)

(to be continued)

① By Western phonetics he means English, French, and German phonetics as can be seen in the following table.

Proposed matches		Examples	Today's translation norm in the mainland of China
4	勃 =b	as *b* in English *Toblen*	易卜生(Ibsen) 杜布森(Dobson) 爱普生(EPSON)
5	特 =t	as second *t* in English *Tatler*	阿姆斯特朗(Armstrong)/杰克—巴特勒(Jackie Butler),希特勒(Hitler)
6	突 =d	as *d* in English *Drayton*	德雷顿(Drayton)/维拉·德雷克(Vera Drake)
7	池 =ch	as *ch* in English *Richmond*	里士满(Richmond)
8	入 =j	as *dg* in English *Dodge*	道奇(Dodge), but 卡斯特桥市长(The Mayor of Casterbridge), 剑桥大学(Cambridge)
9	失 =sh	as *sh* in English *Nash*	纳什(Nash)/布什(Bush)
10	术 =zh	as *g* in French *Rouge*	巴顿鲁治 or 红杖市(Baton Rouge)

As can be seen, Lin Yutang is highly sensitive to this particular problem of translating names. His idea of standardization is still relevant today. The principle of traceability to the source is especially important in bilingual or multilingual communication environments. Matches such as 克 =k and 特 =t have become Chinese transliteration norms. Most of the matches are not used but the idea still works. Generations of efforts toward standardization yielded to various translator's dictionaries of names. Achievements in name standardization are also found in various encyclopedias and bilingual dictionaries. Discussions on the issue are still going on today, particularly on terminology and proper names. Take, for example, articles in the China National Knowledge Infrastructure archive (www. cnki. net), one of China's leading sources of academic magazine articles. From 1961 to 2006 (February), there have been 675 articles about the translation of proper names and from 1981 to 2006 (February) there have been 37 articles about the standardization of names in translation.

Lin Yutang's elaboration of relative standardization of transliteration has been positive for the time in which the article was written. That was a prescriptive age. Today, thanks to the profusion of translations since then, a descriptive approach is possible.

As pointed out in Hu Yilu's article①, the translation of names is much more than transliteration. Names of persons, places, organizations, and whatever need various strategies. Lin Yutang's prescription turns out to be only partially workable (as he honestly predicted). Maybe difference in the translation of names should be tolerated to certain degrees, even in transliteration. There is no absolute authority for the job of standardization. Individuals, governments, organizations, scholars of a certain field, and a small group of people working together on a project shall be allowed to formulate their own standards as they see fit. A good solution is to offer some overall guiding principles while allowing for some form of autonomy in various fields or organizations. Some early or more "authoritative" translations whether they follow any set principles or not may eventually emerge as norms, to be widely accepted by later translators.

III Dimensions of Taste: Translation Criticism in the Framework of Fidelity, Fluency, and Beauty

An important concept in Croce and Spingarn's aesthetic is *taste*. Now that Lin Yutang accepts this aesthetic wholesale, we can also examine his taste by reading his translation criticisms. As a result, we can conclude that his criticism of translations in general follows his theory of translation. The underlying pivotal concepts in his criticism are also *fidelity*, *fluency*, and *beauty*.

In his exposition of *fidelity*, he criticizes what he thinks is license in the translations of Lin Qinnan (Lin Shu) and Yan Jidao (Yan Fu)②, who in his

① Hu, Yilu (1984). "On the Translation of Names". In The Editorial Board of Translation Newsletter of the China Translators Association (Ed.). Articles on Translation (1894 – 1948). Beijing: Foreign Language Teaching and Research Press.

② Interestingly Lin embraced Yan's theory but dismissed his translations. Lin acknowledged that his three principles of fidelity, fluency, and beauty are almost the same as Yan's *xin*, *da* and *ya*.

view have translated English works into the likes of ancient Chinese classics. However, he never dwells much on the faults of other translators. Instead he would like to point out the merits of some translators he likes. His criticism is usually positive and constructive.

He thus speaks of Arthur Waley's translations from the Chinese,

> Among foreign translators of Chinese literature, Arthur Waley of the UK has been the most successful for the simple reason that his English is good. When I was translating the *Dao De Jing* for the Modern Library, I adopted some of Waley's sentences which were very good translations in beautiful English prose. His translations of the Tang Dynasty poems, 19 of the *yuefu* poems and *The Book of Songs* are not restrained by rhyming yet at once faithful, fluent and beautiful. He has occasional lapses. For example, in his translation of *chizu daxian* in the *xiyouji*①, "barefoot" becomes "red foot." Such lapses shall be excused. When they were translating literary allusions they could resort to exegeses but were completely at a loss with words like *chizu*, which cannot be found in the dictionary …
>
> (Lin, 1994h: 318. Translated from the Chinese.)

This is in line with his emphasis of the translator's competence to write well in the target language and to understand the source text. The former competence corresponds to the *fluency* principle and the latter to the *fidelity* principle.

Of Ku Hung-ming's translation of the *Central Harmony* he says,

> … Ku Hung Ming's translation of that chapter is so brilliant and at the same time so correct and illuminating that I am sorry he did not translate more of the Confucian texts. It makes that chapter intelligible to the modern man.
>
> (Lin, 1938: 45 –46)

"Brilliant" describes the beauty of the translation, "correct" its fidelity to the original, "illuminating" and "intelligible" its fluency, notwithstanding some semantic overlapping of the four adjectives.

In translating poetry, the principle of beauty stands out. Lin Yutang takes a particular liking to Helen Waddell's "translation" of a few dozens of poems in the *Shijing*, or *The Book of Songs*. Knowing no Chinese, Helen Waddell entirely relied on James Legge's meticulous scholarly translation. Waddell took the idea

---

① The title was translated by Waley as *Monkey*.

from Legge's work and recreated it as if a sympathetic poet were writing on the same subject. Sometimes, she could reduce six or seven stanzas to one or two. Lin Yutang has a high regard for Helen's method, which portrays the wailing of the widow and the heartless deserter in verisimilitude. Fifteen poems reworked by Waddell are included in *The Wisdom of China and India.* Waddell has employed rhymes but Lin Yutang thinks that her rhymes are natural and unaffected.

IV Lin Yutang's Contribution to Translation Studies

1 The Originality of Perspective

Viewed as isolated remarks, very little in Lin Yutang's discourse had not been said before. Almost nothing was original. The expression theories were nothing new. "translating by the sentence" and "paraphrase" were not his inventions. The concepts of *fidelity*, *fluency*, and *beauty* were virtually borrowed. The comparison of translating to writing was not new. His theory of translation in general echoed or overlapped with those of some of his contemporaries except for some minor differences. The following excerpts from the theoretical discussions of Sheng Yanbing (Mao Dun), Guo Moruo, and Cheng Fangwu, for example, illustrate this point:

Shen Yanbing (1896 –1981) on *letter* and *spirit* in 1921:

> I think that it is better to render *shenyun* (the spirit) while allowing for differences in the letter than otherwise. The function of literature is to move the soul (to win sympathy or to yield pleasure). The power of moving lies more in the spirit than in the physical letter. Once the spirit is lost, much of the power to move is lost. Upon close observation, it may be known that it is easier to keep the physical appearance than the spirit, however hard the translator tries. Therefore, if more attention is paid to the physical appearance, it is more unlikely not to lose the spirit.
>
> (Shen, 1984: 93. My translation.) (Note: Lin will have no objection to this.)

Guo Moruo (1892 –1978) on *form*, *meaning* and *spirit* in 1923:

> "I think that the ideal translation preserves the *ziju* (form) and the *yiyi* (meaning), and especially *qiyun* (the spirit or the feeling tone) of the original. Every physical element in the original should be represented in the translation but word-for-word translation must not be done. Word order may be changed. Either generalization or specification may be done. As long as the meaning is not damaged, freedom is allowed for the attainment of the feeling tone."
>
> (Guo, 1923; *Articles on Translation*: 102. Note: Lin will agree with Guo on the preservation of meaning and feeling tone but not on words and sentences.)

Cheng Fangwu (1897 –1984) on the ideal translation of poetry in 1923:

> The ideal translation of a poem should, first, be a poem in its own right, second, transfer the feeling, third, transform the content and fourth, adopt the original form.
>
> (Cheng, 1984: 202. Note: Lin Yutang won't agree with "to adopt the original form" but he will agree with the rest.)

Scholars of good academic standing often share similar views or concerns about translation whether or not they know or know of each other.

Nonetheless, Lin Yutang is a highly original translation theorist. His originality lies in his grand perspective and the innovation of methodology for the study of translation.

By "grand perspective," I mean his comprehensive synthesis of carefully selected existing ideas with his own ideas into an aesthetic perspective. He integrated existing ideas of art, literature, language, psychology, and translation with his own impressions from practical translation experience. He put all these things in a crucible, and through a process of synthesis came up with a "total concept" (in this case a theory) that is greater than the mathematical sum total of the parts. Nothing he said was new, but when we take all his writings on translation as a whole, there is a great difference. This is a systematic theory with a central proposition and supported with significant details.

2 A Shift from Impressionism to Rationalism

Translational behavior is variegated. Our perception of translation differs from person to person. In a particular time-space, however, exposed to the same manifestations of "truth" and similarly bound by cognitive means available, a typical pattern of method and perspective may emerge. Translation theorists may generally follow a set of assumptions, concepts, values, and practices that constitute a way of viewing translational reality. This typical pattern or example is what philosophers of science speak of as a paradigm. ① Translation theories move with the times. As time passes, the realm of translation assumes new characteristics and consequently the approach to translation changes, i.e., the paradigm of translation research shifts.

In the late nineteenth century and the early twentieth century, as Western science and technology and Western worldviews entered China, the artistic mind met with the scientific mind. The impact of the encounter was also reflected in translation theories. Lin Yutang's discourse on translation happened to symbolize a paradigm shift in approaching translation, a move-away from the traditional method and perspective and the debut of new methods and new perspectives.

The practice of translation is inevitably accompanied by theoretical discussion or reflection by people somehow involved in the business: initiators, translators, editors, project managers, or translation users, etc. However, early theoretical discussions of translation were rather intuitive and fragmentary both in China and in the West. According to Chen Fukang's *A History of Translation Theory in China* (2000), the earliest account of translation in China is found in historical documents such as *Zhouli* and *Liji*. The Confucian dictum: "A proper noun shall be close to its source language and a common noun shall follow the convention of the target language" in *Chunqiu Guliang Zhuan* was but a passing remark. However, as translations increased in quantity, so did theoretical discussions and over time such discussions grew in both scope and depth. Before the May 4 Movement in 1919, China had seen three translation booms: translation of Buddhist sutras from the East Han Dynasty to the Song Dynasty, translation of science and technology in the late-Ming and early-Qing period, and translation of Western learning after the Opium War (Ma, 1998: I).

Early Chinese theories of translation generally very much relied on intuitive judgment on the part of the parties involved in translation. This intuitive pattern

---

① In *The Structure of Scientific Revolutions* (1962), Thomas Kuhn describes a paradigm as a set of beliefs, theories, or a world view that is unquestioningly accepted and has become established as "truth." A paradigm shift is a radical change or transformation.

is termed by Leo Tak-hung Chan (2004) as "the traditional approach" and the theories in the traditional approach as "impressionistic theories". This approach finds its last major exponent in Yan Fu who established the basic tenets for Chinese translators and expressed them in three Chinese characters, which despite the controversies they have caused are still influencing Chinese translators and Chinese theorists today.

The traditional approach, or the impressionistic approach — in a manner of speaking — often appears fragmentary and vague by the modern scientific or pseudo-scientific standards. Take Yan Fu's theory for example. It occurs in a short preface to his translation of *Evolution and Ethics*. In a sketch, Yan outlines three difficult tasks of translation:

> Translation involves three requirements difficult to fulfill: fidelity (*xin*), comprehensibility (*da*) and elegance (*ya*). Faithfulness is difficult enough to attain but a translation that is faithful but not comprehensible is no translation at all. Comprehensibility is therefore of prime importance. ... The *Book of Changes* says: "Fidelity is the basis of writing." Confucius said: "Writing should be comprehensible." He also said, "Where language has no refinement, its effects will not extend far." These three dicta set the right course for literature and the guidelines for translation. In addition to faithfulness and comprehensibility, we should strive for elegance in translation. ①

Such a theory came as a passing comment on translation in general when the translator was addressing problems he encountered in translating the book. The three words *xin*, *da*, and *ya* are direct borrowings from Chinese theories of literature. While they are systematic in a limited sense that they seem to cover the main aspects of transferring a text from language to language, the system is far from complete in that analytical details are lacking. Due to the nature of the Chinese language, the words themselves are vague and prone to various interpretations. These terms are highly ambiguous for it cannot be agreed upon what exactly is *xin*, *da*, or *ya*.

The traditional approach did not end as the May 4 Movement in 1919 ushered in the modern era. It continued in the Chinese theories of translation

---

① For a complete English translation of Yan's preface, see "Preface to *Tianyanlun* (1901)" translated by C. Y. Hsu. In Chan, Leo Tak-hung (2004). *Twentieth-Century Chinese Translation Theory: Modes, issues and debates*. Amsterdam/Philadelphia: John Benjamins.

up to the present day. Theorists of the modern period who have followed the traditional approach include Lu Xun (on literal translation), Qu Qiubai (on the use of the vernacular), Guo Moruo (on the translator as match-maker), Mao Dun (on literary translation), Fu Lei (on *shensi* or likeness in spirit), Qian Zhongshu (on *huajing*, or entering into the spirit, one of the hardest Chinese words to render into English), among many others. Today the traditional approach is represented by the Beijing University Professor Xu Yuanzhong (2003) who terms the Chinese tradition of translation studies "the Chinese School" and claims that literary translation theories of this school are "the most progressive" in the world of the twentieth century.

There have been dialogues between the various theories but the mystic nature of the various impressionistic theories makes the most fundamental issues everlasting objects of contention. No general consensus yet has been reached on Yan Fu's three principles, Fu Lei's *shensi*, and Qian Zhongshu's *huajing*, for example. Because theoretical discussion stops at fundamental issues, the Chinese system of translation theories is seriously flawed by lack of methodology and inadequate attention to detail. Derived from practice, the theories are intended to serve as practical guidelines but operable details are evidently lacking. This shall account partly for backwardness of Chinese translation softwares up to this day.

Alongside the traditional impressionistic approach which is largely artistic we can spot another line of development: a modern approach which is more rational, systematic and operable. Having germinated within the traditional approach, this approach borrows largely from rationalism, systematicity and precision of scientific research.

From Liang Shiqiu's short article "Translation," which was published in 1928, we know that the method of survey was used in the study of translation at that time, though it was used in a crude manner and the article itself on the whole belonged to the impressionistic tradition:

> According to a survey, French and Russian literature has dominated literary translation in recent years. There are very few English masterpieces except the translations by Lin Qinnan. It is a puzzling phenomenon as there are obviously more people who know English than those who know French or Russian.
>
> (*Articles on Translation*, pp. 133 –134. Translated from the Chinese.)

Challenging Yan Fu's impressionistic theory, and dismissing the distinction between *yiyi* (meaning-based translation, free translation, paraphrase) and *zhiyi* (direct translation, literal translation), in 1929 Chen Xiying came up with his own theory of translation (which is on the whole also impressionistic) distinguishing between *xingsi* (likeness in form), *yisi* (likeness in meaning), and *shensi* (likeness in spirit). According to him, spirit is the essence of character and it cannot be grasped without the original feelings of a poet. The rational part consists in that in rejecting Yan Fu's principles Chen is classifying translations into literary and non-literary and saying that the principles apply to neither.

These were just the early rudiments of the modern rational approach to translation. The modern approach did not gain momentum until the last decades of the twentieth century which saw the introduction of Eugene Nida, whose significance lies more in the "scientific" way he treats translation than in how much more truth he holds.

However, the modern rational approach of translation studies in China did not start with the introduction of Nida by the end of the century. Rather, it started with Lin Yutang's "On Translation," in which he took a rational analytical approach to the study of an art. Transcending the politicized debates in the 1920s and 1930s over literalism (the Lu Xun model) versus liberalism (the Lin Shu model), or Europeanization versus Sinicization, Lin Yutang elaborated his aesthetic theory of translation. Such a theory is unambiguously explained in "On Translation" and constitutes the core of Lin's entire discourse on translation.

There are two features that make Lin Yutang's theory of translation symbolic of the paradigm shift in translation studies:

First, a shift from intuitive judgment to theoretical awareness.

The practice of translation has given rise to theoretical speculations about this particular field of human activity. Early theoretical speculations were mainly based on the intuitive impressions of the translator. Broadly speaking, there is no translator who is not a theorist. Every translator, whether good or bad, has a purpose and develops his own understanding of the significance of his work and the procedures to follow in his business. One difference between the translators, however, is that some of them have articulated their theories while others have not.

For Lin Yutang too, translating was a practical activity accompanied by a theoretical activity. While doing the job, he reflected on what to translate and how to do the job well, and was able to spell it out so that experience could be passed on to others. He had a consciousness of controlling output and improving performance. In the different stages of his life as author and translator, he wrote a great deal about the subject.

But many other translators do the same. As the enterprise of translation increases its complexity, theories of simple impressions are no longer adequate. Understanding has to be deepened and one must go beyond those simple impressions. There has to be increased theoretical awareness so that the more complex phenomenon can be better accounted for. In order to see the phenomena in a better light, the theorist must go outside of his experience and impressions. Theory in its Greek origin, *theoria*, means "contemplation" and "speculation." (Pearsall, 1998: 1922). It is "a superstition or a system of ideas intended to explain something, especially one based on general principles independent of the thing to be explained." (ibid.) The theorist has a distance and detachment from his experience and impressions to enable him to get a better view. Such a distance or detachment is what I mean by "theoretical awareness."

It is such theoretical awareness that distinguishes Lin Yutang from many other translators: he not only sees translation from inside but also from the outside with his interdisciplinary perspectives under the grand aesthetic perspective.

This theoretical awareness of his has led to his study of translation based on the following sources:

(1) his experience as a reader in translated literature: Chinese translations of foreign literature such as works of Spencer, Darwin, and Adam Smith, English translations from the Chinese and other languages such as translations of Chinese literature by Arthur Waley, H. A. Giles, Ku Hung-ming, Fitzgerald's translation of Omar Khayyam's *The Rubaiyat*, and Indian literature in English translation; (2) his experience as a reflective translator responding to actual translation problems; (3) attention to and familiarity with translation theories or concepts, both Chinese and foreign, such as in "The Translator's Preface to

Evolution and Ethics" by Yan Fu, "In Reply to Rong Tinggong's Comment on the Translation of Names" by Zhang Xingyan, "On the Translation of Names" by Hu Yilu, and *Recollections of a Translator* by Fu Sinian, "On the Translation of Homer" by Matthew Arnold, as well as fragmentary remarks on translation in the newspapers and prefaces to translations; (4) theories of writing (and fine arts), such as the concept of *xingling* (*hsing-ling*, self-expression) of Yuan Zhonglang and other Chinese artists, and the expressionism of Croce and Spingarn; (5) his knowledge of psychology; (6) his knowledge of linguistics.

Second, a shift from fragmentary formulations to a systematic theory.

Early translation theories were often as fragmentary as they were intuitive. Because of Lin's theoretical awareness, he frequently wrote about translation. In 1933 his translation theory took shape in the famous essay "On Translation," which is his attempt at a systematic study of translation. He continued to write more on the subject and over time his theoretical speculation accumulated to cover various aspects of translation. While some Chinese researchers of translation have noted the significance of this article in certain respects (eg. Zhou, 2004; Chen, 1997), a close examination of all his written discourse over time reveals to us a relatively mature theoretical system.

Briefly stated, the theoretical system of Lin Yutang's discourse on translation comprises the following parts: (1) the function of translation as stipulated by his general poetics; (2) a theory of translation that deals with the nature of translation, translator genius, and principles and procedures of translation; (3) application of the theory in translation criticism. Such a system may be graphically represented in Figure 2.

In this system L. Y. T. combines the artistic approach with the scientific approach. The artistic approach gives the vision and the scientific approach gives the method. Together they are supposed to make translation experience transferable.

However, brilliant and symbolic as it is, in the modern history of translation, Lin Yutang's theory does not sparkle like his translations for the lack of academic promotion like in the case of many in-vogue theories. The symbolic significance of his theory has been insufficiently noted by Xu Yuanzhong but only in that he is one of the pioneering Chinese translation theorists by emphasizing beauty (Xu, 1999). By using the word "symbolic," I mean that

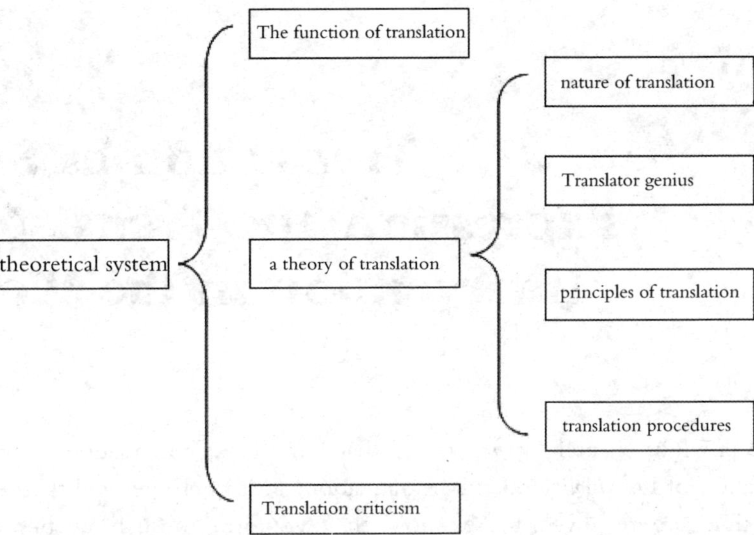

Figure 2 Theoretical System of Lin's Discourse on Translation

Lin Yutang represents a trend in translation studies, or to be more exact, he is one of the representatives of a paradigm shift from the impressionistic to the rational approach to the study of translation. This shift has not been completed, nor is it going to be in the future.

CHAPTER

Three

Translation as Self-Expression: the Translator's Intervention in the World

In the previous chapter, it was found that Lin Yutang's translation theory is an application of his *xingling* poetics in translation. In this chapter and the next, his translations are reviewed to see how they conform to such poetics of self-expression. The review reveals that translation for him is an act of self-expression. In his translations, the translator has a visible presence. He speaks through the translations. His choice of what to translate is not blind. He is often physically visible in the translations either by inserting comments or by writing extended introductions to them, purposefully linking himself and the translated texts. By doing so he distinguishes himself from many other translators. Translator autonomy in his case is maximized. He articulates his own voice by translating and he does things with translations. In other words, he is not a passive translator receiving translation assignments only for livelihood. Translation is one of his ways to intervene in the world.

Translation in Lin Yutang's System of Self-Expression

It is a human habit to flatter or deify the great. Speaking of Lin Yutang as a translator, people tend to unduly over-praise him. They say that his translations are good. By exaggerating the quality of his translations, they in fact belittle him, for they fail to understand the true nature of his greatness as a translator.

There are very few translators in history who have achieved prominence solely through the merit of their translations. On the whole, the translator cannot go very far. We have no evidence that Lin Yutang exceeds his predecessors in excellence, nor do we have proof that his translations are unsurpassed by later translators. An overview of all Lin Yutang's important works reveals that despite his many volumes of translations he is primarily an author, not a translator. The great does not need to be flattered or deified. The true value of Lin Yutang's work as a translator does not consist in how words come beautifully together to form sentences and how sentences in turn marvelously assemble to make a text. Rather, it lies in what they are for and whether they effectively serve that end. Therefore, to get a fair understanding of Lin Yutang's real greatness as a translator one must inevitably understand the nature and constitution of his self-expression.

Sharing the concerns of his age, he intervened in the realities of the times for betterment of the human condition. Too many people are weighed down by the problem of survival so that they do not think, or at least appear not to be thinking. It is a deplorable situation when the soul is entirely kidnapped by the body. An enlightened intellectual, Lin Yutang not only thought. He thought aloud. He shared his thoughts with his fellow beings in various forms. He wrote, he translated, he spoke and he fought. Therefore, his translations do not stand alone. They work together with his writings and other acts of self-expression to make his presence in this world.

1 Seeking Self-Expression as an Author

A well-read man who celebrates life, Lin Yutang's primary approach to the world is authorship by which he creates and disseminates ideas about a reasonable human existence. In the 1920s, under the influence of Lu Xun and other famous men of letters, he quickly matured as a writer of journalistic prose. He became a contributor to the *Yusi* magazine, fighting ferociously in debates with scholars who sided with the warlord government in Beijing. Later, alienated from the Lu Xun camp, he founded *Analects Fortnightly*, *This Human World* and *The Cosmic Wind*. These magazines established his reputation as a writer of *xingling* literature. In the early 1930s, he became a columnist of the English language magazine *The China Critic* and a contributor to the *T'ien Hsia Monthly* — another English magazine — and established a reputation as a prominent English language writer in China.

On the basis of his journalistic writings, two books were published in the mid-1930s that presented his systematic view of the world. *My Country and My People* is an interpretation of Chinese culture from Lin Yutang's perspective. His voice is found in the interpreting. In the book, he talks about China with pride and confidence. It is a candid analysis of China's past and present from the perspective of a Westernized Chinese intellectual in good English prose and with the author's unique personal insights. Criticism and pride are combined in the book. Such a tone has proved to be popular among Western readers. As a result, it turned out to be such a bestseller that it saw seven reprints within four months of its debut. He was famous overnight. The book was translated into various European languages and enjoyed the same success. Then he became a bigger name back in China (Lin, 2002: 131). Encouraged by the first success, he published *The Importance of Living* in 1937. The latter book was intended to introduce to Western readers the ancient Chinese way of thinking and living in comparison with Western thought and Western life. In this book, his emphasis on humanism is amplified. The entire book is about "mankind," "human life," life's philosophy, and life's forms. A sequel to *My Country and My People*, it met with greater success. It was recommended by the Book-of-the-Month Club shortly after its publication, and appeared on top of the bestseller list for fifty-two weeks successively.

He continued to develop his motifs in his novels and other writings, which include *Moment in Peking* (1939), *With Love and Irony* (1940), *A Leaf in the Storm* (1941), *Between Tears and Laughter* (1943), *The Gay Genius: the Life and Times of Su Tungpo* (1947), *The Vermillion Gate* (1953), *Looking Beyond* (1955), *The Chinese Way of Life* (1959b), *From Pagan to Christianity* (1959a), *The Red Peony* (1961b), *Imperial Peking: Seven Centuries of China* (1961a), *The Pleasures of a Nonconformist* (1962), and *The Flight of the Innocents* (1964). His ideas are fairly consistent throughout his works.

In his fiction, the characters often speak his way. In *Moment in Peking* (1939), he incorporates his essays into the novel. The story is told with admiration for Mr. Yao, the Taoist. In *The Vermillion Gate* (1953), we can see his shadow in Li Fei the protagonist who published an essay in the newspaper on the value of kowtowing (Lin, 1994f: 16). In real life, it was Lin Yutang who published the article "The Callisthenic Value of Kowtowing" (Lin, 1940: 159 –163). *Looking Beyond* (1955) describes an imaginary island somewhere in the Pacific. The book was written in 1955 but the story took place in 2004. It might have taken its inspiration partly from Tao Yuanming's *The Peach Blossom Colony*, which he admires. On this island, people are ridden of excessive progress and find their permanent safe haven. The criticism of material civilization in the West is a permanent Lin Yutang theme. *The Gay Genius* (1947), the life story of an ancient Chinese poet-statesman, embodies Lin Yutang's social and artistic ideals.

2 Translator as Part of the Author

There is a phenomenon in Lin Yutang's works: the author and the translator are often present at the same time. In *My Country and My People*, for example, translations appear in three forms: (1) passages translated by the author or other translators, such as excerpts from Su Tongpo, Tao Yuanming, Chuangtse, Liu Yuxi and other Chinese poets and authors; (2) adaptations such as the story of the "Ferry of the Jealous Woman"; (3) embedded translations of Chinese words, idioms, and proverbs such as "For the husband has in her eyes become a 'predestined enemy', and the Chinese proverb says 'predestined enemies will always meet in a narrow alleyway'" (Chu, 2005).

Such a union of the translator with the writer is not just a phenomenon. It is a recurring pattern. In *The Importance of Living*, *The Gay Genius*, *Moment in Peking* as well as in many other books, translations also abound, serving the purpose of the writing. The translations give the English language reader a sense of historical authenticity or a poetic feel.

On a global level, we also find the union of the translator with the author. We have noticed that Lin's Chinese translations fit in well with his conception of a new Chinese literature. His major English translations from the Chinese serve either or both of the two purposes: (1) to give substantial support to his interpretation of traditional Chinese culture; (2) to introduce to Western readers literature at his choice to express his conception of life and the world as expressed in his various writings. How his English translations echo the motifs in *My Country and My People* and *The Importance of Living* may be seen in two anthologies: *The Wisdom of China and India* (1942) and *The Importance of Understanding* (1960). The former is his compilation of his own translations and those of other famous translators. His translations include *Laotse*, *Chuangtse*, *The Aphorisms of Confucius*, *Chinese Tales*, *Parables of Ancient Philosophers*, *One Hundred Proverbs*, *The Mortal Thoughts of a Nun*, *Six Chapters of a Floating Life*, *Family Letters of a Chinese Poet* by Cheng Panch'ao (Zheng Banqiao), and *Epigrams of Lusin* (Lu Xun). While the former collection is largely philosophical echoing the "Bases" in *My Country and My People*, the latter illustrates the second part of the book: "Life" — women's life, social and political life, literary life, artistic life and the art of living. *The Importance of Understanding* is a huge collection of prose and verse, as many as 107 pieces in nearly 500 pages under subtitles like "human life," "love and death," "the seasons," "nature," "human adjustments," "women," "the home and daily living," "art," "literature," "after tea and wine," "ancient wit," "fools to this world," "wisdom," "Zen," and "epigrams and proverbs." It is almost a factbook for both *My Country and My People* and *The Importance of Living*. While trying to introduce a little bit of everything Chinese to the Western reader, in translating he never hid his preference and admiration for Chuangtse (Zhuangzi), Yuang Chuanglang (Yuan Zhonglang), Tao Yuanming, Shen Fu, Su Tungpo (Su Dongpo), Li Mi-an, and Li Liweng, writers of the *literarati* or expressionist tradition, with which he identified himself. Interestingly, the four books are closely related, like siblings. Two of them are more theoretical and the other two are more factual. In the more theoretical books, literary facts are given in small portions of translations. In the anthologies of translations, it is the other way around: literary facts are gathered and grouped only to be explained by brief notes and introductions. Most of Lin Yutang's important English translations appear in the two anthologies. His other English translations, *Letters of a Chinese Amazon and Wartime Essays* (1930) and *The Chinese Theory of Art* (1967), for example, can conveniently find their places in his system of expression represented by *My Country and My People*.

3 Political Involvement and Two Early Translations Inspired by the Chinese Revolution

Lin Yutang was never exactly a statesman in his life but his enthusiasm for politics used to be very strong and never abated. After all, as one of the pioneer thinkers of his generation and as a man of conscience he could hardly cut himself off from the realities of his times and the pangs of the rebirth of a nation. In the preface to *On the Wisdom of America* (1950), he says that whatever he writes he writes for the moderns. As Qian Jun notes, he has never been free from the politics of his day (1996: 50). His political engagement started as early as in the campaign against the warlord government in Peiping[①].

He was as wrathful as any other revolutionary youth in the first years after returning from his studies in America and Germany. In 1923, at the age of 29, he became a professor of English philology at the English Department of the National Peking University and a lecturer of English at the Peking Normal University. It was there in Peking that he started to write and take revolutionary actions. Later he recalled in his autobiographical sketch:

> I was a university professor in Peiping. I used to be very critical of politics and therefore considered one of the radicals in Peking University. At that time, professors of Peking University fell into two relentless and uncompromising opposing groups, one represented by *The Modern Review* weekly with Dr. Hu Shi as the leader, the other by the *Yusi* weekly under the leadership of the Zhou brothers — Zhou Zuoren and Zhou Shuren. I belonged to the second group. The debates on the problem between the Ministry of Education and the Peking Normal University were breathtaking. There, we had a center of free speech for the intellectual circles and a stage for intellectual activities. Inspired by the debates, I joined the students in their protests and fought the police with flagpoles and stones. Half-naked hooligans hired by the police threw bricks at the students

① About Peking, Beijing and Peiping: In modern Chinese history Beijing (北京) has also been known as Peiping (北平, the Wade-Giles system of transliteration), a name used by Chiang Kai-Shek's Nationalist Party and its supporters, for the capital of Chiang's Nationalist government was Nanjing. *Jing* means "capital." Beijing is a contemporary transliteration of the same name. Today, Beijing University still chooses to use its age-old English name Peking University to honor its tradition.

> so that they could not advance any further. And there came the opportunity to use my pitching skills in baseball. This fully made up for the life that I had not enjoyed as a Chinese university student in my overseas years. The Duan Qirui government in Peiping was rather tolerant and respected freedom of speech and assembly. The Kuomintang (the Chinese Nationalist Party) was behind the student movement. Some important members of the Nationalist Government are former student leaders in Peiping.
>
> (Lin, 1994g: 28 –29. Back translation from the Chinese version of Lin's autobiographical sketch.)

In the spring of 1926, Zhang Zongchang, nicknamed the Dog Meat General, entered Peking with his troops and killed two journalists without trial. Lin Yutang's life was also endangered. He was blacklisted by the warlord government under Duan Qirui as one of fifty radical professors to be arrested. In the following years, he taught briefly in Amoy University, worked as a secretary in the Foreign Ministry of the Nationalist Government in Hankow (Hankou) and later, disillusioned with the politics of the Kuomintang (Nationalist Party) moved to Shanghai to devote himself to writing and translating. In the Hankow years, his heart throbbed with revolutionary ardor, wrote for the papers in praise of the Northern Expedition, translated into English the diary of a girl soldier in the Nationalist army, and planned to translate Dr. Sun Yat-sen's works into English.

As mentioned earlier in the book, March to September, 1927, Lin Yutang served as a secretary in the Ministry of Foreign Affairs by presided over Eugene Chen (Chen Youren), who had earlier taken back the British Concession in Hankow. Lin Yutang was also editor of the English version of the literary supplement of the *Central Daily News*, where he published his English translation of the war correspondence from Hsieh Ping-ing (Xie Bingying), then a girl cadet fighting in the revolutionary army. In 1927, as the nationalist army pushed north victoriously, Lin Yutang's heart like many other Chinese hearts "throbbed with ecstatic joy over the birth of a new nation and the dawn of a new day for China."① He considered the Nationalist victory a spiritual act.

> It was the expressed and organized desire of a young nation for a new and modern China, a high resolve to break away from her feudalistic warlords and equally feudalistic

① See "Preface" to *Letters of a Chinese Amazon and Wartime Essays.*

> gentry. It was only through the impetuous genius of Young China, that first, fine, careless frenzy of her young soul — only young China had a soul, for how can you call rickety bones and shaky frames and sticky fingers and green-tinted skins a soul? — yes, it was only through such a tempestuous soul as hers that the desire for a revolution of things was brought near the possibility of [becoming] accomplished fact.
>
> (Hsieh & Lin, 1930: vi)

The taste for Ping-ing's war diary is a sign of his preference for *xingling* in literature, "a high poetic sensitivity to life and nature" (Lin, 1998b: 4). As a beginning writer, the girl did not display mature writing skills. She herself was shy of it, never expected its publication and was unwilling to re-publish it in book form. What he liked about the diary was exactly its *xingling*, an equivalent to Wordsworth's "natural overflow of powerful feeling." He dismissed writing techniques and truly believed in anything from the heart. The diary from the girl in army uniform, written on the knee in her precious leisure time in the intervals of war, was up to the standard. He told the girl when they first met at the editorial office, "As to writing, the most important thing is to write from your heart. Be natural and honest. No dragging on. No vanity. Be practical and then you become a good writer." (Hsieh, 1981. Translated from the Chinese.)

The letters from the girl soldier aroused Chinese interest in their own right. Lin Yutang first translated one of the letters and published it in the English edition of *Central Daily News*. It was equally liked by English-language readers, and an American columnist even bothered to write him a letter requesting more of the kind. This must have reinforced his confidence in translating the rest of the letters and finally putting them in a collection under the title of *Letters of a Chinese Amazon and War-Time Essays* (1930).

Here, Lin Yutang's idea of "writing from the heart" found its parallel in translation. He translated what he liked even though the original was from an anonymous young hand. In his enthusiasm for the revolution, he found a voice in Ping-ing for his throbbing heart. In this sense, Ping-ing's work was his own. His translation was intrusive and helped shape the "original": first, as mentioned above, the writing exercise of the beginning writer was under the direct influence of a famous author's counsel; second, Lin Yutang once and again encouraged the young writer to write more stories and together with the earlier stories publish the diary in book form, which is recorded both in Lin Yutang's preface to the Chinese edition of the war diary and the lady writer's nostalgic article commemorating the eightieth birthday of Lin.

Later Lin Yutang's revolutionary zeal subsided a great deal but not completely, for as late as 1929 he published a translation of *The Chinese Puzzle* by Arthur Ransome, British author and sympathizer of the Chinese Nationalist revolution and critic of British policy in China.

The Chinese Puzzle (1927) was by a British writer and journalist Arthur Ransome (January 18, 1884 – June 3, 1967), who wrote mainly for the famous *Manchester Guardian* (now the *Guardian*). In the winter of 1926, he was appointed by the *Manchester Guardian* and *Baltimore Sun* to travel to China to report on the volatile political situation in the country. He was in China from January to April 1927 and witnessed the turmoil of the Second Revolution. In such a short time, he was able to have a keen insight into the political situation of the country and write a book about it. The Chinese revolution had not bothered the British mind until suddenly they realized that their vital interests in China were in danger and therefore had to be defended. Ransome criticized the British businessmen in Shanghai who asked for strong military intervention because their property needed protection. He believed that the rise of Chinese Nationalist movement should be recognized and that British policy in China should be directed toward building a friendship with the Nationalists. As Lloyd George (former Prime Minister of the United Kingdom) points out in his preface to the book, the British "cannot coerce China into trading with us, therefore we must make friends with her"; "Chinese nationalism is essentially a just cause", British "interests and China's interests are identical", both nations wanting peace and trade; if the British "continue to insult and exasperate each other we are likely before long to have neither" (Ransome, 1927: 11). When the British were writing about the Chinese revolution, there was a tendency to pick out and exaggerate one or other of its many facets:

> ... One party fixes its attention on the factor of foreign privilege, and is thenceforward blind to all aspects of the revolution except that of a struggle against foreign domination in China. Another party is content with the names of generals, and thinks of the struggle merely as one between Chiang Kai-shek and his satellite generals on the one side and Chang Tso-lin, Yang Yu-ting, and their satellites on the other. A third party,

> blinking in the glare of Moscow, sees red everywhere and imagines the struggle as one between Communism and anti-Communism ...
>
> (Ransom, 1927: 33)

In Ransome's view, all these misconceptions honestly held by some people might be exploited by others to justify policies of their own. The British should not ignore the willing support of the different classes of Chinese given to the revolutionary forces. The Chinese revolutionaries were revolting against two things: domination by war-lords and economic encroachment by foreign countries. The Chinese, according to Ransome, were trying to shrug off whatever in their opinion impeded their own economic development and that was a fair definition of the aims of all respectable "bourgeois" revolutions. Both sides of the civil war, revolutionaries and warlords alike, would like to see Chinese control of their own customs. The British therefore should have a sober China policy. In this line of thinking, Ransome gave a detailed account of the then revolutionary China and the parties in the civil war, the Chinese people, foreigners in China and their conflict with the Chinese, and the revolutionary program of the Kuomintang.

The reason for translating the book was given in Lin's preface to the translation: Ransome was an unbiased journalist with an extraordinary insight. He was against the dispatch of more British troops to China, exposing the self-driven motives of the British expatriates in Shanghai and refuting the view that the Nationalist Revolution was another Boxer Rebellion. Ransome regarded the revolution as driven by the popular will of the Chinese people. Naturally he was not liked by the foreign newspapers in Shanghai, but with his stance he unconsciously became an international spokesman for the Chinese revolution.

> ... His condemnation of foreigners in Shanghai is exciting. His praise of the Nationalist Revolution is thought-provoking. Particularly, his analysis of the relationship between extraterritoriality and foreign concessions in China, between the foreign concessions and the Chinese civil war can help Chinese compatriots know better their slogans of 'Autonomous Customs' and 'Take Back the Foreign Concessions' ...
>
> (Ransome, 1929: I)

While appreciating Ransome's insight and able writing, Lin Yutang regretted the lack of criticism of the revolution in the book. In fact, the situation was so bad that in his translation he had to delete words by certain political figures and change the names of some. He seldom used pseudonyms for his translations and writings. This translation was one of the few exceptions. The name he used was Shi Nong (石农). As he almost made no mention of this book in his later works, researchers seldom pay any attention to it. There is no direct link found to identify Shi Nong with Lin Yutang. There is however strong evidence that he did the translation: (1) His daughter included the translation in a brief bibliography at the end of the Chinese language *Biography of Lin Yutang*. She did not mention his pseudonym but she mentioned the publisher. (2) Lin Yutang had an admiration for the style of Ransome and showed great enthusiasm in his recommendation to his readers of a section from *The Chinese Puzzle* in *Readings in Modern Journalistic Prose* (1931). (3) In 1929 and later, Lin Yutang still had a nostalgia for the exciting days of the Northern Expedition of the Nationalist army against the warlords, as revealed in his preface to *Letters of a Chinese Amazon and War-Time Essays* (1930).

Later, disillusioned with politics in the Nationalist government in Hankow, Lin went to Shanghai. There, he was an important member of a civil rights organization led by Mr. Ts'ai Yüan-p'ei (Cai Yuanpei) and Madam Song Qingling. Under the rule of the Kuomintang government, the environment became increasingly hostile to freedom of expression, but he continued to criticize current affairs under the veil of humor and it was through his political criticism in the *Little Critic* essays that Pearl S. Buck "discovered" this extraordinary Chinese writer in the English language①.

During the Second World War, he stood firm against Fascists. He organized donations in the US to contribute to the Chinese resistance and spoke for the anti-Fascist cause by writing the anti-invasion novel *Moment in Peking* (1939) and a number of anti-invasion articles②.

---

① See Pearl S. Buck's preface to *With Love and Irony*.

② Such as "As 'Philosophic China' Faces 'Military Japan'," *New York Times Magazine*, Dec. 27, 1936, p. 5. and "Can China Stop Japan in Her Asiatic March?" *New York Times Magazine*, Aug. 29, 1937, p. 5.

4 Initiating and Patronizing Translations

For many translators, translating either provides them with a livelihood or certain intellectual satisfaction or both. Whether for the meager profit or for the petty enjoyment, they simply translate whatever comes into their hands or whatever they are employed to translate. Lin Yutang never waited for assignment from publishers or other patrons like many translators do. He had his own ideas about what to do and often initiated translation projects. In addition to making translations, he caused translations to be made and even originals to be written. He lent support to translation projects when he regarded them as worthwhile. Even if a translation was made at request from a publisher, it was usually in his own line of thinking.

In 1927, while working for the Nationalist government in Hankow, Lin Yutang and S. F. Durham Chen (Chen Shifo), his former pupil at Tsinghua, conceived the idea of translating Dr. Sun Yat-sen's complete works into English, and Chen actually made a rough draft of some paragraphs and showed it to Dr. Lin, who thought well of his effort and encouraged him to go on. Unfortunately their stay in Hankow was cut short and they had to go their separate ways. "The pet project" they had fondly contemplated was abandoned for ever (Chen, 1974).

Hsieh Ping-ing is a grateful beneficiary of Lin Yutang's initiative and patronage. In "Blessings from Abroad" (1974), which was written for Lin Yutang's eightieth birthday, Ping-ing spoke nostalgically of suddenly finding herself a published author both in Chinese and in English translation by Lin Yutang:

> At the war front in Xinti, my fellow cadets and I were reading the literary supplement of the *Central Daily News*. To my amazement, my "From Kia-yü" letters, which were addressed personally to Mr. Sun Fu-yuan, were published in the newspaper. More unbelievably, Mr. Lin Yutang translated these letters into English and had them published! A girl under twenty, a country bumpkin who had not completed high school and had no knowledge of literature at all, what I had written must have looked awkward. Thanks to the kindness of Sun and Lin, my clumsy handwriting appeared in fine print. It was like a miracle. I could not bring myself to believe it. It was like a dream, a dream in which I was elated and awe-stricken at the same time, a long dream

from which I have not awoken yet.

(Hsieh, 1981. Translated from the Chinese.)

Not only did Lin Yutang translate Ping-ing's letters, he and Mr. Sun also encouraged her to publish her letters in book form. Ping-ing hesitated. She was shy about her writings because she felt herself lacking in writing skill. Lin Yutang told her that he was going to include his English translations of her letters in a collection of his essays to be published soon by the Commercial Press. He said to her, "Don't you make light of yourself. Your war diary, though lacking in writing skill, is a precious record of history. It has a historical and social significance. It will be a pity if the diary is not published. I will write a preface for your book. But you need to write more. There are too few letters." Encouraged and assisted by the two men, Ping-ing published her first book, which she considered her maiden work.

Lin Yutang's help did not stop at this. He and his two daughters were involved in the English translation of Ping-ing's autobiography. The two daughters, Adet and Anor, were responsible for the translation. A world-famous author by then, Lin Yutang did the proof-reading in person and wrote an introduction. In the course of translating the book, the Lins corresponded with Ping-ing from the United States and hoped that when royalties were paid to Ping-ing she could travel to the United States. The book, *Girl Rebel: the Autobiography of Hsieh Ping-ing, with Extracts from Her New War Diaries*, was published in 1940 by the New York-based John Day Company, the same company that had introduced Lin Yutang to Western readers.

In the 1930s, Lin Yutang founded or co-founded several Chinese language magazines: *Analects Fortnightly* (*Lunyu*) in 1932, *This Human World* (*Renjianshi*) in 1934, *The Cosmic Wind* (*Yuzhoufeng*) in 1935, and *Hsi-feng* (*Xifeng*) in 1936. These magazines promoted his literary ideals and his profile as a writer. Meanwhile, through them he became kind of a literary patron. The mission of *Analects Fortnightly* was to promote humor. *This Human World* advocated literature of self-expression in a familiar style. *The Cosmic Wind* was intended to discuss life in a personal way. The *Hsi-feng* aimed to introduce life and society in Europe and America by publishing translations from the Western press. While running the magazines Lin Yutang gathered around him a group of writers with a similar intellectual bent. He was such an established leader of the so-called Analects School of writers that in a letter to him Lao Sheh respectfully addressed him as *yushuai* (literally Language Marshal or Marshal of *Analects Fortnightly*). Among the important contributors to his magazines were Lao Hsiang (Lao Xiang), Lao Sheh (Lao She), and Yao Ying. Lin Yutang was eager to introduce their best writings to English language readers.

In 1933, Lao Sheh contributed a social satire "Talking Pictures" to *Analects Fortnightly* (No. 29). Lin Yutang liked this piece so much that he not only published it but also translated it into English. In his brief introduction to the translation he hails Lao Sheh as "one of the most distinguished humorist writers living" (Lin, 1936: 115). His translation was to show "the spirit of fun that some Chinese writers possess" and "also the quality of one type of light sketches that are appearing in the Chinese humorous magazine." (ibid.) Indeed, Lao She's stories can be quite humorous. In "Talking Pictures", for example, the first person claims that his second elder sister, having never seen a sound movie, had a theory about it, "as we all do about the things we haven't seen." Other light and acid remarks include "The less facts there are, the more theories there must be" and "Like great men discussing politics, she also indulged in making up a theory about something she did not quite understand." The sister's theory was that "sound pictures" derived the name from the noise the projector made and from the laughter the kissing scenes drew from the audience. The story that follows is full of fun and satire.

The *Analects Fortnightly* also published "Ah Chuan Goes to School!" a short story by Lao Hsiang①. The story reveals in a subtle manner the conflict between the modern school and the ancient level of life in the Chinese countryside. Ah Chuan's family was forced by law to send him to school. The family sold their precious possessions to buy the expensive textbooks. The first lesson consisted of four Chinese characters which means "This is mamma." The mother and the family could not understand because the picture was not that of his mother. The second lesson is "This is papa." Again it could not be understood. The kid went to ask the teacher, who said, "What is in the book is not real." When the boy recited "In the family, there are a papa, a mamma, and brothers and sisters," The grandmother felt slighted and furiously smashed a

---

① Real name Wang Hsiang Ch'en (王向辰)

cooking pot. Then Ah Chuan had to quit school whatever the consequence.

The second number of *This Human World*, which was devoted to familiar essays, published Lao Hsiang's "Salt, Sweat and Tears," a criticism of the proposed increase of salt tax. Lin Yutang translated the article to show the extraordinary refinement in the expression of ideas, "thanks to the censorship on literature and the great attempt for the 'centralization of ideas.'" (Lin, 1936: 115) He translated the article because he felt that it was "literature in the true sense of the word" as it throbbed "in harmony with the heart-beats of the poor peasants in China." (ibid.)

Lin's translations in such cases involve his identification of himself with writers sharing the same views. His translation is voluntary and spontaneous. He particularly likes Yao Ying, a lady writer who in her article airs the same views of reading and arranging books and magazines. In "On My Library," Yao talks about her way of cataloguing — the natural way: "there are books and magazines all over the place, on the sofa, in the dining room, in the side-board, near the wash-stand in the lavatory, etc." In such a method of cataloguing, there are three advantages: first, "there is beauty of irregularity"; second, "there is a richness and variety of interest" when books of different kinds stand side by side; third, "this system has the advantage of obvious convenience." The way of arranging books so much resembled his so that Lin Yutang would have accused her of stealing his ideas had he ever published a word on the same subject. The man loved the article so much that he wrote a long editorial postscript to it. When his rough English translation was published he wrote an introduction and translated his own postscript (Lin, 1936). In this case, Lin Yutang was translating himself by translating Yao Ying.

II The Translator's Intervention in the World for Change toward the Better

There are translators and translators. The mediocre translator receives an assignment, completes it, gets paid, and that is it. He usually passes in oblivion whether he wants fame or not. The good translator has been able to attain excellence in her work, enabling the translations to have some original artistic value. Her name comes only next to the original author(s) of famous works. And this is usually the best a translator can do. Only rarely do we see a translator win a reputation as a great translator and ignore what particular author or authors he has translated. Of the first category we see too many. To the second belong Zhu Shenghao, canonical Chinese translator of Shakespeare, and Fu Lei, hailed Chinese translator of French authors like Balzac and Roman Roland. Lin Yutang is the third type, the type of Lu Xun and Mao Dun. His translations are only part of the textual realities he has created and belong with his other texts to a vision beyond the translated texts.

Yet, in a manner of speaking Lin Yutang is one of a kind, in terms of the matter translated and the language direction of translation. On the one hand, his translations come together to support his general theme of expression in the way other author-translators translate to express themselves. On the other hand, he is a bilingual author and a two-way translator, switching between languages for the best expression. In the early years of his creative life, he worked mainly in Chinese. Then his work became bilingual. And then for a good part of his life, he was solely working in English. In his old age, he retired to the Chiang Kaishek-controlled province of Taiwan and his expression was found in Chinese again with occasional exceptions. Compared with author-translators who are only capable of production in the mother language, Lin Yutang has an additional channel of expression and an obvious advantage. When both his Chinese and his English translations are aligned, we see clearly his concerns about the modern world and his ideal of a better human world.

1 Chinese Translations: Translating the New

Guo Zhuzhang, a Wuhan University Professor (1999), says that in *Studies on Famous Translators* that to study Lin Yutang as a translator the first thing is to know what he has translated. Prof. Guo's words may ring hollow in the ears of many people because they are commonsense not to be said, but if we consider today's academia where people do not address the real issue, Guo becomes quite profound. He is talking commonsense but there *are* scholars who study translators without reading their texts or without knowing exactly what has been translated. To decide what has been translated by Lin is by no means an easy task, especially in deciding what has been translated into Chinese. Lin Yutang himself, while including his major English translations in the list of his own works, excludes all his Chinese translations (See *Memoirs*). In *Biography of Lin Yutang* Lin Taiyi, his second daughter, has made an incomplete and inexact but relatively reliable list of all the books he has written, translated, or edited in person. On Taiyi's list① are such Chinese translations as

The Chinese Puzzle (around 1928, Beixin)
Hypatia, or Woman and Knowledge (around 1929, Beixin)
A Critical Biography of Henrik Ibsen and His Love Letters (1929, Chunchao)
Pygmalion (1929, Kaiming)
The Diary of a Communist Schoolboy (1929, Chunchao)
New Criticism (1930, Beixin)

In the leading Chinese libraries and bookstores we can find other Chinese translations accredited to Lin Yutang: *The Autobiography of a Super Tramp*②, *Keeping Mentally Fit*, *The Road to Success*③, and *A Plan for Self-Management*. Not all the accreditations are correct. At least one book is falsely attributed: strong evidence points to fake translatorship in the case of *The Road to Success*. Besides, in the available biographical information on the man and in his own writings, little is found to reveal the authenticity of a so-called Lin Yutang version of *A Plan for Self-Management*.

Despite the problem of authenticity, two things are revealed by a glimpse of the titles of Lin Yutang's Chinese translations: first, his Chinese translations are about the new and the modern; and second, the name of Lin Yutang sells so well that publishers would like to share the profit generated by that name.

Feminism: *Hypatia, or Woman and Knowledge*

---

① Taiyi could not provide the exact years for the first two books.

② Completed in July, 1935 and published in March, 1941.

③ Marden, O. S. 1939. *The Road to Success*. Trans. Lin Yutang. Shanghai: *Zhongguo Zazhi*. [罗杰·马尔腾著. 1939.《成功之路》. 林语堂译. 上海中国杂志公司(1939年10月增订再版).] The book includes two of Marden's books: *Training for Efficiency* and *Every Man a King*.

This is a thesis published as a booklet by Dora Russell (1894 – 1986), second wife of the British philosopher Bertrand Russell. Hypatia (370 – 415) was a legendary woman scholar in ancient Egypt, famous for her learning, eloquence, and beauty. She was persecuted and killed by Christians who deemed her philosophical views unacceptable. Despite the title, the book is not about Hypatia in ancient Egypt. Dora was a hard-edged feminist and social campaigner. Hypatia is a symbol of a woman seeking knowledge and emancipation. Believing her work will also be denounced by Christians and torn into pieces, Dora named her book *Hypatia*.

Hypatia starts with the description of a sex war between men and women: In the past, man and woman, represented by Jason and Medea, measured their strength against one another as individuals. Though each voiced the wrongs and the naked brutality of their sex, it did not occur to either to seek in politics or in social reform a solution or a compromise. Jason, faced with a turbulent and insurgent female, resorted to the powers of kingship and the state — to suppress and exile, but not to remedy. Medea, driven mad by the contempt and ingratitude of men as individuals or in the mass, and aware that the law did not protect her, expressed herself in savage protest. Dora points out the modern injustices for women. In the modern era, women have won the right to vote in politics, but their victory is only partial. Men, unable to launch open warfare with women, take to sniping. A man, in spite of legal protection granted to married women, snipes the married women out of those posts for which they are peculiarly fitted — as teachers or maternity doctors. Dora Russell criticizes early feminists for abstaining from sex and advocates the enjoyment of bodily pleasures on the part of women: "I would hazard a guess that, relatively to the population, fewer women retain their virginity till death than in the Victorian period or the Middle Ages. In all probability it is sex, not sexlessness, which makes women cling so tenaciously to the right to earn their living." (Russell, 1925: 29) Dora herself did not quite believe in marriage although she did get married (Russell later divorced her because she gave birth to two children fathered by somebody else):

> Marriage brings a jealous intolerant husband, children, prying and impertinent neighbors — degraded and humiliating slavery for the vast majority of women. Thirty shillings a week and typing or working in a shop, a still tongue, or a toss of the head and

> the assertion that independence is the best; and, in the background a lover with whom somehow evenings are spent — a lover who has no claim and cannot tyrannize. A lover, perhaps, who pleads to become a husband, but has no chance unless his income is good or secure. Marriage would change him: Aspasia knows it. Marriage would also rob her of that thirty shillings a week, which alone stands between her and the abyss of primeval submission.
>
> (ibid: 30)

Dora thinks that both modern women and men should openly and shamelessly enjoy sexual love. She is not concerned with the morals of convention or superstition, but with the morals of experience. To the modern women, sex is an instinctive need as it is to men, and further, the prevention of conception brings to them no loss of poise, health, or happiness. Contraception is a blessed safeguard to health and recovery in the periods of rest between pregnancies. Sex information should be given. The beauty of sex and maternity should be taught to boys and girls at an early age in the same way science and physiology are taught. Sex information should be provided in lessons in physiology and taught as something natural, as botany or nature-study is taught: "One straightforward lecture of concise information could have dispelled the lurking mystery once and for all and imparted a sense of magic and wonder and ambition." (Russell, 1925: 45) Dora also encouraged the application of science and nature to maternity to avoid suffering in childbirth.

In real life, both Dora Russell and Bertrand Russell held similar views on sex and marriage. Both believed in free sex and they could excuse each other for occasional affairs. They got married but later divorced.

Interestingly, Lin Yutang approved of the idea of equality between women and men but not what the Russells were doing. On hearing the divorce of the Russells, he wrote "On Bertrand Russell's Divorce"① in both English and Chinese. This article shows that his view of marriage is essentially conservative.

---

① English version: Lin, Yutang (1935c). "On Bertrand Russell's Divorce." *The Little Critic, Essays, Satires and Sketches on China* (*Second Series: 1930 –1932*). Shanghai: The Commercial Press, Limited; Chinese version: Lin, Yutang. "On Bertrand Russell's Divorce." *This Human World* (XI). September 5, 1934. [林语堂. "罗素离婚. "《人间世》第 11 期,1934 年 9 月 5 日.]

Aware of the natural inequality between men and women, he believes that it is impossible to establish complete equality between the sexes. In his view, the wife is always the losing party in case of a divorce. His own marriage is a proverbial story of love and devotion. Here we come across one of his "bundle of contradictions" mentioned in *Memoirs of an Octogenarian* (1975). In his view, ideal and reality must be compromised. He translated Mrs. Russell's booklet because "she is a woman of new ideas." Either because her ideas were too new for China then, or because the translation was too poor, or both, the booklet was "almost never read" (Lin, 1994a: 41).

New Education: *The Diary of a Communist Schoolboy*

The Diary of a Communist Schoolboy was the English translation of Nikolai Ognyov's *Diary of Kostya Ryabtsev*. The novel shows the goings-on at a Soviet high school, which is like a miniature revolutionary republic with the students in charge. Its author went through several arrests under Czarist rule for his revolutionary activities. He was an exile abroad for quite some time. He mobilized workers and soldiers. The novel was applauded both in Russia and elsewhere. Within one year after its publication, it became known all over the world in German, English and Japanese. The title of the German version was closest to the Russian original. *The Diary of a Communist Schoolboy* was the English title. The Japanese translation of the title was *The Diary of a Soviet Student* (The Japanese version was a translation of the English version). Interestingly, three Chinese translations were published almost simultaneously with two bearing the same title *Xin'e Xuesheng Riji* (*The Diary of a Student in New Russia*), which was an adaptation of the Japanese title. Another Chinese translation — by Cha Shiji — was entitled *The Diary of a High School Student in Soviet Russia* (Ognyov, 1929c). Dan Ling's *Translator's Note* to his version of *The Diary of a Student in New Russia* (Ognyov, 1929b) helps us understand why Chinese publishers and translators took a liking to the novel:

The setting of the novel was Russia in 1923 and 1924, when the country was beginning its post-war reconstruction. Educational reform was going on in the schools. The new was battling with the old. Great vigor and creativity were seen in the young liberated Russians. At the threshold of a new epoch, Russia faced great difficulties against which its people fought. China had a similar background. The Chinese school system was also going through reforms. The Dalton Plan, which was adopted in the Soviet schools, had been introduced into the Chinese education system seven or eight years earlier. Constantine, the protagonist of the novel was a daring progressive boy. He observed life as it was and took positive steps to fight against the odds of life, instead of daydreaming, loitering, dissipating, or pursuing selfish ends. "This can be a great model for Chinese students today so that instead of dissipating their talents they can be devoted to the Nationalist government and work for the construction of the motherland." (Ognyov, 1929b: 3)

Lin Yutang's version (Ognyov, 1929a) is a collaboration with Zhang Yousong. The translation of this novel shows how as a translator he was sensitive to issues of his time.

New Drama: Ibsen and Shaw

Introducing Ibsen: *A Critical Biography of Henrik Ibsen and His Love Letters*

Historically China had no drama in the Western sense of the word. The translation of Western drama in the early decades of the twentieth century "provided a model for the Chinese *huaju*" (Qin, 1997: 28). Ever since then, the new art form has played an important part in the dissemination of new ideas, the country's resistance against foreign invasion, and the reform of Chinese society.

Lin Yutang's interest in modern Western drama is found in his translation of Georg Brandes' study of Ibsen and his translation of some of Ibsen's letters (1929). Ibsen is a revolutionary Norwegian playwright, who produced a number of plays that "changed the entire course of Western drama" (Simpson, 1998). His plays include *A Doll's House* and *An Enemy of the People*, among many others.

A friend of Ibsen's, Georg Brandes (1842 – 1927) was an influential Danish literary critic who influenced Ibsen's writing and wrote about the man. By translating Brandes, Lin Yutang was translating Ibsen. And more interestingly, by translating the artist, Lin Yutang came to resemble the artist: both left their home country and became, if we do not take the word "exile" literally, exiles (the difference lies in the degree of being an exile), won a name abroad and retired home with glory in old age. Such a similarity is more than a coincidence. If we compare Lin Yutang's later popularity with what he had translated from Brandes' discussion of Ibsen, we cannot help but think that his cosmopolitan idea of writing has much in common with Ibsen's:

> For most writers, it is bad luck to be born in a country whose language is not spoken in other countries. Becoming world-famous is easier for a mediocre writer who writes in a popular language than for a genius who has to speak through a translator.
>
> First, the essence of the writer's art is lost in translation and this is not only true of poetry. Second, the reader's knowledge and experience that the original writer appeals to are common sense at home but in translation become alien to foreign readers. The works of a writer are consistent with the intellectual context of the writer and are created for the context, which is different from contexts elsewhere.
>
> Ibsen has overcome these difficulties because for one thing his modern prose drama has been written in brief and concise conversations and, for another, as his art improves he has started to write for the world audience instead of readers at home in Northern Europe (He is ignoring factual accuracy. For example he imagined a Rosemersholm Castle, which has never existed in Norway), and third, he was the inventor of a new art — reputed German playwrights such as Alexandre Dumas and Emilie Angier [Note: here Alexandre Dumas and Emilie Angier are taken for Germans by mistake] have become old-fashioned because of his plays.
>
> (Lin, 1994d: 51. Translated from the Chinese.)

Lin might have been inspired by Ibsen. Had Lin not written in the English language and had he not written in a next-to-conversation style, he would not have enjoyed such great international popularity as he had. However, there is a difference between Lin and Ibsen. What Lin presented was a modern perspective to interpret existing knowledge. Ibsen was a fiery revolutionary.

Pygmalion

It is said that Chinese drama (*huaju*) started in 1907 with a partial and experimental performance of Bernard Shaw's *Pygmalion* by a group of Chinese students in Japan①. Lin Yutang was the first translator of the complete manuscript of the play ever published in Chinese. His translation, renamed *The Girl Who Sells Flowers* was published in 1929 as bilingual reading for Chinese learners of English and reprinted in 1931, 1945, and 1947. His version was 27

---

① In 2007, the Chinese are celebrating the centennial of this art form in China.

years ahead of a later influential version by Yang Xianyi under the title *Pikemeiliang*, a transliteration of the original title.[①] Yang's version completely employs the vernacular and because of this has almost replaced its predecessor among the general reading public of today. Interestingly, it has adopted the Chinese title by Lin Yutang in its later editions. This shows the influence of the Lin Yutang version.

The play is a story of a professor of phonetics who believes that one's accent has a great deal to do with his social position and sets out to prove that he can turn a girl selling flowers on the streets into a lady by simply improving her way of speaking. He does it, but the girl refuses to be dominated by the condescending professor. According to Margery M. Morgan (1983), "*Pygmalion* examines the assumptions of social superiority and inferiority that underlie the class system, and demonstrates how unconsciously regulated patterns of social behavior (etiquette, opposed to more spontaneous manners) help preserve class distinctions."[②]

Bernard Shaw, author of the play, was the creator of "a new art of drama in the 1890's" and "remained the vigorous center of the British theater for half a century" (Morgan, 1983). His ideas and the pungency of his pen were popular among the Chinese progressive intellectuals. When he visited Shanghai, he was greeted with a warm welcome from the enlightened intellectuals. Lin Yutang, then member of a progressive organization — China Civil Rights Alliance[③], took part in the enthusiastic reception of Bernard Shaw in the house of Madame Song Qingling, widow of the late Dr. Sun Yat-sen in February, 1933. Also present were the other leading figures of the civil rights organization, including Lu Xun and Ts'ai Yüan-p'ei (Cai Yuanpei) as well as two international friends Harold Robert Isaacs (chief-editor of the *China Critic*)

---

① In Shaw, Bernard. 1956. *Selected Works of Bernard Shaw*. Trans. Yang Xianyi. Beijing: People's Literature Press. [肖伯纳著. 1956.《肖伯纳选集》. 杨宪益译,人民文学出版社:1956.]

② Morgan, Margery M. (1983). GEORGE BERNARD SHAW. British Writers Vol. 6. British Council: Pages 101 –132. Retrieved from Literature Resource Center: http://galenet.galegroup.com

③ 中国民权保障同盟

and A. Smedley, both progressive journalists. This in some way shows where Lin Yutang's ideological sympathies were at that time. In fact, Lin Yutang was so interested in Shaw's humour and wisdom that the Englishman appeared in a number of his writings. ①

Shaw, with his two qualities of truthfulness and humor, represents for Lin Yutang a new way of thinking and an interesting way of writing:

> Bernard Shaw has been well known in China for some time, though he has not been much translated. This is deplorable because among our compatriots there are still a lot whose minds are confused. Shaw's dissension or heresy can be enlightening and thought-provoking. Doolittle the cleaner in *Pygmalion* is the incarnation of Shaw. The man's attack on middle-class mentality is exactly part of Shaw's ideology. Why the attack, the irony and the satire? This cannot be understood by the worldwise hypocrites with their middle-class morality. The hypocrites have been moralists throughout history, but it is lamentable that the educated should have confused minds. The vulgar philosophy of "don't know life, how know death [Note: Lin's favorite way of translating the Confucian maxim]" has done a great deal over the past two thousand five hundred years, which is so evident that it requires no more explanation from me.
>
> The hypocrites neither understand nor can bear the sting of Bernard Shaw's tongue. Therefore they dismiss him by calling him "a funny guy." This is absurdity in its extremity. As Shaw puts it himself, "My way of joking is to tell the truth; it is the funniest thing in the world." Shaw is joking again by mating truth with joke and this is a maxim from Shaw. Shaw's humor, in fact, any humor, is dedicated to the telling of truth, to the disclosure of all truths in life, society, education, politics, marriage, medicine, religion, etc. Such is the secret of Shaw's art and the essence of humor. Those who are accustomed to a peep show — naturally "the majority" — regard the show as the truth and have to dismiss a guy who discloses the nature of the show as a funny guy. In case the fault is with somebody else, it can be smiled away. In case the fault is one's own, he flies into a rage, defends himself and accuses the trouble-maker. In this play, Eliza says that when she was a poor flower girl she could make a living by selling flowers but six months later she becomes so destitute that the only thing she can do

---

① These include "Random Thoughts on Reading Biography of Bernard Shaw" (读《萧伯纳传》偶识), "More on Shaw" (再谈萧伯纳), "A Talk with Bernard Shaw" (*With Love and Irony*), "Corrections of 'Welcome to Bernard Shaw'" (欢迎萧伯纳文考证), "Bernard Shaw and the Rotary Club of Shanghai" (萧伯纳与上海扶轮会), "Bernard Shaw and America" (萧伯纳与美国).

is to sell herself by marrying a man after having corrected her pronunciation and learned the manners of a lady. Is this truth or a joke? ...

(Lin, 1994d: 87 –88. Translated from the Chinese.)

Lin Yutang believes in the new way of thinking and the interesting way of writing, and he has been famous for the same.

New Criticism: Benedetto Croce, J. E. Spingarn, Oscar Wilde, E. Dowden and Van Wyck Brooks

As has been pointed out in Chapter Two, Lin Yutang identifies himself with Western theories of expression by critics like Croce and Spingarn. Such identification is borne out by his translator's notes to his anthology of Chinese translations entitled *Xinde Wenping*, or *The New Criticism* (1930). His translation of the New Criticism literature consists of excerpts from Benedetto Croce's *Aesthetic as Science of Expression and General Linguistic*①, selected translations of some American and European critics, which include an excerpt from "Creative Criticism: Essays on the Unity of Genius and Taste" and "Seven Arts and Seven Fallacies" back translation of the Chinese title) by J. E. Spingarn, "The Critic as Artist" from *Intentions* by Oscar Wilde, "French Criticism" (back translation of the Chinese title) by E. Dowden and "The Critics and Young America" by Van Wyck Brooks.

Lin Yutang welcomes the New Criticism of the expressionists because it does away with all restrictions and archetypes. The expressionists, according to Lin Yutang, believe that literature and all other fine arts "are unbounded expression of individuality" (Lin, 1994d: 194). Therefore, archetypes cannot be constructed.

New Scholarship: *Keeping Mentally Fit*

This is a book on popular psychology by Joseph Jastrow (1863 –1944), American psychologist. The author is concerned with the psychology of the average reader. It is intended to "meet the needs of the popular reader who

---

① The excerpts were first published in the *Yusi* magazine (《语丝》) in 1929 and then published again in *New Criticism* (《新的文评》) in 1930.

catches the quarry on the wing, and reads as it runs or rides (Jastrow, 1928, Preface viii)." It concerns itself with the application of psychology to achieve mental health, as mental fitness is a worthy ideal and must be made a practical reality for most people to retain their jobs and their content. Jastrow (1928) deals with such topics as "Keeping Happy," "Starting Early — With the Child," "Delicate Questions," "Tricks of the Mind," "How Queer We Are," "The Cult of Beauty," "The Psychology of Sport," "Reading and Judging Character," "Choosing and Holding Your Job," and "'Personal': A Few Typical Cases." Through a survey of human interests, an analysis of the surface of things, the author arrives at the simply stated nature so that his reader can "get the point and carry away an impression." Quite unlike a psychology textbook, the book is in a journalistic style to be read by the laymen of psychology.

New Experience: *The Autobiography of a Super Tramp*

First published in 1908, this is an autobiographical novel by W. H. Davies (1871 –1940), tramp, poet, and autobiographer, who was active from 1905 to 1939 in England, America and Europe. This biography is a glorification of his personal experience as a tramp, particularly in America — then a fast-developing continent fascinating to many — working, begging, stealing and doing everything that decent people would not do. It was nothing conventional both in content and style so that Bernard Shaw wrote in the preface: "... If he is to be encouraged and approved, then British morality is a mockery, British respectability an imposture, and British industry a vice. Perhaps they are: I have always kept an open mind on the subject; but still one may ask some better ground for pitching them out of the window than the caprice of a tramp." (Davies, 1963: 5) Shaw did not see some of the doings of the beggars as immoral. In his eyes, it was simply a matter of bad luck: "I suppose every imaginative boy is a criminal, stealing and destroying for the sake of being great in the sense in which greatness is presented to him in the romance of history. But very few get caught. Mr. Davies unfortunately was seized by the police; hauled before the magistrate and made to expiate by stripes the bygone crimes of myself and some millions of other respectable citizens. That was hard luck, certainly." (Davies, 1963: 10) On the one hand, it is the candid narration of one man's story. On the other, it is "a fascinating picture of a vast, bustling continent intent on its own affairs" as the publisher of the 1963 edition says in the back cover.

With genuine appreciation, Lin Yutang translated the novel. He thus says of the author and the book in "The Translator's Preface" (Lin, 1941):

> W. H. Davies, a one-legged British poet, is a world-famous author. Earlier in his life, he traveled as a tramp across the Atlantic, in America and in Europe. A beggar, a rogue and a thief, he and his kind lived a life free from worries for food and clothing. He enjoyed free train rides and took the prison for a hotel. His life, miserable in appearance, was poetic: romance, abandonment, pleasures, excitements ... and humor. Even the veteran writer Bernard Shaw admires his freedom in the preface.
>
> Davies' writings are mostly poetry. This book is an exception. It is a candid, vivid and humorous account of his tramping stories. Upon publication, the literary world was moved and it is considered an unprecedented masterpiece.
>
> Sure enough, here is the hard evidence.
>
> Therefore, I dare to strongly recommend this writing by the one-legged author.
>
> (Preface dated July, 1935. Translated from the Chinese.)

He likes the novel and recommends it to his readers.

The Authenticity of *The Road to Success*①

In 1994, the Northeast China Normal University (NCNU) published supposedly Lin Yutang's translation of sixty-three chapters of O. S. Marden's *Training for Efficiency* under the title *Cheng Gong Zhi Lu* (*The Road to Success*) in its Lin Yutang collection, which remains the largest in Chinese and a major source of reference for Chinese readers and researchers. In 2003, the Shaanxi Normal University (SNU) published the same title but mixed up the sixty-three chapters with twenty-two chapters of *Every Man a King*②. The SNU edition dates back to the 1939 edition of the same title by the Shanghai-based China

① Marden, O. S. 1939. *The Road to Success*. Trans. Lin Yutang. Shanghai: *Zhongguo Zazhi*. [罗杰·马尔腾著. 1939.《成功之路》. 林语堂译. 上海中国杂志公司(1939年10月增订再版).]

② *Every Man a King* is an inspirational masterpiece by Orison Swett Marden and *Training for Efficiency* is a selection from the Marden books.

Zazhi Company.

The NCNU edition is definitely mistaken about the translatorship whatever original source it may have. It is in fact an early work of a young man and a later educationist Cao Fu, prior to his enrollment in Fudan University. Cao's translation was published in 1932 by the Kaiming Bookstore①. The two versions do not differ significantly from each other. The changes in the so-called Lin Yutang version are no more than editorial in nature.

The 1939 *Zhongguo Zazhi* edition and the 2003 SNU edition are absurd. Had Lin Yutang been the translator, he would have known that the author's name is Orison Swett Marden instead of Roger Marden! Besides, the "Translator's Preface" lies when it says that Lin Yutang has "improved" the translation because "the book has been translated by Cao Fu but Cao's translation is not good enough for popularization." In fact, Cao's translation was one of the most popular readings among senior high students of that time according to a survey by Mr. Gong Qichang (Cao, 1943). The minor changes in the so-called Lin Yutang version are not significant enough to support the claim of improvement. What is astonishing is that "Lin Yutang's" preface is almost an exact copy of Cao's preface except for the addition of the statement:

> "The book has been translated by Cao Fu but Cao's translation is not good enough for popularization. I have made some corrections of Cao's version and put it together with *Every Man a King*, another book by Dr. Marden under the new name *The Road to Success*."
>
> (Lin, 2003. Translated from the Preface)

and the deletion of the last paragraph:

> Part of the book has been published in the *Juewu* (*Awakening*) column of *Minguo Daily*. Confined by newspaper space, the translation suffered from omissions. Here in this book, omissions are restored and some revisions are made.
>
> (Cao, 1932. Translated from the Preface.)

Elsewhere in the preface, there are only slight changes in tone as befits a master. For example, where "Lin" says,

---

① Marden. O. S. 1932. *Motivational Philosophy*. Trans. Cao Fu. Shanghai: Kaiming Bookstore. [O. S. Marden 著，曹孚译.《励志哲学》. 开明书店，1932.]

> I have experienced the same gloom and depression as young people today are going through. Marden's writings have lifted me out of it all and changed my attitude toward life. All the gloom, depression, despair and despondency are gone. Now what faces me is a world and a life full of sunshine. I am therefore recommending this book to young people with whom my sympathies go and who hopefully might be inspired and affected.
>
> (Lin, 2003: Translator's Preface, Translated from the Chinese.)

Cao says almost the same. The only difference is deletion by "Lin" of Cao's "as a young man" in the first sentence. Given Lin's stature and achievements, it is unlikely for him to plagiarize a young man who was going to college. As Cao was translating he published parts of the book in a newspaper in 1931. In the following year the complete translation was published in book form. The earliest version of "Lin's" *The Road to Success* was in 1939, three years after his departure from China. Lin became a world-famous author in 1935. It might have been the publisher's trick in a highly competitive book market for motivational books.

Lin Yutang's busy schedule after 1936 did not seem to allow for translating books from English to Chinese for domestic readers. In 1936, he left China for the U. S. In 1937, he published his second important book in English: *The Importance of Living*. In 1938, he went in Europe and planned for his first novel *Moment in Peking*. In 1939, *Moment in Peking* was published. In 1940, he paid a brief visit to Chiang Kai-shek in Chongqing and then left China again. In the same year, he published *With Love and Irony*, a collection of his *Little Critic* essays in the *China Critic*, as well as his early translations from the Chinese in *The Travels of Mingliaotse* and *Guwen Xiaopin* (*Ancient Vignettes from the Chinese*). For this reason only, it is doubtful whether he has translated another book *A Plan for Self-Management* by Everett William Lord.

What is confusing and leaves the problem of authenticity inconclusive is that the Marden style of writing is a familiar style that appeals to a mass audience and so is Lin's style of writing in both English and Chinese. While Marden's writings are psychologically therapeutic, some of Lin's English writings and translations are also intended for mental health such as *The Importance of Living* and *The Importance of Understanding*.

2 English Translations: Translating the Old

In comparison with Lin Yutang's Chinese translations, his English translations are very easy to cite. They start with literature of his day by authors such as Hsieh Ping-ing and Laoshe but are mainly from pre-modern Chinese literature. As he became an expatriate and the physical distance increased between himself and his country, and as he grew older, he became more and more interested in the translation of old literature of the old country.

His early English translations are concerned with the problems and aspirations of the Chinese in the modern era. However, he did not translate much of modern Chinese literature. The diary of Ping-ing for him represents the modern spirit of the Chinese to renovate the country. "Talking Pictures" by Lao Sheh (Lao She), "Ah Chuan Goes to School!" and "Salt, Sweat and Tears" by Lao Hsiang (Lao Xiang), with their humor and satire, represent the state of being of the Chinese caught between the old and the new. While modernity and tradition constitute the two themes of his English translations, we can perceive a shift from the former to the latter with the passage of time.

A Story of Chinese Life: *Six Chapters of a Floating Life*

The book was translated in the spring and summer of 1935. In this autobiographical narrative, Shen Fu (1763 –?), recorded the story of life with his wife. The two lived a simple yet beautiful life. Lin Yutang finds two things that make the booklet worth translating: the heroine is "one of the loveliest women in Chinese literature" (Lin, 1942: 965), and "in this simple story of two guileless creatures in their search for beauty, living a life of poverty and privations, decidedly outwitted by life and their cleverer fellowmen, yet determined to snatch every moment of happiness and always fearful of the jealousy of the gods," he "seemed to see the essence of a Chinese way of life as really lived by two persons who happened to be husband and wife. Two ordinary artistic persons who did not accomplish anything particularly noteworthy in the world, but merely love the beautiful things in life, lived their quiet life with some good friends after their own heart — ostensibly failures and happy in their failure." (ibid: 966) Lin Yutang found in the couple "the spirit of truth and beauty and the genius for resignation and contentment so characteristic of Chinese culture." (Shen, 1999: 22) There should have been six chapters of the book but the extant version (dating back to 1877) contains only four chapters. Lin Yutang once tried to find the missing chapters without success. He even went to find the grave of the hero and heroine. Fascinated by the story, he decided to render it into English, "so that the world will know how a Chinese couple lived a simple, quiet and adorable life (ibid: Postscript)." First serialized in the *Hsi-feng Monthly* (*Xifeng Monthly*) in 1935, Lin's English version was the first to have ever been done.

Despite his experience in translating and writing, Lin Yutang was extremely meticulous in his translation of the booklet. Before publication in the *T'ien Hsia Monthly* (*Tianxia Monthly*), he had made over ten revisions and continued to improve his work after publication. The story was also published in the *Hsi-feng Monthly*. Already an accomplished author in English, he was modest enough to have his friend Zhang Peilin make some corrections. As he said in his postscript, "English readers were particularly fond of it." (Shen, 1999) Two things are meant here: The story was intriguing enough, and the translation was good enough. Later, a book edition was published by the Shanghai-based Hsi-feng She in 1941. The story is also an important part of *The Wisdom of China and India* (1942). Today, it still enjoys popularity among English language readers and English learners in China. From February 1999 to June 2003, the new FLTRP edition underwent four prints with a circulation of 32,000. Interestingly, the book as of date has never been published overseas in an independent volume. Nonetheless, through today's international book marketing network, we know for sure Lin Yutang's translation of the story is reaching a yet larger world audience.

Lin Yutang thus explains why this story of Chinese life represents the spirit of Chinese civilization:

> ... For the answer to the question "What is the spirit of Chinese civilization?" is to be found in the *Six Chapters*, in the picture of Chinese life, not as Chinese thinkers thought life ought to be lived but as the actual common people have lived it. The *Six Chapters*, as well as the *Family Letters of a Chinese Poet*, gives us some intimate glance into Chinese life, valuable because it was autobiography and not fiction, and was written by a Chinese for Chinese readers. The beauty and ugliness of Chinese family life are there,

> and there are both good and bad characters in it. But the fundamental temper of the Chinese spirit, its struggles, its longings, its resignations, and its causal glances along the wayside of life, are all there, written down sincerely by a common medium-educated Chinaman who made not too great a success either with his paintings or with his small trade as a commercial traveler.
>
> (Lin, 1942: 576)

This booklet can give Western readers an intimate understanding of the spirit of Chinese culture through a lifelike story.

Chinese Wisdom in the Wisdom Books

Lin Yutang has six "wisdom" books to his name. Four of them are about the wisdom of China in translation accompanied by his interpretations. The other two wisdom books are respectively about India and America. His selected translations of Chinese philosophy and the Chinese way of life form a coherent discourse in itself. The wisdom books were born at an age in which the world was aspiring for mutual understanding between the peoples. Westerners, especially Americans as their imperialist expansion went on, needed a broader global vision. In such a context, there was a hunger for the wisdom of other peoples: the wisdom of China, the wisdom of India, the wisdom of Israel, etc. Lin's selections gave the English reader a quick understanding of Chinese culture in one book. Thanks in part to market demand, his translations underwent several expansions or reorganizations under different titles to cater to different readerships. The four books on China can almost be considered one book if we examine their relationships:

> The major part of *The Wisdom of Confucius* (1938) can be found in "The Wisdom of China" in *The Wisdom of China and India* (1942);
>
> *The Wisdom of China* (1948) is a reprint of "The Wisdom of China" section in *The Wisdom of China and India* (1942);
>
> *The Wisdom of Laotse* (1948) is an expansion of his translation of *Laotse* and *Chuangtse* in *The Wisdom of China* (1948).

Therefore, a study of "The Wisdom of China" in *The Wisdom of China and India* (1942) is a study of almost all his books on the wisdom of China, including Chinese ideals of life and how the Chinese have lived them. "The Wisdom of China" follows Lin's basic conception of Chinese ideals of life: The

Confucian plus the Taoist views and ways of life[1]. The Confucian view is concerned with how to get along well in this world while the Taoistic view tells how to get away from the cares of the world and enjoy life. Such a conception was explained in *My Country and My People* and reiterated in *The Importance of Living*. Consistent with his earlier ideas, "The Wisdom of China" logically contains three major parts: (1) Taoist classics (*Laotse*, *the Book of Tao* and *Chuangtse*, *the Mystic*); (2) Confucian classics including *The Book of History*, *Mencius*, selected translations of *The Analects* entitled *The Aphorisms of Confucius*[2], and *The Golden Mean* of Tsesze; (3) the practical side of life as the Chinese have lived it, which includes some Chinese poetry, Chinese tales, his earlier translation of *Six Chapters of a Floating Life*, some parables of ancient philosophers, some family letters of Chen Panch'iao, a Chinese poet, some epigrams of Lusin (Lu Xun) and one hundred proverbs. The poetry section consists of works by other translators and one piece by himself — "The Mortal Thoughts of a Nun." This section was meant "for the West to appreciate something of the spirit of the Chinese poetic genius" (Lin, 1942: 867). "The Mortal Thoughts of a Nun," his own translation included in this section, was meant to show "the typically humorous common-sense and irreligious attitude of the Chinese people." (ibid: 870) The Chinese tales are mainly fairy tales. They are intended to be a cure for the loss of naiveté of the Western modern man who only believes in verifiable truth and confuses it with poetic truth or truth of imagination. In the family letters, proverbs, and particularly in the *Six Chapters of a Floating Life* can be found "the true spirit of Chinese culture" (Lin, 1942: 576). The core of the wisdom books on China is Chinese philosophy. Lin Yutang has made a somewhat systematic translation of the classics of the major Chinese schools of thought and provided his interpretations. Although most of the works had been translated before him, he made a

---

① Other schools of thought are not mentioned except for the inclusion of Motse.

② The selected translations from *The Analects* were classified into "description of Confucius by himself and others," "the emotional and artistic life of Confucius," "the conversational style," "the Johnsonian touch," "wit and wisdom," "humanism and true manhood," "the superior man and the inferior man," "the mean as the ideal character and types of persons that Confucius hated," and "government."

difference by making the abstruse Chinese texts transparent to English readers in simple English.

Classic Chinese Literature of the Soul: *The Importance of Understanding*

A major volume is *The Importance of Understanding* (1960), which contains many of his English translations over the years and serves as a source book for *The Importance of Living*. 107 gems of Chinese literature are included. The idea of compiling such a book came after he wrote the bestseller *The Importance of Living*. He says in the "Preface" to the book,

> Since I wrote *The Importance of Living*, quite some time ago, I have promised myself that I would one day translate some of the best Chinese writings on this Chinese and peculiarly human outlook and understanding of life which are the sources of my own thinking. I did not know what I was doing when I wrote in that book all that I thought of human life and human subjects from the biggest to the smallest. My readers' reactions always surprised me, as if I had something new to say. It did not seem so to me; I was talking a lot of platitudes, which are called in Chinese *lao sheng chang tan*, or "old man's old rubbish."
>
> (Lin, 1960: 17 –18)

These translations, the "snapshots of truth," representing "the sentiment, the mood, the thought of the moment," according to the editor-translator, are meant to provide nourishment for the soul and to be read in a casual way.

3 Linking the Two Largest Language Communities: Chinese-English Dictionary of Modern Usage①

In 1967, Lin Yutang could finally put into practice his idea of compiling a Chinese-English dictionary, which he considered "a pleasurable job of discovering truth like cattle roaming a mountain slope to feed themselves" (Ma, 1981).

The dictionary used his Chinese "Instant Index System," which he had

① Strangely, the hard copy of the dictionary I have borrowed from a professor does not have a copyright page. So I do not know which edition it is.

designed for the Chinese typewriter he had invented and the "Romanized Index of Characters," of which he had been a co-author[①]. He had a project team to assist him. As he promised the publisher that he would translate all the entries by himself, he carefully checked and revised again and again every word in the dictionary, both Chinese and English. With three years of hard work, he crowned his translating career with the colossal work: *Chinese-English Dictionary of Modern Usage*. This is not a one-way dictionary. Every English word is listed in the "English Index" at the end of the dictionary. His dictionary views the meaning of a Chinese character or a word as changing in different contexts and translates the same character or word into a different word or different words depending on its usage. To achieve clarity of meaning, various contexts of usage are provided as examples. For example, the entry for the Chinese character 低 is as follows:

低
91A.71 -9
di.
V. i. & t. To lower, bend, bow: 低首 bend one's head; nod as consent; 低首無言 bend one's head, silent; 低首下心 be servile, submissive.
Adj. Low, opp. 高 high: 高低不平 uneven; 低價 low price; 低一格 one notch (class) lower: 低聲 low voice, whisper; 低音 bass, low octave; 低潮 low tide; 低原 low plain; 低三下四的 low, menial person or job; 低賤 —*jiahn* ↓; low in grade, inferior: 低貨 inferior goods; 低級趣味 (of writing, entertainment) catering to cheap, lower tastes.
低昂 *di-arng*, v. i. & adj., (of singing, prices) swing up and down, soar and dip.
低沉 *dichern*, adj., deep and low (voice).
低回(徊) *dihueir*, v. i., loiter, linger, sunk in thought.
低賤 *dijiahn*, adj., cheap in price; low-class.
低空 *di-kung*, n., low altitude (flying).
低眉 *di-meir*, adj., looking downward in submission or (of Buddha) kindly.

① As a linguist, in 1923 - 1924, Lin was a co-worker on the official GR (Guoyuu Romantzyh), a romanization system of the Chinese language and first proposed the basic form (a-ar-aa-ah) and its modifications. To avoid confusion, he returned to the basic pattern in the dictionary.

低迷 *dimir*, adj., confused in thinking, dazed.
低能 *dinerng*, adj., stupid, incompetent: 低能兒 n., stupid person, an imbecile.
低聲 *di-sheng*, adj., soft-voiced, low-voiced.
低下 *dishiah*, adj., low, lowly.
低首 *di-shoou*, v. i., bend one's head.
低頭 *di-tour*, v. i., bend one's head (in thought, submission, in silence), also 低首 [*di1shou3*] ↑.
低窪 *diwa*, adj., low, low and damp (of place).
低微 *diweir*, adj., lowly, humble (birth, character); weak and small (voice).
低溫度 *di wenduh*, n., low temperature.
低啞 *diyaa*, adj., low and hoarse (voice), creaking noise of oars.
低音部記號 *diyinbuhjihhauh*, n., (mus.) F clef.
低音大提琴 *diyindahtirchirn*, n., contrabass; double bass.

Wherein 91A. 71 −9 is the position of the character in the dictionary according to the Instant Index System. *To lower*, *bend*, *bow* is the definition of the character. 低首, 低首無言 and 低首下心 are the contexts to which such a definition applies. The same character with the same meaning has to be translated in the same or a different way in a different context; *low* is the definition of the character as an adjective but the examples show that the same *low* may either appear as a *low* in *low price* for 低价, *low voice* for 低声, or disappears in *whisper* for 低声, *bass* for 低音 and *inferior* for 低贱, etc. At the end of each entry, if applicable, the conventional combinations (words, phrases or idioms) are listed and translated in the same way as in the examples for each definition. Lin's Chinese-English dictionary exactly complies with his earlier views of a good dictionary in his discussion of translation and language learning. Words change their meanings according to contexts and every word has its individuality.

III Supra-Textual Unconventionality

When translation is used as a tool and translations as material for the author-translator's self-expression, both conventional and unconventional ways of treatment of texts can be expected. In many respects, Lin Yutang is highly unconventional due to the subordination of the translator to the author. The unconventionality is usually supra-textual. It involves manipulation or tailoring of translations to suit the author's self-expression. In his books, he modestly borrows translations wholesale from predecessors if he thinks they are good enough. He improves upon existing translations if he thinks that they are good but somewhat defective for his purpose. He imposes himself on the texts with introductions or interspersed explanations. He chooses the matter at his free will, highly selective in most cases. He adapts the source text to make new stories. His iconoclastic strategies of translation handling, roughly categorized, include creation of hypertexts, borrowing translations, re-use of translations and dramatic rewriting.

1 Creation of Hypertexts

Translation studies often focus on the concept of equivalence. Lin Yutang's own theory of translation also stresses the importance of resemblance of a translation to its original although the word *equivalence* is absent. If we consider translation as a craft according to New Mark's definition that translation "is a craft consisting in the attempt to replace a written message and/or statement in one language by the same message and/or statement in another language" (Newmark, 2001: 7), equivalence does dominate the attention of the translator as a craftsman in a text-to-text transfer. Therefore, Nida says that the translator must strive for equivalence rather than identity, or the reproduction of the message rather than the conservation of the form of the utterance (Nida, 2003: 12). Baker (2000) has made a detailed study of equivalence at different levels (the word level, and above the word level: collocations, idioms and fixed expressions) and in different dimensions (grammatical equivalence, textual equivalence in terms of thematic and information structures, textual equivalence in terms of cohesion, and pragmatic equivalence in terms of coherence and implicature). Based on the concept of equivalence, some other researchers are concerned with instances of non-equivalence as evidence to the ideological manipulation of translations by the famous "invisible hand" (Venuti, 2000;

Robinson, 2001). While it is reasonable to study equivalence in a cross-lingual text-to-text transfer, for Lin Yutang, translation is not all about such equivalence.

Equivalence presumes symmetry. On the input side of the translator is a source text and on the output side is the translation. If we study an individual poem, an essay, a drama or a story translated by Lin Yutang we may easily establish a text-to-text equivalence. For example, *Six Chapters of a Floating Life* in the English language is symmetrical with its Chinese original *Fu Sheng Liu Ji*, but such symmetry is not always established. In practice, Lin Yutang often breaches this symmetry and transcends the conventional text-to-text equivalence. For Lin, text-to-text equivalence is not all the translator's story nor is it compulsory. His basic commitment is not to the text nor to its author. Believing in self-expression he handles translations whatever way he likes. In this light, all translations in his books are but transitory texts to the truth he conceives.

The prototypical concept of translation is linear. Speaking of a translation we instinctively see in our mind's eye a one-to-one correspondence: Text A is a translation of Text B or Book A is a translation of Book B. Unfortunately this is not always the case, especially as far as Lin Yutang's translations are concerned. While Text A may be a translation of Text B, Text A may be a translation of a selection from Text B. It may be a text that is not called a translation but contains a translation of B. It may be a text that is made up of a translation of Text B and other translations. If we regard a book as a text, we have the same picture on a higher level. We can say:

> *Nüzi Yu Zhishi* is Lin Yutang's complete translation of Dora Russell's *Hypatia, or Woman and Knowledge.*
>
> Lin Yutang's *Chuangtse* is a partial translation of the original Chinese *Chuangtse.*
>
> *The Wisdom of Confucius* is not called a translation but it contains selected translations from *The Book of History* and the Confucian classics.
>
> *Xinde Wenping* (*The New Criticism*) is made up of a translation of "The New Criticism" by Spingarn and other Chinese translations.

Lin Yutang has translated a few books but most of his translations are very short and can only appear in magazines or collections. The stand-alone translations include: *The Autobiography of a Super Tramp*, *Keeping Mentally Fit* —

A Guide to Everyday Psychology, *The Diary of a Communist Schoolboy*, *The Chinese Puzzle*, and *Hypatia or Woman and Knowledge*. Into English, he has translated a Chinese booklet *Six Chapters of a Floating Life*, which can hardly stand alone as a book if not in a bilingual form. His usual practice was to translate and publish little pieces. These little pieces often grew to form books, which include the following: *Xinde Wenping* (*The New Criticism*) — a collection of selected Chinese translations in expressionist criticism, *A Nun of Taishan* (*a Novelette*) *and Other Translations*, *The Chinese Theory of Art: Translations from the Masters of Chinese Art, The Wisdom of Confucius,* "*The Wisdom of China*" in *The Wisdom of China and India, Widow, Nun and Courtesan: Three Novelettes from the Chinese,* and *The Importance of Understanding: Translations from the Chinese.*

Very often a collection of translations has a theme. *The New Criticism* is a carefully selected collection of Lin's own translations in the expressionist criticism of Croce and Spingarn. *The Wisdom of China* deals with Chinese thought, and *The Importance of Understanding* deals with Chinese life that has given rise to Chinese thought, especially Taoist thinking. Sometimes, Lin Yutang has something to say on a theme.

In his way of handling translations in the books, we can distinguish two interrelated strategies: hybridization of translations with his own writings and anthologizing translations by himself or other translators. Both strategies more or less exist in many other books by the author-translator. The result of hybridization and/or anthologizing is an independent *hypertext*, a text born out of texts with links to different sources.

Some of his "original" works are also such hypertexts. *My Country and My People*, and *The Importance of Living* are generally regarded as his original writings. Little has been said by researchers about large portions of translations they contain. Intermingling translations and original writings these two books have put him at the height of his fame and won him international reputation. Both enjoyed immediate success on the international book market upon publication in the US and are still widely read today. The writer skillfully makes use of the translator in the writing of the books and the latter by virtue of the former has become widely known to the English-reading public and beyond. The two books appropriate translations in three ways:

(1) English translations from Chinese texts, including his previously

published self-translations.

(2) English adaptations of Chinese texts.

(3) Embedded words, phrases and sentences from the Chinese.

In the first category only, we find at least 64 translated passages in the Foreign Language Teaching and Research Press (FLTRP) edition of *My Country and My People* (Lin, 1998a), and at least 67 in the FLTRP edition of *The Importance of Living* (Lin, 1998b). Some passages comprise a few lines while others are as long as a few pages.

Perfect hybridization is achieved in *The Wisdom of Confucius* published by Ramdom House. Nearly one fifth of the book is devoted to the "Introduction" in which he introduces the system of Confucian thought: the character of Confucian ideas, *li* as the rationalized social order, Confucian humanism, personal cultivation as the basis of a world order, the intellectual upper class as the result of the theory of imitation or the power of example. Also in the "Introduction" is a brief estimate of the character of Confucius who had a charming personality, a high moral idealism and led a full, joyous life — the full human life of feelings and artistic taste — and who was a great scholar and a great humorist. After the "Introduction" is a translation of Confucius' biography from *The Book of History* by Szema Chi'en (Sima Qian), the great Chinese historian (Lin Yutang claims this to be the first English translation of the biography) of all time. The remaining nine chapters are selected translations from the Confucian classics, arranged in a way that they form a somewhat connected discourse granting English language readers easy access. The chapters are given modern English headings that bring out the meaning of the Confucian texts, which are from many classical sources: "Central Harmony," "Ethics and Politics," "Aphorisms of Confucius (mainly from the *Analects*)," "First Discourse: Education Through the Six Classics," "Second Discourse: An Interview with Duke Ai," "Third Discourse: The Vision of a Social Order," "On Education," "On Music," and last "Mencius." Particularly worth noting is his placement of "The Aphorisms of Confucius" after "Central Harmony" (Ku Hung-ming's translation of the Chungyung edited by Lin Yutang, the other translations in the book are all by himself)" and "Ethics and Politics" (his translation of *Tahsueh*, *Liki*). The traditional Chinese approach to Confucianism is to start with *The Analects*, which consists of out-of-context aphorisms. It is a very difficult approach and more difficult for Western readers who expect connected discourse. This kind of rearrangement caters to reader psychology. Apart from the general introduction in the beginning of the book, a translator's note is provided to open each following chapter, giving comments or background information on the text. This is an ingenious way of making literature. The Confucian classics had been translated before, but in an unprecedented way Lin Yutang was bringing the awesome sacred texts close to English readers. Hybridization gives the book originality. Even the Chinese find the book interesting. As a matter of fact, it has been translated into Chinese by Mr. Huang Jia-de. The Chinese version of the book also brings the reader closer to Confucian texts and Confucian ideas. In this case, the form and the content are in perfect harmony.

Another typical example of hybridization is *The Wisdom of Laotse*, which hybridizes Lin's interpretations with his translations of *Laotse* and *Chuangtse*. Neither is Lin the first translator of *Laotse* (or the *Dao De Jing*), which he calls *The Book of Tao* (Previously there had been twelve other translations), nor is he the first to translate *Chuangtse*. His translation of *Chuangtse* is not even complete (11 chapters only). By no means could he or can we claim his translation of the two Taoist classics to be superior to any other translation. His translations nonetheless have made a strong presence. The secret lies in the manner that has made the difference. The book is intended to interpret Taoist thinking to Wesern readers. Lin Yutang chooses the *Dao De Jing* as the central text and starts interpreting. Believing that "Laotse's gems of oracular wisdom lend themselves to diversified interpretations, even in Chinese" he devises a method of reading *Laotse* with *Chuangtse* and claims that this is something that has never been done before. His critics disagree but he is the first to do so at least to the ken of his knowledge) (Lin, 1948: 6). He culls passages from *Chuangtse* to illustrate each chapter of *The Book of Tao*. Thus we have a book with Laotse's pedagogic epigrams supported by Chuangste's vivid allegories. Further, he writes a long introduction to Taoist philosophy, summarizing its gist, and relating it to Emerson and Tolstoy as well as to modern life whose spirituality is being deprived by the progress of scientific thought. For a better understanding of Laotse, he puts him in contrast with Confucius by translating and putting together seven of the eight dialogues (from *Chuangtse*) between Confucius and

Laotse in the last part of the book headed "Imaginary Conversations Between Laotse and Confucius." This is his monopoly. Through his new perspective, his interpretation and his innovative method of organizing the translations, he gives the book great original value, making Taoist texts more accessible to Western readers. The Chinese translation of the book is also enlightening for the average Chinese reader.

The Importance of Understanding is an anthology of prose and verse (largely *belles lettres*), as many as 107 pieces in nearly 500 pages. These are passages that once inspired him in the course of reading. The book is intended for casual dipping, for the nourishment of the human spirit. He did all the translations except for the two Buddhist sutra selections. Believing that there should be no order of arrangement, he nonetheless has made a rough classification so that the reader can conveniently go for what he wants to read. In the selection of materials to translate, he follows an internal order: what expresses the sentiment; what describes scenes; what pleases the senses; what titillates the understanding; what frees the spirit; what nourishes the mind. In the actual presentation of translations, he follows a surface order as shown in the Contents: how some of the best poets and writers saw the problem of human life with its implied conflicts; their thoughts on love and death; what they felt and called beautiful in nature and the seasons; how they managed to compromise and make adjustments in human society; a few selections on women; how to order the home and daily living; how the writers beautified their existence by art and literature; how the ancients talked and joked "after tea and wine," how some eccentric poets and artists became "fools to the world"; how some of the best philosophized and thought about the whole mess of human life and how they went back to the simple life of contentment; and finally, some independent short lines or pithy paragraphs, epigrams and some proverbs.

The Chinese Theory of Art, *Translations from the Masters of Chinese Art* (1967) is an anthology of historical writings on Chinese art. The volume is intended to be a source book on Chinese theory of art and as a help to fuller appreciation of the goal of Chinese painting and its trends and development. It consists of translations from writings by 23 Chinese artists and art critics on problems and techniques, style and taste. The translated authors include Confucius, Chuangtse, Han Fei, Ts'ao Chi, Ku Kai-chih, Tsung Ping, Hsieh Ho, Wang

Wei, Chang Yen-yüan, Ching Hao, Kuo Hsi, Kuo Jo-hsü, Su Tung-p'o, Mi Fei, Chao Meng-fu, Ni Tsan, Huang Kung-wang, Kao Lien, Ku Ning-yüan, Yüan Hung-tao, Hsieh Chao-cheh, Shi-tao, and Shen Tsung-ch'ien①. According to Lin Yutang, prior to him there had only been one translator that covered this field: Osvald Sirén with the book *The Chinese on the Art of Painting*. In Lin's opinion, "Sirén's translations are cumbersome, hard to digest, and sometimes miss the point" (Lin, 1967: 17). Lin Yutang puts the translations in chronological order and connects them in his "Introduction," which gives the historical background, introduces the schools, styles, influences of artists on one and another, and provides a chart of development and a chart of derivations. Furthermore, editorial comments, something rather extended, are provided proceeding or following each selection to give the reader a fair idea of the historical development of Chinese art. The book has 25 illustrations of Chinese works of art, a list of artists in Chinese and English and a Table of Dynasties. On publication, the publisher claimed that the book was "the definitive single-volume source book on its subject" (See back cover to the 1967 edition).

These books are the typical hypertexts created by Lin Yutang.

2 Borrowing Translations

This is the appreciative appropriation of the works of earlier translators. The spirit of appreciation is lacking among many translators. A translator can be a very conceited individual. His conceit usually comes from the failures of other translators who, coping with an impossible task, are prone to errors. The delight of discovering and criticizing the mistakes or absurdities of fellow translators can easily give a translator an illusion that he is better for he can "see clearly" and laugh at the mistakes his folks make. With an understanding of the impossibility and possibility of translation, Lin Yutang is generous enough to accept what is reasonably good and even enthusiastically hails some of his predecessors. He gladly admits that he can do no better and borrows their translations where they are needed instead of attempting a new version. He

① These names are as originally spelt in *The Chinese Theory of Art*.

appreciates the seriousness in the Chinese translation of Buddhist sutras by ancient translators and among the English translators of Chinese classics he cannot hide his admiration for Ku Hung-ming, Arthur Waley, James Legge, Witter Bynner, and Hellen Waddell.

In case that a piece of writing is particularly useful but he cannot come up with a better translation, Lin's solution is not to translate! He simply borrows the existing translation.

In *The Importance of Living*, he quotes the following passage and others from Arthur Waley's *Taotehching*, *the Way and Its Power* and says that the translation is "excellent":

> The best charioteers do not rush ahead;
> The best fighters do not make displays of wrath.
> The greatest conqueror wins without joining issue;
> The best user of men acts as though he were their inferior.
> This is called the power that comes of not contending,
> Is called the capacity to use men,
> The secret of being mated to heaven, to what was of old.
> He who by Tao purposes to help a ruler of men
> Will oppose all conquest by force of arms;
> For such things are wont to rebound.
> Where armies are, thorns and brambles grow.
> …
>
> (Lin, 1998b: 101 – 102)

In *The Importance of Understanding*, two of the translations are not by himself: a selection from the *Lankavatra Sutra* translated from the Sanskrit by Professor Suzuki who made use of three Chinese versions① and a selection from

① *The Lankavatara Sutra — A Mahayana Text* by Suzuki Deisetz Teitaro. London: Routledge, 1932. [Reprints Taipei: SMC Publishing, 1994. Delhi: Munshiram Manoharlal, 1999] Mainly done from the Sanskrit, the Translator makes extensive use of the three Chinese versions. See also Suzukis: *Studies in the Lankavatara Sutra*. London: Routledge, 1930. [Reprint Taipei: SMC Publishing, 1994.] In: *A Buddhist Bible* by Goddard, Dwight (Ed.). Boston: Beacon Press, 1938 [1970, 1994], 277 – 357. Many other editions.

the *Surangama Sutra* translated from the Chinese by Wai-tao①. The two sutras are favorite readings of the Chinese Shan (Japanese Zen)② Buddhists. Believing that they are essential for the understanding of Buddhism in China and that their absence would make his anthology seem incomplete, he happily includes selections of the two sutras into his book. Longer selections are included in *The Wisdom of China and India* (1942), which is an anthology of Chinese and Indian literature translated by himself and other translators.

An able translator as he is, in anthologies of Chinese literature that he has compiled, he frequently refuses the temptation to translate certain texts by himself. Translations by other translators stand side by side with his own. In "Wisdom of China" (a part of *The Wisdom of China and India*), for example, apart from his own translations, he includes works by the following translators:

James Legge:

(1) *Mencius*. The revised translation of 1874. Lin Yutang does not change Legge's text except for the correction of Cantonese spelling of certain proper names. On the one hand, he admires Legge's "inestimable service" by single-handedly translating all the important Chinese classics in a conscientious and scholarly way. On the other hand, he regrets that Legge's translation is too literal to make easy reading.③ (2) *The Book of*

---

① *Surangama Sutra* (*Leng Yen Ching*, Chinese Rendering by Master Paramiti of Central North India at Chih Chih Monastery, Canton, China). In: *A Buddhist Bible* by Goddard, Dwight (Ed.), Bhikshu Wai-tao and Dwight Goddard (Transls.). Boston: Beacon Press, 1938 [1970, 1994], 108 -277. Many other editions.

② 禅宗

③ "His methods amounted to translating every single word, even when two words formed a combination with a new meaning." (Lin, 1942: 745) For a Chinese sentence which means (in fighting a war) "Weather is less important than terrain, and terrain is less important than the people's unity," Legge's translation was "Opportunities of time (vouchsafed by) Heaven are not equal to advantages of situation (afforded by) the Earth, and advantages of situation (afforded by) the Earth are not equal to (the union arising from) the accord of Men." In his opinion, there was still no good translation of such an important work of art but he did not have the time to make a new translation. The Book of History by Legge, undertaken twenty years later, was much better.

History. Here Lin Yutang uses Legge's translation "whose somewhat pretentious and quaint diction seems to suit these ancient documents well. I have made changes only in the spelling of proper names to conform with the current Wade romanization. Legge would spell, for instance, the name of the Chou Dynasty as 'Kâu'. His curious spelling is due to the uniform spelling system of the Sacred Books of the East and to his Cantonese pronunciation" (Lin, 1942: 706). (3) 13 poems under "Poems Translated by James Legge," and two sacrificial odes under "Odes Translated by James Legge": "The Tsai Shu" and "The Ch'u Ts'e." Lin Yutang thinks that "Dr. Legge's translations in regard to diction, rhythm and general effect, often fall short of the true poetic level, but he did not mistranslate, and his work gives us the means of getting a glimpse of the scope and variety of the *Book of Poetry*. He has translated the Book complete, and some of his verses are certainly successful."

(ibid: 868)

Y. P. Mei

The Works of Motse. Lin Yutang has selected Chapters 4, 13, 15, 16, 17, 18, 19, 26, 27, 28, 39, and 46. Mei's translation made use of the best text of Sun Yi-jang. "The baldness of the style is original, consonant with Motse's teachings on simplicity and frugality."

(Lin, 1942: 787)

Helen Waddell

15 poems under "Poems Translated by Helen Waddell," from Waddell's *Lyrics from the Chinese* (Holt). "She based her translations on James Legge's translation and his notes, and her translations are far from literal." (ibid: 868). Of all the translations of Chinese poetry, Lin Yutang thinks that Helen Waddell's is the best.

Herbert A. Giles

Two poems translated by Herbert A. Giles: "To a Young Gentleman" and "To a Man." "Herbert A. Giles' two poems are quite charming," says Lin Yutang

(Lin, 1942: 868).

Arthur Waley

"The Great Summons" by Ch' ü Yüan. In the section headed "Ch' ü Yüan."

Witter Bynner

20 Li Po poems translated by Witter Bynner from the texts of Kiang Kang-hu. Lin Yutang considers Bynner's translation the best of all translations of Li Po.

Genevieve Wimsatt

> A selection from Genevieve's *The Lady of the Long Wall* (Columbia University), renamed "The Tale of Meng Chiang — a 'drum story' in five cantos." "Miss Wimsatt's admirable verse rendering gives the reader a sense of the varied rhythm and dramatic intensity of the original."
>
> (ibid: 870)

However, not all his borrowings are so direct. Sometimes, he makes some corrections or revisions which he thinks necessary or makes changes to other translators' texts so that they fit in with his own work. A case in point is the borrowing of Ku Hung-ming's English translation of the *Chung Yung: The Conduct of Life, or The Universal Order of Confucius* (Ku, 1928), which appears in *The Wisdom of Confucius* (1938) as *Central Harmony* (*Chungyung:* originally Liki, Ch. XXXI), and in *The Wisdom of China and India* (1942) as *The Golden Mean of Tsesze.* While declaring Ku's translation to be perfect, he makes quite a number of changes to Ku's text: first, leaving out Ku's own comments bringing Goethe and Matthew Arnold and the Proverbs from the Christian *Bible* to elucidate the meaning of Confucianism; second, he makes changes where he thinks that Ku has departed slightly from the Chinese text; third, he reorganizes the text and gives the sections headings like "The Central Harmony," "The Golden Mean," "Moral Law Everywhere," "The Humanistic Standard," "Certain Models," "Ethics and Politics," "Being One's True Self," "Those Who Are Absolute True Selves," "Eulogy on Confucius" and "Epilogue." In Lin's words, "These renderings are essentially correct; some are even brilliant. I have, however, found it necessary to add, delete and substitute phrases or lines, bringing about, I believe, a closer adherence to the original, and have naturally changed certain spellings of Chinese names to make them uniform with the rest of the book." (Lin, 1938: 102)

In Lin's text, the majority of Ku's sentences are borrowed "as is", but changes can be spotted almost on every page. A minor change involves substitutions of a few words while the structure of Ku's sentence is not touched:

Original：天命之谓性，率性之谓道，修道之谓教。

(Zhu, 1987: 25)

Lin: <u>What is God-given</u> is what we call <u>human nature</u>. To fulfil the law of our <u>human nature</u> is what we call the moral law. The <u>cultivation of the moral law</u> is what we call culture.

(Lin, 1938: 104)

Ku: The ordinance of God is what we call the law of our being. To fulfil the law of our being is what we call the moral law. The moral law when reduced to a system is what we call religion.

(Ku, 1928: 14)

Or the structure of Ku's sentence is changed for better coherence, without fundamental change of wording and meaning:

Original: 子曰:"中庸其至矣乎! 民鲜能久矣!"

(Zhu, 1987: 28)

Lin: Confucius remarked: "To find the central clue to our moral being which unites us to the universal order, that indeed is the highest human attainment. For a long time, people have seldom been capable of it."

(Lin, 1938: 105)

Ku: Confucius remarked: "To find the central clue to our moral being which unites us to the universal order, that indeed is the highest human attainment. People have seldom been capable of it for long."

(Ku, 1928: 16)

By proof-reading Ku's translation against the Zhu Xi version of the text, Lin Yutang has made some corrections which involve a content change:

Original: 武王末受命,周公成文武之德,追王大王、王季,上祀先公以天子之礼。

(Zhu, 1987: 38)

Lin: The Emperor Wu received Heaven's mandate to rule in his old age. His brother, Duke Chou, ascribed the achievement of founding the Imperial House equally to the moral qualities of the Emperors Wen and Wu. He carried the Imperial title up to the Great emperor (Wen's grandfather) and the Emperor Chi (Wen's father). He sacrificed to all the past reigning Dukes of the House with imperial honors.

(Lin, 1938: 114)

Ku: The Emperor Wen never actually ascended the throne. But his son, the Duke of Chow, ascribed the achievement of founding the Imperial House equally to the moral qualities of the Emperors Wen and Wu. He carried the Imperial title up to the Great emperor (Wen's grandfather) and the Emperor Chi (Wen's father). He sacrificed to all the past reigning dukes of the House with imperial honors.

(Ku, 1928: 41)

Some corrections involve great semantic changes although seemingly it is just a matter of word substitution:

Original: 在下位不获乎上,民不可得而治矣;获乎上有道:不信乎朋友,不获乎上矣;信乎朋友有道:不顺乎亲,不信乎朋友矣:顺乎亲有道:反诸身不诚,不顺乎亲矣;诚身有道:不明乎善,不诚乎身矣。

(Zhu, 1987: 44)

Lin: If the people in inferior positions do not have confidence in those above them, government of the people is an impossibility. There is only one way to gain confidence for one's authority: if a man is not trusted by his friends, he will not have confidence in those above him. There is only one way to be trusted by one's friends: if a man is not affectionate toward his parents, he will not be trusted by his friends. There is only one way to be affectionate toward one's parents: if a man, looking into his own heart, is not true to himself, he will not be affectionate toward his parents. There is only one way for a man to be true to himself. If he does not know what is good, a man cannot be true to himself.

(Lin, 1938: 121)

Ku: If those in authority have not the confidence of those under them, government of the people is an impossibility. There is only one way to gain confidence for one's authority. If a man is not trusted by his friends, he will not gain the confidence for his authority. There is only one way to be trusted by one's friends. If a man does not command the obedience of the members of his family, he will not be trusted by his friends. There is only one way to command the obedience of the members of one's family. If a man, looking into his own heart, is not true to himself, he will not command the obedience of the members of his family. There is only one way for a man to be true to himself. If he does not know what is good, a man cannot be true to himself.

(Ku, 1928: 36 -37)

Where Ku departs too far from the Chinese original, a new translation is found:

Original: 其次致曲。曲能有诚,诚则形,形则著,著则明,明则动,动则变,变则化。唯天下至诚为能化。

(Zhu, 1987: 47)

Lin: The next in order are those who are able to attain to the apprehension of a particular branch of study. By such studies, they are also able to apprehend the truth. Realization of the true self compels expression; expression becomes evidence; evidence becomes clarity or luminosity of knowledge; clarity or luminosity of knowledge activates; active knowledge becomes power and power becomes a pervading influence. Only those who are absolutely their true selves in this world can have pervading influence.

(Lin, 1938: 123 –124)

Ku: The next order of the process of man's mind is to attain to the apprehension of a particular branch of knowledge. In every particular branch of knowledge there is truth. Where there is truth, there is substance. Where there is substance, there is reality. Where there is reality, there is intelligence. Where there is intelligence, there is power. Where there is power, there is influence. Where there is influence, there is creative power. It is only he who possesses absolute truth in the world who can create.

(Ku, 1928: 45 –46)

In case a predecessor has had evident strength in a translation but the translation is not what Lin Yutang exactly desires, he preserves that strength and changes the part that he does not like. On the shoulders of giants, he makes a new version. Such a practice has made the translation very competitive. Typical examples are *The Book of Tao*, which was based on Arthur Waley's version and some other versions, and *Chuangtse*, *the Mystic*, which was based on Herbert A. Giles' translation. In such instances, he does not dismiss the works of his predecessors altogether and start from scratch. Rather, he evaluates them and tries to preserve their strength. This practice is especially valuable for translators who are trying to create new versions of classics. Ignoring the achievements of previous translators, many try to create new versions that are better but end up with something not any better. However good a translator is he has his limitations. It requires a confident and generous personality for a translator to use what is valuable in the old translation for the creation of a new version. In this regard, Lin Yutang has set a good example for later translators.

The following excerpt from "Horses' Hooves" of *Chuangtse* shows how he builds on H. A. Giles' version of *Chuang Tzu*.

The original:

吾意善治天下者不然。彼民有常性,织而衣,耕而食,是谓同德。一而不党,命曰天放。故至德之世,其行填填,其视颠颠。当是时也,山无蹊隧,泽无舟梁,万物群生,连属其乡;禽兽成群,草木遂长。是故禽兽可系羁而游,乌鹊之巢可攀援而窥。夫至德之世,同与禽兽居,族与万物并,恶乎知君子小人哉?同乎无知,其德不离;同乎无欲,是谓素朴。素朴而民性得矣。

(Zhuang Zi, 1998: 120)

Lin's and Giles' translations:

Table 4 Lin Yutang and H. A. Giles in the English Translation of Zhuangzi

From "Chuangtse, Mystic and Humorist" in *The Wisdom of China and India* (1942) by Lin Yutang: Horses' Hooves	From H. A. Giles' translation of *Chuang Tzu*.① Chapter 9: Argument: Superiority of the natural over the artificial. Application of this principle to government.
I think one who knows how to govern the empire should not do so. For the people have certain natural instincts — to weave and clothe themselves, to till the fields and feed themselves. This is their common character, in which all share. Such instincts may be called "Heaven born." So in the days of perfect nature, men were quiet in their movements and serene in their looks. At that time, there were no paths over mountains, no boats or bridges over waters. All things were produced each in its natural district. Birds and beasts multiplied; trees and shrubs thrived. Thus it was that birds and beasts could be led by the hand, and one could climb up and peep into the magpie's nest. For in the days of perfect nature, man lived together with birds and beasts, and there was no distinction of their kind. Who could know of the distinctions between gentlemen and common people? Being all equally without	Now I regard government of the empire from quite a different point of view. The people have certain natural instincts: to weave and clothe themselves, to till and feed themselves. These are common to all humanity, and all are agreed thereon. Such instincts are called "Heaven-sent". And so in the days when natural instincts prevailed, men moved quietly and gazed steadily. At that time, there were no roads over mountains, nor boats, nor bridges over water. All things were produced, each for its own proper sphere. Birds and beasts multiplied; trees and shrubs grew up. The former might be led by the hand; you could climb up and peep into the raven's nest. For then man dwelt with birds and beasts, and all creation was one. There were no distinctions of good and bad men. Being all equally without knowledge, their virtue could not go astray. Being all equally without evil desires, they were in a state of natural integrity, the

(to be continued)

① The excerpt is taken from the Galileo Hyperbook of *Chuang Tzu*, translated by Herbert A. Giles, first published in 1889; Galileo Hyperbook of Chuang Tzu created and edited by Michael Presky, 1995. The hyperbook editor claims that this book contains the complete and exact text of the Chuang Tzu as translated from the Chinese by Herbert A. Giles, excluding his notes. The Galileo Library: http://www.galileolibrary.com/ebooks/as07/chuangtzu_toc.htm

From "Chuangtse, Mystic and Humorist" in *The Wisdom of China and India* (1942) by Lin Yutang: Horses' Hooves	From H. A. Giles' translation of *Chuang Tzu*. Chapter 9: Argument: Superiority of the natural over the artificial. Application of this principle to government.
knowledge, their virtue could not go astray. Being all equally without desires, they were in a state of natural integrity. In this state of natural integrity, the people did not lose their (original) nature. (Lin, 1942: 670)	perfection of human existence. (Giles, 1889)

Here almost every sentence of Giles' is somewhat changed while we can still see the close connection between the two versions.

When translating *The Book of Tao* he did not start from scratch. He learned from Arthur Waley and Isabella Mears to create his own version. Because Mears' version is unavailable, I cannot decide exactly how much is borrowed from each of the two predecessors. There is very little physical resemblance between Lin's version and that of Waley. In this case, Waley's translation merely serves as a reference:

The original:
道冲,而用之或弗盈;渊兮,似万物之宗。锉其锐,解其纷,和其光,同其尘。湛兮!似或存;吾不知谁之子,象帝之先。(第四章)

(Lao Zi, 1998: 7)

Lin's and Waley's translations:

Table 5 Lin Yutang and Arthur Waley in the Translation of the Dao De Jing

From "Laotse, the Book of Tao" in *The Wisdom of China and India* (p. 585)	From *Tao Te Ching* translated by Arthur Waley (1998, p. 9)
The Character of Tao Tao is all pervading①,	The Way is like an empty vessel

(to be continued)

① "Tao is a hollow vessel." in *The Wisdom of Laotse* (Lin, 1976: 63).

From "Laotse, the Book of Tao" in *The Wisdom of China and India* (p. 585)	From *Tao Te Ching* translated by Arthur Waley (1998, p. 9)
And its use is inexhaustible! Fathomless! Like the fountain head of all things, Its sharp edges rounded off, Its tangles untied, Its light tempered, Its turmoil submerged, Yet crystal clear like still water it seems to remain①. I do not know whose Son it is, An image of what existed before God. (Lin, 1942: 585)	That yet may be drawn from Without ever needing to be filled. It is bottomless; the very progenitor of all things in the world. In it all sharpness is blunted, All tangles untied, All glare tempered, All dust soothed. It is like a deep pool that never dries. Was it too the child of something else? We cannot tell. But as a substanceless image it existed before the Ancestor. (Laozu, 1998: 9)②

Such a practice of borrowing very rarely appears in his Chinese translations. This may be because he can translate into Chinese as a mother tongue with relative ease despite the awkwardness or great syntactic similarity between his Chinese translations and their originals.

3 Re-Use of Translations

Reading Lin Yutang one is sometimes perplexed by his repetitions. One the one hand, there seems to be a high level of consistency in his writings and translations in terms of what he wants to express to his readers; it seems as if he is proud of his views and never wants to modify them or change them. What

① "Yet dark like deep water it seems to remain." in *The Wisdom of Laotse* (Lin, 1976: 63).

② The excerpt is proof-read against Arthur Waley's *The Way and Its Power: A Study of the Tao Te Ching and Its Place in Chinese Thought*, Allen & Unwin, London, 1934. *The Way and Its Power* is electronically reproduced at the Association Francaise des Professeurs de Chinois website: http://www.afpc.asso.fr/wengu/wg/wengu.php?l=Daodejing

was written and translated becomes his facts and he will without hesitation re-use them as the occasion rises. On the other hand, a lover of Lin Yutang books eager for more writings by the author may bear a secret grudge: as he reads more of Lin Yutang he has to live with familiar passages here and there. A question then arises: Is this a mark of the exhaustion of his genius or is there more to this practice of repetition than it appears? One may criticize his repetitions but it is found that they are often not as simple as they seem.

Many of his major English translations have been re-used in part or in full, sometimes more than once. For example, the following translations keep recurring:

"Laotse, the Book of Tao" (*The Wisdom of China and India*, *The Wisdom of China*, *The Wisdom of Laotse*), "Chuangtse, the Mystic" (*The Wisdom of China and India*, *The Wisdom of China*, *The Wisdom of Laotse*, *Chuangtse*), "Aphorisms of Confucius (*Analects*)" (*The Wisdom of Confucius*, *The Wisdom of China and India*), Lin Yutang's revised version of Ku Hung-ming's translation of *The Golden Mean of Tsesze* (*The Wisdom of China and India*, *The Wisdom of China*, *The Wisdom of Confucius*), *Six Chapters of a Floating Life* (*Tien Hsia Monthly*, *Hsi-feng Monthly*, single volume by the Hsi-feng She in 1939, *The Wisdom of China and India*, *The Wisdom of China*, selected passages in *My Country and My People*, *The Importance of Living* and *The Importance of Understanding*), *A Nun of Taishan* (*A Nun of Taishan and Other Translations; Widow, Nun and Courtesan*), "The Tale of Chi'enniang" (*My Country and My People*, *The Wisdom of China and India*), *The Mortal Thoughts of a Nun* (*My Country and My People*, *The Importance of Understanding*, published in a newspaper in 1957), "Taiyu Predicting Her Death" from the *Hongloumeng* (*The Importance of Understanding*, *Wu Suo Bu Tan He Ji*), "The Half-and-Half Song" of Li Mi-an (*The Importance of Living*, *The Importance of Understanding*). This is not an exhaustive list of his repeated use of his own translations.

In many cases, when a work or part of a work is re-used, it is modified or revised, and almost every time a work is re-used, there is a different context to achieve a new meaning. For example: the translation of *Chuangtse* is expanded in *The Wisdom of Laotse* through the translation of more chapters. The arrangement is also changed in the translation. It is cut into pieces to explain the chapters of *Laotse*). If we compare "The Half-and-Half Song" in *The Importance of Understanding* (1960: 187 –188) with its earlier version in the *Importance of Living*, we can find the following revisions as shown in the brackets:

a. By far the greater half have I seen through
This floating life — Ah, there's a (the) magic word —
This "half" — so rich in implications.

b. Have servants not too clever, not (nor) too dull;
A wife who's not too simple, nor too smart (who is not too ugly, nor too dull) —

c. So then (— So then), at heart, I feel I'm half a Buddha ...

The same translation, re-used in part or full, revised or not, sometimes takes on a different meaning in each different context. In *My Country and My People*, the excerpts from Chapter II of the *Six Chapters of a Floating Life* are used to illustrate the aesthetic principle of "concealment and surprise" in the designing of the Chinese house and garden. In *The Importance of Living*, the passages from Chapter I contribute to the theme of the Chinese enjoyment of nature with Yün the heroine as one of the two Chinese ladies Lin Yutang selected for this purpose. The complete early editions (in the *Tien Hsia Monthly*, the *Hsi-feng Monthly* and the 1939 single-volume edition) are meant to let English readers know the adorable simple life of a Chinese couple. In "The Wisdom of China," the book is re-used in full to show the spirit of Chinese civilization. It is offered as a sketch of Chinese life. In *The Importance of Understanding*, Lin Yutang considers *Six Chapters of a Floating Life* "one of the tenderest tributes to a woman," and includes the beginning and the end of the story under the title "In Memory of a Woman." The excerpts belong to the theme of "love and death." In all these contexts, the same material is tailored to different ends of expression. The meanings in different contexts are closely related and we cannot exactly tell one from another; but each context does offer a different perspective. Or, it may be said that the meaning of a translation depends as much on its context and interpretation as on what it is standing alone.

Lin Yutang is profusely fond of his own translation of "The Mortal Thoughts of a Nun," a selection from a popular Chinese drama (anonymous, before 1700) in which a young nun of 16 is bored with monastic life and yearns for secular love. She just cannot concentrate on her Buddhist practices:

While I say mitabha,

I sigh for my beau,
While I chant saparah,
My heart cries, "oh!"
While I sing tarata,
My heart palpitates so!

And her maiden's heart rebels against her religion:

Whence comes this burning, suffocating ardor?
Whence comes this strange, infernal, unearthly ardor?
I'll tear these monkish robes!
I'll bury all the Buddhist sutras;
I'll drown the wooden fish,
And leave all the monastic putras!

This translation first appears in *My Country and My People*. As a revised version in *The Wisdom of China and India* it becomes a gem of Chinese dramatic poetry, which "shows the typically humorous, common-sense and irreligious attitude of the Chinese people" (Lin, 1942: 870). In *The Importance of Understanding*, it becomes part of the "love and death" theme. In a bilingual version published in a Chinese language newspaper in 1968 (Lin, 1994h: 335 – 343), Lin Yutang says that this piece represents the type of Chinese literature that is expression of the heart and non-classicist. In his opinion, classicist Chinese poetics lays more emphasis on the literary form than on the content. Unfortunately by this re-publication he outraged the Chinese Buddhist community in Taiwan and Hong Kong.

Such re-use of earlier translations may be justified considering the expansions, revisions and shifting of perspectives. Meanwhile, it is dubious because of its excessively high frequency. One cannot help but suspect that as the later Lin Yutang was a famous man there were too many requests from the publishers who wished to publish anything that he handed them. There is no way to know whether he got more royalties through the re-use of his many translations as a freelance author-translator who could not afford stopping publishing.

Lin Yutang views a piece of work as an epitome of the nation's culture in general and therefore he can always find a different point of view to look at the work and a different way to use it. He can always move his translations about in different publications. Every time a translation is used, it is in a different context with a different perspective and consequently a new meaning. To Lin, the translations are just like the builder's bricks and tiles with which he can build whatever structure he wants.

4 Dramatic Rewriting

While partial adaptations or rewritings exist in many of Lin Yutang's translations, some of his narratives are very peripheral cases of translation by being whole-sale adaptations or rewritings. He does not always transfer the exact content of the original to the target language version. Sometimes, he makes changes in the target text, changes that can be as dramatic as to redesign the structure or the entire plot of a story. In so doing he challenges the borderline between translation and writing, for such works are neither prototypical translations nor prototypical writings. Because of the large scale of rewriting to the degree that the target language texts bear very little physical resemblances to their source materials in terms of verbiage and plot, this kind of peripheral translating may be called *dramatic rewriting*. Works of this kind include *Miss Tu* and some of the pieces in *Famous Chinese Short Stories*.

Miss Tu is based on a popular legend told in Feng Menglung's *Ching Shih T'ungyan* (*Jing Shi Tong Yan*). Lin Yutang uses the outline and the main characters of the story and all the rest is his own writing. "Miss Tu" is Lin's translation of the name Du Shiniang. Du's story is a Ming Dynasty story of love, betrayal and retribution. She became a courtesan at 13, and, betrayed by her lover (who sold her) drowned herself at the age of 19. The original Chinese story as it appears in the *San Yan* is very concise and can be told in a dozen pages. It has no superfluous words irrelevant to the development of the story and every word is a visual picture and strikes a chord of the heart. Figuring that Western readers are used to reading long sophisticated stories, Lin Yutang changes the presentation by putting the narration in the mouth of an "I" gradually discovering the tragic love story, then he waters it down to make it a novelette by adding various details that are his imagination. Meanwhile, almost no visible physical correspondence can be found between his English presentation and the original story by Feng. Lin Yutang employs some techniques of Western fiction such as flashbacks and descriptions of psychological workings of the characters. He philosophizes through the mouth of "I" while telling the story, giving the story a mysticism by an inconclusive ending, a hint at something but a hint that cannot develop into a clue. The story unfolds itself piecemeal to "me" and the unfolding itself is a new story by Lin Yutang: the suicide of the courtesan, "my" conversation and later involvement with the young man's servant who was looking for his young master (Mr. Li) who disappeared after the incident, the love story before the death of the courtesan as related to "me" by Mr. Liu (a close friend of Mr. Li who had helped the young lovers to buy the girl's freedom from the bawd), and a mystical ending: appearance and death of a white-haired mad monk at Miss Tu's memorial temple, who nobody knew and was thought to be the missing lover of Miss Tu. The original storyline is dissected and assimilated into Lin's new story. Fortunately for the English reader, though the story has duly or unduly lost all its Chineseness, they still get the rough outline of the famous Chinese story.

Famous Chinese Short Stories Retold by Lin Yutang claims to be an anthology of Chinese stories in translation but the reteller does not confine his duties to those of a translator. In most of the stories he makes some changes. While there are only a few changes in some stories greater ones take place in others. The very titles of the stories themselves betray the reteller's strategy of adaptation or rewriting:

> "Curly-Beard" (虬髯客传), "The White Monkey" (白猿传), "The Stranger's Note" (无名信), "The Jade Goddess" (碾玉观音), "Chastity" (贞节坊), "Passion" (莺莺传), "Chienniang" (离魂记), "Madame D." (狄氏), "Jealousy" (西山一窟鬼), "Jojo" (小谢), "Cinderella" (叶限), "The Cricket Boy" (促织), "The Poet's Club" (东阳夜怪录), "The Bookworm" (书痴), "The Wolf of Chungshan" (中山狼传), "A lodging for the Night" (李卫公靖), "The Man Who Became a Fish" (薛伟), "The Tiger" (张逢), "Matrimony Inn" (定婚店), and "The Drunkard's Dream" (南柯太守传).

Many of the above titles literally do not have much to do with their original titles. They are just new titles given to the stories.

From his "Introduction" we can find two reasons which are essentially one for the adoption of such a strategy. One is about his basic idea of a short story:

> The purpose of a short story is, I believe, that the reader shall come away with the

> satisfactory feeling that a particular insight into human character has been gained, or that his knowledge of life has been deepened, or that pity, love or sympathy for a human being has been awakened, nothing in the reader's basic assumptions should stand in the way, requiring elaborate explanation, in order that this desired effect may be achieved. I have chosen stories which present no such difficulties and which make the achievement of this effect easy or possible, although I recognize that some of these stories will appeal to the reader because of the strangeness and exotic charm of a remote atmosphere and background.
>
> (Lin, 1952: xi)

The other is about the impossibility of translation, the various differences that challenge the translator:

> I have sometimes found translation impossible. The differences in language, customs and practices that could be taken for granted and those which have to be explained, in the reader's natural sympathies for this or that character, and above all in the pace and technique of modern story-telling — all these make it necessary that the stories be retold in a new version.
>
> (ibid: xvi, xvii)

He claims to have preserved the universal interest in the stories and done away with what is going to hinder universal understanding. The selection of the stories itself is based on his estimation of a story as having "a nearly universal appeal" (Lin, 1952: xi).

The way to adapt each story is different from the way to adapt another as if each story has its individuality. Lin Yutang tells his reader about what he has done in the prefatory notes to the stories:

In some cases, minimal adaptation takes place. He sometimes tries to produce exact translations, such as in the case of "Cinderella" (though in fact it is not exact) and the shorter stories at the end of the book. To some stories he just adds some details, such as Curly-Beard. In many other stories, the "originals" only serve as sources out of which he builds new stories or new themes. In the prefatory notes he lists some of the changes he has made to the original stories:

> In "White Monkey" the story is changed to make the Chinese general's humiliation in losing his wife to the monkey the main theme.
>
> The original of "The Stranger's Note" shows the "stranger" as a thorough cheat and villain disguised as a monk, while his version, besides omitting and supplying some

details, switches the reader's sympathy to the stranger and makes the wife stick to him instead of going back to her first husband, the original solution being more satisfactory to a Chinese audience. In the original, the wife is a suffering, submissive woman, doing nothing on her own initiative.

"The Jade Goddess" is based on a story bearing the same title in the *Chingpen T'ungshu Shiaoshuo* (*Jingben Tongsu Xiaoshuo*). He says, "The original story ends quite differently. The jade carver's wife was discovered by an officer and buried alive in a garden, but she appeared as a ghost to effect her revenge. I have followed the first part of the story only, and developed the story according to the simple theme of whether a great artist should destroy his art to cover his identity, or let his art betray him."

(Lin, 1952: 67)

To make a short story long, "Chastity" is developed from a short anecdote in popular Chinese books of jokes and anecdotes. The anecdote tells how a widow, on the eve of receiving a memorial arch erected in her honor, was tempted by a servant, lost the arch, and hanged herself.

In "Passion," or "The Western Room," his version follows closely the original story by Yuan Chen until the point where the lover (Yuan Chen himself) abandons the girl and proceeds to make ridiculous excuses for himself and the rest is Lin's invention. In rewriting the story, Lin Yutang has used Yuan Chen's poems to fill out the gaps in the original.

In "Madam D.," he fills in the details about the students' movement for recovery of national territory, which are historical facts, based on such works as Chou Mi's *Kweihsin Tsachih*①.

In "Jealousy" he omits the ending where a Taoist priest is called to exorcise the spirits.

In "The Poets' Club," he rewrites the story, for the verses written by the animals have little meaning in translation. He feels compelled to translate the names of the poets into English, for the names in the original contain hints as to the true character of the poets.

However, a closer look at the works shows that the rewriting is often more sophisticated than the changes he lists.

"The White Monkey" is approximately eight times as long as its original. In the Chinese story, General Ouyang's young beautiful wife was kidnapped by the White Monkey. The General and his men found the place where the wife and other kidnapped women were kept. Then, the women and the General's

① 周密《癸辛杂识》。

gang worked together to kill the White Monkey. One year later, General Ouyang's wife gave birth to the White Monkey's son, who looked like a monkey but was exceptionally brilliant and talented. The boy grew up to be a great man of letters and a great calligrapher. The story was an insinuated insult to Ouyang Xun, the famous Tang Dynasty calligrapher. In Lin's version, the White Monkey kidnapped women so that they could bear children for him and his tribesmen, but he never took mothers away from their children. He believed that children "are the real reason for marriage, and the husband is the excuse" (ibid. 39). Here Lin Yutang makes the ancient Chinese monster speak the way of a modern Western intellectual, almost the same way as Dora Russell talks about free sex and free love in *Hypatia, Women and Knowledge*, a feminist booklet that Lin Yutang has translated from English to Chinese. Lin's description of the customs of the aborigines led by White Monkey is based on the much rumored customs of some minority ethnic groups in China's southwest and Hainan Island:

> He explained. Among these tribes, a girl chooses a man at the annual courtship dance, goes with him to the mountains, and lives with him afterward. If, after a year, a baby is born, she goes with him to see her parents. Then she is considered married. If not, the match is broken, and next year she selects another man at the New Year dance. This goes on until she has conceived, or becomes a mother.
>
> (Lin, 1952: 38)

The Lin Yutang ending, which goes well with Dora Russell's philosophy, is more unexpected to the Chinese than that of the original. General Ouyang lost the contest with the White Monkey and therefore had to leave his wife with the monster. However, the White Monkey agreed that if the woman did not bear a child the next year he would give her back to the General. The next year, the General came back to get his wife, only to find her happy with a new-born baby and the White Monkey, refusing to go back with him.

Stories like "Jo Jo," "Chienniang," and "The Cricket Boy" have not undergone plot or thematic changes as in "The White Monkey" but their expansion has gone through great changes.

In "Jo Jo" (Lin's version of *Xiao Xie*), as in some other stories, the adaptation is several times the length of the original. The storyline is followed, but not all the details of presentation. The original story of *Xiao Xie* begins with something like:

> Mr. Chiang of Weinan County had a haunted house. Annoyed, he evacuated it. A servant was left to take care of the house but soon died. None of the other servants survive who were later sent to keep the door. Mr. Tao Wangsan was a romantic guy with a mania for prostitutes, but as soon as he was drunk, the girls were asked to leave. His friends used to send him girls. He gladly accepted them but never really did anything to them. He often slept in the house of Mr. Chiang and was approached by Mr. Chiang's maids at night. He refused the temptation and therefore Mr. Chiang thought highly of him. A poor man and newly widowed, he could not bear the heat in his own thatched house. He asked Mr. Chiang to lend the deserted house to him. The latter turned down the request because he did not like to see his friend's life at risk in the haunted house. To persuade Mr. Chiang, Mr. Tao wrote a dissertation entitled "Sequel to 'On the Non-Existence of Ghosts'." "What can ghosts do?" he said. Moved by his persistence, Mr. Chiang assented.
>
> (Pu, 1997: 977. Translated from the Chinese.)

Lin Yutang omits some details and adds details that are his imagination while following the original storyline. The result is an extended story. The beginning of the story in Lin's version is:

> "I don't believe in ghosts," said Tao, a young man of thirty and a recent widower. He spoke in a tone of cocky confidence. His friend Chiang who knew him quite well did not mind it at all. He knew Tao was eccentric and brilliant. Tao had come to ask if he could live in his friend's house. It was summer, and his own house, which consisted only of one room, a kitchen, and a very small garden, was hot and oppressive. Flies swarmed around the place. Chiang had a garden residence in the suburb which was cool and shaded, but which had been abandoned because it was haunted.
>
> "Now look here," said Chiang with a kind smile, "worthless as you are, I love you too much to want you to risk your life. In two and a half years, three successive caretakers have died."
>
> "It could be a coincidence."
>
> "No, no, don't tell me that. One or two deaths could be a coincidence, but not three."
>
> Tao produced from his pocket an essay, entitled "An Expansion on Yuan Chan's Theme Disproving the Existence of Ghosts."
>
> "Read it," he said. "I have lived thirty years without seeing a ghost and, if there is one, I would love to meet her. The ghosts I read about are usually so charming anyway."
>
> (Lin, 1952: 193-194)

Then, Lin Yutang invents the content of the essay besides making the conversations as detailed as possible. By so doing, he seems to have given the story more blood and flesh. However, in the development of the story, he does not altogether cast away the original author's way of story-telling. From time to time, we find him following the story by the sentence.

"Chienniang" is an adaptation of a Tang Dynasty tale. The Chinese *Li Hun Ji* means "Story of the Departed Soul." Interestingly, Lin Yutang rewrites the same story twice. The earlier version as in *The Wisdom of China and India* is called "The Tale of Ch'ienniang." A little bit longer than the original, it basically follows the outline of the Chinese story and does not purposefully depart very far from its storyline despite some slight changes and unconscious deviations. The later version as in *Famous Chinese Short Stories* is much longer, over ten times as long as the original and full of narrative details. "The Tale of Ch'enniang" is a rough translation of the original:

> Ch'ienniang was the daughter of Mr. Chang Yi, an official in Hunan. She had a cousin by the name of Wang Chou, who was a brilliant and handsome young man. They had grown up together from childhood, and as her father was very fond of the young boy, he had said that he would take Wang Chou as his son-in-law. This promise they had both heard, and as she was the only child, and they were very close together, their love grew from day to day. They were now grown-up young people, and even had intimate relationships with each other. Unfortunately, her father was the only man who failed to perceive this. One day a young official came to beg for her hand from her father, and, ignoring or forgetting his early promise, he consented. Ch'ienniang, torn between love and filial piety, was ready to die with grief, while the young man was so disgusted that he decided he would go abroad rather than stay and see his sweetheart become the bride of another person. So he made up a pretext and informed his uncle that he had to go away to the capital. As the uncle could not persuade him to stay, he gave him money and presents and prepared a farewell feast for him. Wang Chou, sad to take leave of his lover, was thinking it all over at the feast and he told himself that it was best to go, rather than remain to carry on a hopeless romance.
>
> (Lin, 1942: 943 –944)

But compared with the following version (excerpt) called "Chienniang," the above rough translation is a very close one:

> Wang Chou, a young boy of seventeen, had lost his father and was now alone. Steady and more mature than his age indicates, he was old enough to shift for himself.

> His father had told him on his deathbed that he should go to live with his aunt, who was living in the south at Hengchow, and had reminded him that he was betrothed to his cousin. This was a promise between his father and the father's sister when the babies were being expected; they had said that in case one was a boy and the other a girl, they would be betrothed to each other. Wang Chou disposed of the house and set out to the south accordingly. The young boy's mind was enlivened by the hope of seeing a girl cousin whom he had not seen since the age of six when his father received an appointment in the north. He wondered how she had grown and whether she was still the fragile, affectionate child who used to cling to him as a play companion and wonder at all his doings. He had better hurry, Wang Chou thought, for a girl of seventeen might be betrothed to someone else if he did not show up. But the voyage was slow, and it took him a full month to come down the Hsiang River and then the Tungting Lake and finally reach the mountain city of Hengchow. ...
>
> (Lin, 1952: 129 -130)

This is just the beginning of the story. In this version, a great many narrative details are added.

This super-textual unconventionality characterizes Lin Yutang's translations and is a hallmark of the hovering spirit over all his works.

CHAPTER
Four

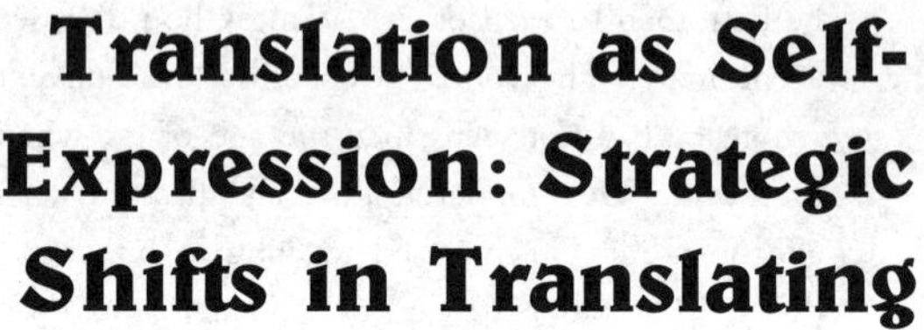

Translation as Self-Expression: Strategic Shifts in Translating

Despite Lin's theoretical soundness, the problems he encounters are no less complicated than those confronting other translators. A theory as a simplified view of the nature of facts is but a theory. There are always aspects of translation that are not fully revealed by a theory. In this chapter, Lin Yutang's process of translating is studied by observing his products (translations). Texts are analyzed to reveal his methods of translation, which are matched against the translation continuum from the most literal to the most liberal.

I The Translation Continuum: a Framework of Observation

1 Inseparability and Conflict — Semantic Correspondence and Verbal Correspondence in Translation

An ideal process of translating is the construction of both semantic and verbal correspondence, but this is not always possible. It is possible only by dint of luck or by flashes of the translator's genius. In one language, a message may manifest itself in various linguistic forms and each linguistic form may be used to express various messages. Polygamy is the most common type of relationship between messages and linguistic forms. When transferred into another language, the same polygamy no longer abides, for the target language has its own polygamical relationships. Where a similar form is found in the target language to express the same message, the translator translates with ease; where a similar form is lacking, the translator has to fumble among the available linguistic devices for an acceptable solution to generate the message, disregarding verbal correspondence to the source text.

Virtually no translation can be restored by the method of back-translation to its original despite the traces the translation bears of the original. The message may be basically the same but the language has been irrevocably and fundamentally changed. Even the message itself has been changed in one way or another as its medium changes. The new text has to stand alone, independent of the former text. It is going to function in a different setting with different readers of a different background.

2 The Translation Continuum

Due to the inseparability of sense and sign or content and form in the making of a text and inseparability of semantic correspondence and verbal correspondence in cross-lingual transfer, even the extreme liberalists in translation cannot disregard the original forms altogether and even the extreme literalists cannot feel comfortable with 100% word-for-word solutions. The translator's solution is always somewhere on a translation continuum, on which Dryden's three categories of translation (metaphrase, paraphrase and imitation) spread. On the one end of the continuum is *metaphrase*, or word-for-word translation, in the middle is *paraphrase*, or translation with latitude, and on the other end is *imitation*, the creation of the same meaning or spirit with entirely new devices. In a meaning-oriented translation, semantic correspondence is obligatory while verbal correspondence optional.

Lin Yutang's Strategic Shifts along the Translation Continuum

Denouncing any single formula for translation Lin Yutang's *xingling* poetics concentrates on the transfer of meaning. What is implied by such a poetics is that, as long as meaning is realized, any method may be used. When Lin Yutang emphasizes the "total concept" of a sentence, it seems that content can exist without form in the translator's mind or meaning can be deprived of its carrier. His theory of translation seems to suggest that meaning is extractable from its body. This must not be taken literally. In fact, "total concept" itself is vague, for we can hardly know exactly what a total concept of a sentence is, and the parts of a sentence are always significant clues for the construction of a similar sentence meaning. Therefore, in practice, his primary strategy is to reconstruct the "body parts" which often resemble their original counterparts and work together to generate the meaning in the translation. However, such a strategy does not always work without producing awkwardness or unintelligibility because two languages do not have equivalent sets of signs for the construction of the same meaning. From time to time other less close strategies have to be followed.

Neither "literal" nor "free" can categorize Lin Yutang's strategy of translating. Viewed in terms of formal and semantic correspondence, there is always some verbalism and semanticism at the same time. It is a matter of balance. While semantic correspondence is the inner law Lin's translation method falls somewhere in a continuum whose one end is total verbal correspondence and whose other end is total absence of verbal correspondence. The existence of verbal correspondence does not necessarily negate that of semantic correspondence and vice versa. Among Lin's translations, there is hardly one which consists of either total verbal correspondence or total non-correspondence. There are no set ways for translating. Any decision by the translator is a function of his intuition at the moment.

Perfect translation is not possible but the translator has to try because he is committed to share something with a different linguistic community. Predestined to lose part of the battle, as long as he can gain some ground and effect that sharing, we shall consider his effort a victory. Lin Yutang experiments with any solution that may get the message across linguistic barriers. His strategic shifts are the results of his sensitivity to make sense of sign in translation.

1 Lost in Translation

Among the recently published academic journal articles on Lin Yutang's translations, the general tone is one of praise. The translator is worthy of praise of course given the influence he has created through his translations. However, any praise should be to the point.

Due to the great differences between Chinese and English, we shall expect no saint that does not err. Everybody attempting a translation may get caught up and lost between the languages. Even a successful writer does not always guarantee successful translation. An able writer in the Chinese language, Lin Yutang has also experienced the misery that other translators have been through. By the late 1920s, he as a writer had already had a sizable readership in China. In 1928, he published a tragicomedy *Zi Jian Nanzi* (*Confucius Saw Nancy*)①, whose enacting by a group of students outraged the Confucian clan and caused quite a stir. In December of the same year, his collection of earlier essays was published as the *Da Huang Ji*. However, when it came to translating, the language was not as readable as his original Chinese writings of the same period. His Chinese translation in 1929 of Dora Russell's *Hypatia, Woman and Knowledge* will shock the present-day reader for its awkwardness and translationese. I have shown the following excerpts from his translation to a number of my colleagues, all of whom were astounded②:

---

① 《子见南子》

② The Chinese translations are from the following pages of *Hypatia, Henrik Ibsen: a Critical Study, Pygmalion, New Criticism* (Complete Masterpieces of Lin Yutang. Vol. 27): (1) p.4; (2) p.5; (3) p.6; (4) p. 30; (5) p.33; (6) p.33; (7) p.36; (8) p.38; (9) p.38; (10) p.42. The English excerpts are from the following pages of *Hypatia, Woman and Knowledge* (Russell, 1925): (1) p.1; (2) p.2; (3) p.3; (4) p.46; (5) p.51 -52; (6) p.53; (7) p.59; (8) p.63; (9) p.63; (10) p.69 -70.

(1) 在往时 Jason 及 Medea 两人互相角斗而两位都不是十分模范人品，虽然各方表示他所代表性别的男性①及所受的冤屈，他们两位都未曾想到用政治或社会改良方法来求一解决或是协调。In the past, Jason and Medea, neither of them quite an exemplary character, measured their strength against one another as individuals; and, though each voiced the wrongs and the naked brutality of their sex, it did not occur to either to seek in politics or in social reform a solution or a compromise.

(2) 所谓性的战争起源于最近二十或二十五年间，女子为他们的国民选举权及正当发育而奋斗之时。During the last twenty or twenty-five years, when women were struggling for their right as citizens to a vote and to a decent education, began what has been called the sex war.

(3) 平均起来，女子爱她的情人比爱她的儿女还要强烈。(If honesty of thought, speech, and action were made possible for women, it might transpire that) on the average a woman's love for her mate is more compelling than love for her offspring.

(4) 有益的是训练女子使有知识，有勇毅，有强健体魄，其余的可随她的本性与心智去告诉她，创造新的人类是值得所必经过的不便与苦痛。Everything is to be gained by training a woman in knowledge, courage, and physical strength, and leaving it then to her own instinct and her mind to tell her that to create new human beings is worth the discomfort and the suffering which she must necessarily undergo.

(5) 到今日为止，医生及牙医还不肯用麻药于妊娠的女人，替她拔起一根使她日夜痛楚伤损气力的坏牙。To this day most doctors and dentists refuse to give an anaesthetic and draw a rotten tooth which is wearing down a pregnant mother's strength by sleepless nights and days of agony.

(6) 她应当姑息时忍心，应当忍心时姑息；她不是饱餍儿女，便是使养料不足，或是饮食失宜。She would coddle when she should have hardened, harden when she should have coddled; she would over-feed and underfeed, or give the wrong kind of food.

(7) 固然，她不能养育多数儿女：我们听到各方面的诉声，说现代中等阶级要使儿女得到正当教育真不容易。She cannot have a large family, it is true, and the cry goes up on all sides that it is very hard for the middle-classes to pay for the proper education of their children.

(8) 如果丈夫死，她便永远不停地更勤苦地工作，否则将她的儿女送到贫民院。Should the husband die, she must work continually and harder or send her children to the workhouse.

(9) 战争的罪恶已令我们已经够受。<u>The crime of war is bad enough</u>: this butchery of hope and promise and human lives is one so black that the heart and mind of every woman who has borne a child should revolt against it until it is tolerated no more. (The underlined part.)

---

① 男性 might be a print error for it makes no sense here.

(10) 所以两年以上无子的结婚，如有一方愿意，即可解除婚约。Therefore marriages which after two years did not result in a child should be dissoluble at the wish of either party to the contract.

In the above examples, there are three outstanding problems:

(a) A false equivalent is used where a close equivalent is available, e.g.

"sex war" in (2): 性的战争 (false equivalent), 两性的战争 (close equivalent)

"proper education" in (7): 正当教育 (false equivalent), 良好教育 (close equivalent)

(b) English grammar is squeezed into Chinese without making proper adaptation to Chinese conventions, e.g.

"she would over-feed and underfeed, or give the wrong kind of food" in (6): The Chinese (她不是饱魇儿女，便是使养料不足，或是饮食失宜) is ungrammatical.

"Should the husband die" in (8): The monosyllabic word 死 is awkward in the Chinese vernacular. 死亡 would be more appropriate.

"marriages which after two years did not result in a child" in (10): The average Chinese will say something like 结婚两年没有孩子.

(c) The translator is unable to find an appropriate Chinese expression, e.g.

In (9) "The crime of war is bad enough" is translated flexibly but the Chinese is not acceptable.

The basic cause of the problems is excessive verbal adherence to the original. The ten examples are not isolated cases. Such problems abound in the entire text. Fortunately, after publication the book was not much read nor criticized. In his other Chinese translations of the same period, e.g. in *The New Criticism* and *Pygmalion*, similar problems more or less exist.

The above examples are not to prove that Lin Yutang is an unqualified translator. They are just to disperse the mystery of translational genius and show that the distance between a famous translator and an average one is not so great as might have been expected. To start with, geniuses and average translators may be on a par with each other in the face of the same problems. Everybody may get lost. From the perspective of pure craftsmanship, Lin's early Chinese translations are far from perfect. As his experience increased, he might have been able to do better given his proficiency in Chinese. Unfortunately for today's researchers, Lin Yutang did not translate much into Chinese beyond this period. Little is available for us to make a linear comparison between his early Chinese translations and his later ones so that we could find if he made any significant progress in his way of translating after he wrote "On Translation" in 1933. His Chinese translation of *The Autobiography of a Super Tramp* in 1935, excerpts from which will be discussed shortly in this chapter, employs a more liberal strategy and may be considered a tentative modification of his earlier direct approach. What is interesting is that in his earlier translation of a few quatrains of the *Rubayat* he does not follow a close strategy either and that the direct or literal approach is often present in his later English translations despite his frequent employment of approaches other than literal. Therefore, we are justified to ignore the time dimension and focus on a holistic view of his translations in general in our effort to perceive the strategies underlying his translations. Perplexed as any other translator, he has tried desperately to find a way out, shifting between strategies across texts and within a text.

2 The Metaphrase End of the Continuum

On the metaphrase end of the continuum is Lin Yutang's primary strategy of establishing close verbal correspondence. Such a strategy is apparent in his Chinese and English translations alike and it has not changed over time. It can be perceived in most of his Chinese translations, such as *The Chinese Puzzle, Pygmalion, Hypatia, or Woman and Knowledge*; essays in *New Criticism*, or *Keeping Mentally Fit*. The same basic strategy is found in his English translations such as "*Laotse, the Book of Tao,*" "*Chuangtse, the Mystic,*" *Six Chapters of a Floating Life, The Chinese Theory of Art: Translations from the Masters of Chinese Art* and the miscellaneous essays as in *The Importance of Understanding*. Close verbal correspondence is attempted inasmuch as it does not harm semantic correspondence.

A close verbal correspondence is one in which most linguistic segments (words or natural word clusters) in the original have counterparts in the translation, counterparts that are both linguistically and semantically close. In the translation of *Hypatia, or Woman and Knowledge*, for example, we find that the sentence "*When she has found a husband the community denies them a decent house*" (Russell, 1925) is actually divided into five segments:

①When + she + has found + a husband + ②the community + ③denies + ④them +⑤ a + decent + house

And in the translation "待她找到一位丈夫之时,社会不给他们一间成样的房屋。" each of the segment is represented in Chinese as follows:

① When she has found a husband: 待她找到一位丈夫之时; ② the community: 社会; ③ denies: 不给; ④ them: 他们; ⑤ a decent house: 一间成样的房屋

In this case, the Chinese sentence is so close to its original that ① is subdivisible into:

When: 待……之时; she: 她; has found: 找到; a husband: 一位丈夫

In this subdivision of segment ①, "a husband" is also respectively represented by two Chinese words.

Segment ⑤ has three words and none of them disappears in the translation:

a: 一间; decent: 成样的; house: 房屋

The translation of this sentence is almost a metaphrase.

However, the translator does not always follow the syntactic order of the original. In the translation of the following sentence,

① The life of the working woman ② who intends maternity ③ is becoming well-nigh impossible, ④ and she knows it. (现在预备做母亲的劳动妇女的生活,已经将近于不能维持,这一点她也自己知道。)

In the translation, the numbered segments appear in a slightly different order:

② who intends maternity + ① the life of the working woman (the working woman's + life) + ③ is becoming well-nigh impossible + ④ (and) it + she + knows

and within segments ① and ④, there is an order change, the former a product of grammatical difference and the latter because of a difference of linguistic convention.

However, closeness is a relative concept. Close correspondence is not exact correspondence. Exactitude is not possible, as even the original writer is not sure whether he has used an exact word or phrase, among the choices that have opened to him. It is a matter of convenience and adequacy. So it is up to the translator, who can say a sentence this way or that, or prefers one word or phrase over another without much reason. As long as a word or phrase fits in with the rest of the sentence and contributes to the objective of the sentence it has fulfilled its mission. In the Chinese translation of "The life of the working woman who intends maternity is becoming well-nigh impossible, and she knows it." Here we see how the five segments in the original are represented by another five corresponding segments with a flexible choice of words. While the majority of words like *life*, *working woman*, *intends*, *maternity*, *well-neigh*, *impossible*, *it*, *she*, *knows* find their counterparts in the translation, no one prevents the translator from choosing 准备/想/想要/计划/打算 etc. instead of 预备，要孩子/生孩子/当妈妈 instead of 做母亲，差不多/快要 instead of 将近于，坚持不下去/举步维艰 instead of 不能维持，明白/心里有数 instead of 知道. And by no means can we know that this particular solution of Lin's makes him an excellent translator. If we can, he is just one of the thousands who can do equally well on this sentence.

The following random selection of an excerpt from Lin Yutang's translation of the *Liki* in *The Wisdom of Confucius*① shall suffice to show that, in his English translations, he also follows a similar basic strategy of trying to establish a close verbal correspondence without damaging semantic correspondence. For the convenience of comparative study, the excerpt is broken down into sentences. The matching segments in the English are underlined and in the Chinese are separated by +'s.

(1) 古之欲明明德于天下者先治其国。

The ancients who wished to preserve the fresh or clear character of the people of the world, would first set about ordering their national life.

古 + (之) 欲 + 明明德 + 于天下(者) + 先 + 治 + 其国

(2) 欲治其国者先齐其家。

Those who wished to order their national life would first set about cultivating their family life.

---

① From *Ethics and Politics* (《礼记·大学》) (Tahsueh, Liki, Chapter XLII), *The Wisdom of Confucius* (Lin, 1938: 139 -140).

欲治其国者 + 先 + 齐其家

(3) 欲齐其家者先修其身。

Those who wished to regulate their family life would set about cultivating their personal life.

欲齐其家者 +(先)修其身

(4) 欲修其身者先正其心。

Those who wished to cultivate their personal lives, would first set about setting their hearts right.

欲修其身者 + 先 + 正其心

(5) 欲正其心者先诚其意。

Those who wished to set their hearts right would first set about making their wills sincere.

欲正其心者 + 先 + 诚其意

(6) 欲诚其意者先致其知。

Those who wished to make their wills sincere would first set about achieving true knowledge.

欲诚其意者 + 先 + 致其知

(7) 致知在格物。

The achieving of true knowledge depended upon the investigation of things.

致知 + 在 + 格物

(8) 物格而后知致。

When things are investigated, then true knowledge is achieved;

物格 + 而后 + 知致

(9) 知致而后意诚。

when true knowledge is achieved, then the will becomes sincere;

知致 + 而后 + 意 + 诚

(10) 意诚而后心正。

when the will is sincere, then the heart is set right (or then the mind sees right);

意 + 诚 + 而后 + 心 + 正

In the above examples, the translation and its original are related by a basic sentence-to-sentence correspondence. In the translation of each sentence, traces of the original can be found in segment-to-segment correspondences. Most of the words that are not underlined serve to fill either grammatical gaps or semantic ones. Within each segment, the translator is free to prefer one word to another. There are short segments and longer ones. The longer segments are usually more freely translated.

The above excerpt from *The Wisdom of Confucius* is an example of close verbal correspondence. The equal devotion to both content and form is found in Lin's translation of other Chinese sacred texts. Despite his claim that his translation method in the book is *paraphrase*, which means a meaning-based method of translation, he does not try to deviate far from the original wording and structure. The following sentences from a chapter of *Mencius* (Mengzi) as appears in the same book, are also examples of close verbal correspondence:

①性,②犹③杞柳也;④义,⑤犹⑥桮棬也。

(孟子·告子章句上)

①Human nature ②is like ③the willow tree, and ④righteous conduct or character ⑤is like⑥a wicker basket (made of the willow branches)

(Lin, 1938: 276)

①以人性②为仁义,犹以杞柳为犹桮棬。

(孟子·告子章句上)

①To make human nature ③follow benevolence and righteousness ②is like ④making willow branches ⑤into wicker baskets. (ibid.)

In Lin Yutang's English translation of narratives we can also perceive his method of establishing close verbal correspondence between the original and the translation. The following sentence from *Six Chapters of a Floating Life*① is a good example of close verbal correspondence.

①I am ②by nature ③fond of ④forming ⑤my own opinions ⑥without regard for what others say.

(Lin, 1942: 1024)

①余 + ②凡事 + ③喜 + ④(独)出 + ⑤己见 + ⑥不屑随人是非

Here, the translator has tried to match every word or word cluster with a corresponding word or word cluster. Segments ①, ③, ④, and ⑤ are perfect cases of both verbal and semantic correspondence.

Likewise, in the following sentence from the same translation, all eight segments in the Chinese have found their counterparts in the English version:

③For thirty years ①I ②worked as a government clerk ④in different yamens and practically visited every province except ⑤Szechuen, ⑥Kweichow ⑦and ⑧Yunnan.

(ibid: 1023 -1024)

---

① From "Chapter IV The Joys of Travel," *Six Chapters of a Floating Life*, in *The Wisdom of China and India* New York: Random House, 1942: 1023 -1024.

①余②游幕③三十年来,④天下所未到者,⑤蜀中、⑥黔中⑦与⑧滇南耳。

Despite the paraphrasing in the translation of segments ② and ④, and the slight semantic changes in the translation of segments ⑥, ⑦ and ⑧, as the translator is so bound by the segments of the original, on the whole we can still regard this sentence pair as an instance of close verbal correspondence.

3 Paraphrase: the Middle Part of the Continuum

Now that meaning is pivotal the translator may opt for a loose verbal correspondence, which we may call a paraphrase, in which much of the original wording or structure is disregarded. Lin Yutang experiments with such a strategy in his 1935 translation of *The Autobiography of a Super Tramp*. The way he treats the following sentence is typical of how he treats the whole text:

①Although ②I had at this time become lazy, ③losing almost all sense of respectability, ④I often reproached Brum for ⑤the aimlessness of this existence; ⑥telling ⑦him ⑧we must work ⑨and attend to ⑩other wants than those of the body.

(Davies, 1963: 55)

懒,使我丧失了一切人生的意志,但我虽是这样无目的的过去,有时,我总谴责波伦的。我劝他必须起来后找工作做,注意解决膳宿以外的问题。

(Lin, 1986:52)

Here, it is very difficult to match segments in the Chinese with their possible counterparts in the English. The original sentence becomes two in the Chinese and segment matches can be very vague as in ①, ②, ③, ⑤, ⑧ and ⑩:

①Although: (…,但); ②I had at this time become lazy: 懒; ③losing almost all sense of respectability (使我)丧失了一切人生的意志; ④I often reproached Brum (有时,我总谴责波伦的); ⑤for the aimlessness of this existence (我虽是这样无目的的过去); ⑥telling (劝); ⑦him (他); ⑧we must work: (必须起来后找工作做); ⑨and attend to: (注意解决); ⑩other wants than those of the body: (膳宿以外的问题)

In other translations, latitude can be perceived from time to time. The following sentence pair can be considered an instance of loose verbal correspondence. Here, in the longer segments, the translator concentrates on the total meaning of each segment and expresses it in a way not confined by the original wording and structure:

> Unfortunately, I was not free to wander where I liked, inasmuch as I was always attached to some office, and could therefore only hastily enjoy such natural scenery as came my way, getting at most a general impression of things without the opportunity to explore the more unfrequented and out-of-the-way spots.
>
> (Lin, 1942: 1024)
>
> 惜乎轮蹄征逐,处处随人,山水怡情,云烟过眼,不道领略其大概,不能探僻寻幽也。

Wherein "I was always attached to some office" is not a close rendering of 轮蹄征逐 (travel on wheels), "I was not free to wander where I liked" is not a direct translation of 处处随人 (everywhere following others), and "could therefore only hastily enjoy such natural scenery as came my way" discards the original images in 山水怡情,云烟过眼 (the enjoyable landscape was like clouds and mists that pass the eye).

It shall be pointed out that Lin's paraphrase does not exclude metaphrase. In the translation of some segments or sentences he uses metaphrase, while he employs paraphrase in other segments or sentences.

The following is from the English translation of Ping-ing's letter "At Kiayü" dated May 27, 1927:

> I have decided not to keep a diary any more, but to write whatever I please. But where shall I keep it? I have already told everybody that I have lost everything except myself and the medicine box. The only way for me is to send it to you as I have done with the "diary."
>
> I sent you a letter on the morning of the twenty-sixth from Puchi — an unfinished letter, which I hope you have already received.
>
> (Hsieh and Lin, 1930: 23 -24)
>
> 此后的计划我决计改变方针不写《从军日记》而写随意记罢了。然而写的这些东西放在什么地方呢?我已经告诉了大家说所带的东西通常丢完了,剩下的只有一个我和一个药箱。现在只好和《从军日记》一样寄给你,而且这些东西我是希望你介绍给大众知道一知道的。
>
> (Hsieh, 1999: 13.)

Wherein three sentences are examples of close verbal correspondence bordering on metaphrase:

> But where shall I keep it? 然而写的这些东西放在什么地方呢?

I have already told everybody that I have lost everything except myself and the medicine box. 我已经告诉了大家说所带的东西通常丢完了，剩下的只有一个我，和一个药箱。

I sent you a letter on (the morning of) the twenty-sixth from Puchi — an unfinished letter, which I hope you have already received. 二十六号由蒲圻发来的信——一封未完的信——想必已收到了吧？

And two sentences are examples of paraphrase in which the translator has great latitude in the target language wording:

I have decided not to keep a diary any more, but to write whatever I please. 此后的计划我决计改变方针不写《从军日记》而写随意记罢了。

The only way for me is to send it to you as I have done with the "diary." 现在只好和《从军日记》一样寄给你，而且这些东西我是希望你介绍给大众知道一知道的。

Sometimes latitude takes place in the form of omission. As long as the spirit of the writing is preserved, the translator chooses to ignore some details. Following the above excerpt is an omission of two paragraphs. Here is my translation of the omitted part:

But please do not laugh at me as if I were a kid who wants attention or who is extremely proud of her own writings. I have indeed a lot of funny stories to tell everybody. However, I have to beg you not to "laugh off" your teeth and beard. A stomachache from your roaring laughter is no big deal, though.

Dear F —①, my war diary is dull and uninteresting. Perhaps nobody would read it. I know this well but I cannot write anything better. I don't know why I cannot write beautifully and I know my future writings will be the same. Nevertheless, I am not too worried about my writing skill because what I write is life as it is. It is candid truth without any untruth.

(Xie Bingying, 1999: 13)

Some words may have been regarded inessential and their omission is justified as the "total" concept of the sentence is not impaired. Here is an example taken from his translation of Spingarn's "New Criticism":

At the end of the last century, France once more occupied the center of that stage

① Lin's way of translating "Mr. Fuyuan."

whose auditors are the inheritors of European civilization.

(Spingarn, 1917: 4)

上世纪之末，法国重新站立于欧洲文化的舞台上的中心.

(Lin, 1994d: 200)

4 The Imitation End of the Continuum

Poetry is the field where the greatest latitude takes place. Because of the importance of form, Lin Yutang tries to catch the spirit and recreates images and sounds to bring out that spirit. The following two quatrains are from his translation of Fitzgerald's English translation of the *Rubaiyat* by Omar Khayyam:

Fitzgerald's English version	**Lin Yutang's Chinese version**
Come, fill the cup, and in the fire of Spring	来，在这春日和风里斟个满大杯，
The Winter Garment of Repentance fling:	把岸然道貌的空架子一齐都丢开。
The Bird of Time has but a little way	时光的鸟已鼓翼前去了，
To flutter — and the Bird is on the Wing.	而这鸟并没有很长的路可以飞。
(Quatrain 7)	(Lin, 1994i: 20)
And those who husbanded the Golden grain,	无论是那些守财如命吝啬的老太太，
And those who flung it to the winds like raindrop,	或者是那些挥金似土慷慨的少奶奶，
Alike to no such aureate earth are turned	都不能变成个甚么香土堆，
As, buried once, Men want dug up again.	瘗埋后还有人愿意挖他出来。
(Quatrain 15)	(Lin, 1994i: 20 -21)

A general correspondence is found between the Chinese and the English but they are different. In Quatrain 7, "the fire of Spring" becomes "the warm breeze of Spring" in the translation, "the Garment of Repentance" becomes "the hollow air of hypocrisy," and in the original, "in the fire of Spring" modifies "fling" but its translation modifies both "fill" and "fling." In Quatrain 15, the first *those* becomes what literally means "the stingy old ladies" and the second becomes what means "the extravagant young ladies." Responding to criticism from his readers, he broke down his translation into three components: Lin Yutang: 65%; Fitzgerald: 25%; Omar Khayyam: 10%. Total: 100% (Lin, 1994i: 25). The ratios shall not be taken seriously, for in this case, Lin just wants to reiterate that translation of poetry is impossible.

When translating Chinese poems into English, Lin also aims at reproduction of the spirit:

译《乐隐词》八首（四）	**(4)**
懒散无拘	And how about a quiet life leading?
此等何如	From balcony watch the fish feeding,
倚栏杆临水观鱼	And earn from moon and flowers a leisure life!
风花雪月	Have friendly chats —
赢得功夫	Some incense —
好炷些香	And some reading.
说些话	(Lin, 1994h: 325)
读些书	

While such images as "balcony," "watch the fish," "moon and flowers," "chats," "reading" correspond to original images, information in general is reorganized in the translation. There are very few other physical resemblances between the two versions.

In order to foreground the form to create rhyme he has to rephrase the original words and add two rhyme words "leading" and "feeding." When the rhyme is created, the rhyming scheme (a, a, b, c, d, a) is quite different from the original scheme (a, b, a, c, d, b, e, f, g, b). In fact, it is another poem which has borrowed the spirit from the original, of which it is an imitation. This translation is one of eight poems translated in his early days and was republished upon request from the *Central Daily News* when he came back to Taiwan after decades of staying in the United States①.

5 Mobility along the Continuum

As a translator Lin Yutang is by no means bound to one particular way of translating. He is always open to a number of choices and his decision is always a decision of the moment. In another moment he may happen to favor another way. For example, in the translation of Chang Ch'ao's epigram 多情者必好色；好色者未必多情, he has decided to make the word 情 (*qing*) visually present in the discussion of the Chinese concept of *qing* (which he equates with *passion*) in *The Importance of Living*:

① He hand-copied the eight poems and mailed them to the *Central Daily News* (Lin, 1994h: 328).

A passionate nature always loves women, but one who loves women is not necessarily a passionate nature.

(Lin, 1998b: 94)

Whereas in a complete translation of the *Quiet Dream Shadows* under the category of "human life," the word *passion* practically disappears:

A great lover loves women, but one who loves women is not necessarily a great lover.

(Lin, 1960: 39)

It is so much a momentary decision that I believe if he had been asked to talk about romance and sex, he might have translated the same into:

A romantic individual is in want of sex but one who is in want of sex is not necessarily a romantic individual.

What matters in the decision is the translator's sensitivity to the issue on hand. There is always a preference of the most obvious and convenient solution, a natural inclination toward verbal correspondence, which is the most time-saving solution. A word-for-word solution is good enough as long as it does not alter the meaning of the sentence and does not bring grammatical awkwardness. In an earlier discussion, it was noted that Lin Yutang's translation of the following sentence is an instance of close verbal correspondence:

①性,②犹③杞柳也;④义,⑤犹⑥桮棬也。

(孟子·告子章句上)

①Human nature ②is like ③the willow tree, and ④righteous conduct or character ⑤is like⑥a wicker basket (made of the willow branches)

The next moment, when faced with another issue, he intuitively embarks on a different solution. The sacred Chinese text is marked by a terseness which the Chinese can understand but too much is behind the words that simply substituting a word for a word or a phrase for a phrase will not work even if English connectives are provided to make the translation less fragmentary:

食色,性也。仁,内也,非外也;义,外也,非内也。

(孟子·告子章句上)

Food (and) sex (are) nature. Benevolence (is) inside, not outside. Righteousness (is) outside not inside.

His solution in this case is a loose verbal correspondence, foregrounding the meaning of the sentence and backgrounding the original words that generate the sentence meaning:

> The desires for food and sex are born in us. Benevolence comes from within and is not something external, while righteousness is something external, and does not come from within.
>
> (Lin, 1938: 277)

Such a movement from the close end of the continuum to the loose end is also evidenced by the following excerpt from Lin Yutang's *Six Chapters of a Floating Life*:

> 余笑曰:"女先生且罢论,我有一言作譬,即了然矣。"芸曰:"君若何譬之?"余曰:"鹤善舞而不能耕,牛善耕而不能舞,物性然也,先生欲反而教之,无乃劳乎?"素云笑捶余肩曰:"汝骂我耶!"芸出令曰:"只许动口,不许动手。违者罚大觥。"素云量豪,满斟一觥,一吸而尽。余曰:"动手但准摸索,不准捶人。"芸笑挽素云置余怀,曰:"请君摸索畅怀。"余笑曰:"卿非解人,摸索在有意无意间耳,拥而狂探,田舍郎之所为也。"时四鬟所簪茉莉,为酒气所蒸,杂以粉汗油香,芳馨透鼻,余戏曰:"小人臭味充满船头,令人作恶。"素云不禁握拳连捶曰:"谁教汝狂嗅耶?"
>
> (Shen Fu, *Fu Sheng Liu Ji*)

> Then I laughed and said, "Will the lady teacher please stop a moment? I have a parable for explaining it, and she will understand at once." "You try it, then!" "The stork," I said, "can dance, but cannot plow, while the buffalo can plow, but cannot dance. That lies in the nature of things. You are making a fool of yourself by trying to teach the impossible to her." Su-yün pummelled my shoulder playfully, saying, "You are speaking of me as a buffalo, aren't you?" Then Yün said, "Hereafter let's make a rule: let's have it out with our mouths, but no hands! One who breaks the rule will have to drink a big cup." As Suyün was a great drinker, she filled a cup full and drank it up at a draught. "I suggest that one may be allowed to use one's hands for caressing, but not for striking," I said. Yün then playfully pushed Suyün into my lap, saying, "Now you can caress her to your full." "How stupid of you!" I laughed in reply. "The beauty of caressing lies in doing it naturally and half unconsciously. Only a country bumpkin will hug and caress a woman roughly." I noticed that the jasmine in the hair of both of them gave out a strange fragrance, mixed with the flavour of wine, powder and hair lotion and remarked to Yün, "The 'common little fellow' stinks all over the place. It makes me sick." Hearing this, Suyün struck me blow after blow with her fist in a rage, saying, "Who told you to smell it?"
>
> (Shen, 1999: 67)

In the translation of most sentences his method is fairly direct, moving meaningful units into English and reorganize them according to English grammar and English way of writing, trying to keep track of the original words as far as he can provided the translation does not look weird. For example, the effort at close verbal correspondence is fairly clear in the following sentence pair and many others:

> Then I laughed and said, "Will the lady teacher please stop a moment? I have a parable for explaining it, and she will understand at once." 余笑曰:"女先生且罢论,我有一言作譬,即了然矣。"

I: 余; laughed and said: 笑曰; the lady teacher: 女先生; please stop a moment: 且罢论; I: 我; have: 有; a parable for explaining it: 一言作譬; and she will understand at once: 即了然矣.

Meanwhile, a lower level of verbal correspondence is found in the following sentence pair, which we consider an example of loose correspondence:

> You are making a fool of yourself by trying to teach the impossible to her. "先生欲反而教之,无乃劳乎?"

You: 先生; are making a fool of yourself: 无乃劳乎; by trying to teach the impossible to her: 欲反而教之

Sometimes the translation is so free that there is no verbal correspondence at all. For example:

> You try it, then! 君若何譬之?

In this example, "You try it then!" does not literally correspond to 君若何譬之 but its meaning is bound by its immediate context. Therefore, "You try it, then!" means "What is your parable?"

Another example of latitude in the same excerpt is:

> You are speaking of me as a buffalo, aren't you? 汝骂我耶!

Here, "speaking of me as a buffalo" is taken from the context. It is a form of insulting to compare a person to a beast. A close rendering will be something like "You are insulting me!" or "That is derogatory!"

In practice, the types of correspondence can be intertwined. At one level it is one kind of correspondence and at another level, it is another kind of correspondence. For example, the following sentence can be roughly divided into two segments:

①只许动口,②不许动手(A close correspondence: Only mouth. No hands!)

Lin's translation:

③ Hereafter let's make a rule: ① let's have it out with our mouths, ② but no hands

At the segment level, we can regard ① and ② as instances of close correspondence, but ③ is an instance of verbal non-correspondence. At the sentence level, this is an instance of loose correspondence.

In the general pattern of verbal correspondence, close or loose, verbal correspondence is frequently absent at the lower levels of the text. It is particularly so in the translation of poetry. The following is one of his English translations of which he has been proud:

声声慢	**Forlorn**
李清照	Li Yi-an (1081 –after 1141)
寻寻觅觅,	So dim, so dark,
冷冷清清,	So dense, so dull,
凄凄惨惨戚戚。	So damp, so dank,
乍暖还寒时候,	So dead!
最难将息。	The weather, now warm, now cold,
三杯两盏淡酒,	Makes it harder
怎敌他晚来风急!	Than ever to forget!
雁过也,	How can a few cups of thin wine
正伤心,	Bring warmth against
却是旧时相识。	The chilly winds of sunset?
满地黄花堆积,	I recognize the geese flying overhead:
憔悴损,	My old friends,
如今有谁堪摘?	Bring not the old memories back!
守着窗儿,	Let fallen flowers lie where they fall.
独自怎生得黑!	To what purpose
梧桐更兼细雨,	And for whom should I decorate?
到黄昏,	By the window shut,
点点滴滴。	Guarding it alone,
这次第,	To see the sky has turned so black!
怎一个愁字了得!	And the drizzle on the kola nut
	Keeps on droning:
	Pit-a-pat, pit-a-pat!

Is this the kind of mood and moment
　To be expressed
　　By one word "sad?"

(Lin, 1960: 143－144)

First, there is a general pattern of verbal correspondence between the original and the translation at three levels: segment to segment, sentence to sentence and text to text. Close verbal correspondences are found in the following:

"How can (怎) a few cups of (三杯两盏) thin wine (淡酒)/Bring warmth against (敌他)/The chilly winds of sunset (晚来风急)?"

Loose verbal correspondences are found in the following:

"The weather, now warm, now cold,/Makes it harder/Than ever to forget!" (乍暖还寒时候,最难将息).

In order to build the general sentiment of the poem, sometimes the translator sacrifices verbal correspondence at lower levels of the syntactic and semantic hierarchy. Take the following:

"So dim, so dark,/So sense, so dull,/So damp, so dank,/So dead!"

Here traces of original words can hardly be found as the English language cannot achieve the same feeling of sadness by repeating words. A rendering like the following would definitely sound unpoetic:

"Search search/Lonely lonely/Sad sad sad."

As the English language does not have the same device, Lin Yutang has to come up with a solution that conforms to norms of the English language. His solution is the use of alliteration, a rhetorical device in English. By alliterating *dim*, *dark*, *dense*, *dull*, *damp*, *dank*, and *dead*, he tries to build a feeling of sadness. The alliteration, however, is criticized by Xu Yuanzhong, who says that despite its success in recreating the beauty of sound it "renders the spirit at the cost of meaning" (Xu, 1999)①.

① Xu proposes two versions in its stead: (1) I look for what I miss,/I know not what it is,/I feel so sad, so drear,/So lonely, without cheer. (2) I seek but seek in vain,/I search and search again.

Thus, there is no single way to translate. In the same text or across texts, Lin Yutang employs different strategies. Such strategic shifts are manifestations of the translator's sensitivity at various moments to the variegated textual landscape.

6 Self-Translations: Semantic Fidelity and Verbal Liberty Magnified

Many of Lin Yutang's writings have appeared in both Chinese and English. In some cases we know exactly which version is a translation, for example, *Confucius Saw Nancy* is his own English translation of a tragicomedy, and he has translated into Chinese 11 of the 24 chapters of *Between Tears and Laughter*①. Many of his essays however were published almost simultaneously in Chinese and English and we cannot decide from the publication dates which are the originals. In such cases, we need to take into consideration two important factors: first, since most of the essays are about the Chinese experience, the English writings themselves are translations even if they were written prior to the Chinese versions; second, both versions of the same title are almost of equal status because they both directly represent the thought of the author. Therefore, the twin texts form the perfect basis for the study of Lin Yutang's ideal translation in practice. He is in a better position than anybody else to know what is exactly semantic fidelity to his own text and what verbal liberties he can take.

Some of the twin texts are mentioned in the section headed "Nine Years of Experiment: 31 –39", here are more:

(1) "*Shanghai Zhi Ge*" (上海之歌), *Xing Su Ji* (1934)/"A Hymn to Shanghai," *The Little Critic, Essays, Satires and Sketches on China (First Series: 1930 –1932)* (1935)

(2) "The Little Critic: On Bertrand Russell's Divorce" (罗素离婚), *The China Critic*, VII (September 6, 1934)/"*Luosu Lihun*," *This Human World*, No. 11 (September 4, 1934)

(3) "*Yipian Meiyou Tingzhong De Yanjiang — Hunli Zhici*" (婚礼致词), *Analects*

① Lin Yutang. *Between Tears and Laughter*. New York: The John Day Company, 1943. Lin Yutang translated the first 11 chapters into Chinese and Xu Chengbin translated the rest of the book. The Chinese version was published by the Commercial Press in January, 1945 and saw several reprints shortly after its publication.

Fortnightly, No. 53 (November 16, 1934)./"The Little Critic: A Lecture Without an Audience — A Wedding Speech," *The China Critic*, VII (October 11, 1934)

(4) "*Zhongguo Wenhua Zhi Jingshen*" (中国文化之精神), *Da Huang Ji*, (1934a)./"The Spirit of Chinese Culture," *The China Critic*, V (June 30, 1932)

(5) "*Hunjia Yu Nüzi Zhiye*" (婚嫁与女子职业), *Xing Su Ji* (1934b)/"Marriage and Careers for Women," *The Little Critic, Essays, Satires and Sketches on China (First Series: 1930 –1932)* (1935)

(6) "*Lun Zhengzhi Bing*" (论政治病), *Xing Su Ji* (1934)/ *The Little Critic: On Political Sickness. The China Critic*, V (June 16, 1932)

(7) "*Jiading Wo Shi Tufei*" (假定我是土匪), *Analects Fortnightly*, No. 44 (July 1, 1934)/"If I Were a Bandit," *The Little Critic, Essays, Satires and Sketches on China (First Series: 1930 –1932)* (1935)

(8) "*Tan Yanlun Ziyou*" (谈言论自由), *Xing Su Ji* (1934)/"The Little Critic: On Freedom of Speech," *The China Critic*, VI (March 9, 1933)

(9) "*Si Mandaren*" (思满大人), *Xing Su Ji* (1934)/"The Little Critic: The Lost Mandarin," *The China Critic*, V (November 17, 1932), 1219 –1220. Also included in *Asia*, XXXIV (June, 1934)

(10) "*Wode Jieyan*" (我的戒烟), *Xing Su Ji* (1934)/"My Last Rebellion Against Lady Nicotine," *The Little Critic, Essays, Satires and Sketches on China (First Series: 1930 – 1932)* (1935)

(11) "*Wo Zenyang Mai Yashua*" (我怎样买牙刷), *Xing Su Ji* (1934)/"The Little Critic: How I Bought a Toothbrush," *The China Critic*, V (August 18, 1932)

(12) "*Lun Woshou*" (论握手), *Analects Fortnightly*, No. 72 (September 16, 1935)/"On Shaking Hands," *The China Critic*, X (August 22, 1935)

Two versions of the same text often bear similar titles, but sometimes the Chinese and English titles can be as dissimilar as most of the following titles in *Between Tears and Laughter*:

(1) A Confession 前序第一
(2) Karma 业缘篇第二
(3) The Emergence of Asia 时变篇第三
(4) The Suicide of Greece 述古篇第四
(5) Churchill and Pericles 证今篇第五
(6) World War III 果报篇第六
(7) The "White Man's Burden" 排物篇第七
(8) "Government by Music" 明乐篇第八
(9) Mathematics and Peace 卜算篇第九
(10) Defense of Courtesy 明理篇第十

(11) Europeanization of the World 欧化篇第十一

Both versions represent the same author. They are both responsible for the same idea but have no responsibility to each other. In perfect communion with the author, the translator is now at large. The devotion is to the content that the translator conceptualizes, not exactly what has been materialized in the other text. If there is devotion to form, it is not the form of the firstborn text (whichever of the two is the firstborn), rather, it is the inner form as he thinks fit for the text, or in other words, the original form of the new text. Thus we can explain the drastic differences in both form and content of the two versions in "Zarathustra and the Jester," a self-translation of "*Satianshi yu Dongfangshuo*" (萨天师与东方朔)①. Putting his own ideas in the mouth of Nietzsche's Zarathustra, he creates his own allegorical social satire:

> Zarathustra had just been to the court of fools, had spoken with His Majesty the King, the Prime Minister, the Archbishop, and the King's Jester, and had found the Jester the wisest of them all. He alone saw what was happening in the Kingdom; he alone did not take life as a jest. There were tears in his laughter, and laughter in his tears. The Jester had spoken to him who was the Understanding One: —
>
> (Lin, 1935b: 220. Lin Yutang's self-translation.)
>
> 萨拉图斯脱拉来到鹘突之国鲁钝之城,拜见国君俑,太子俑,宰相颛蒙,太傅鹿豕.主教安闲及御优东方曼倩,觉得这鹘突国中鲁钝城里.只有曼倩一人最聪明,只有他尚分得青红皂白,只有他不玩世盗名,游戏人生;他的笑中有泪,泪中有笑,东方曼倩对萨天师说:
>
> 萨天师! 慈悲长老! …
>
> (Lin, 1994f: 18. Chinese original.)

In the English version, the proverbial Chinese jester Dongfang Shuo is simply reduced to "the Jester." In the Chinese, the King, the Prime Minister and the Archbishop each have a name too. Lin Yutang must have thought that these names are irrelevant to the English reader and unduly add to their comprehension load. The cross-linguistic marks are erased by the translator so that either the English or the Chinese does not have a cross-flavor.

While Lin Yutang's original writings are often delightful reading, many of his translations read with some awkwardness, especially many of his Chinese

① In *Yusi*, Vol. 4, No. 33, 1928.

translations (See the section headed "Lost in Translation"). Such awkwardness does not exist in either the Chinese or the English version of "Zarathustra and the Jester."

> 也许你是来探访佩嘉禾章的痨病胸膛,或是来献勤于吃燕窝粥的小姐?
>
> 也许你要来访问善做讣闻的稳健青年,或是来问候长髯老爷,在玩弄他们的徽章?不然,或是你来瞻仰登天鸡犬的风采,及亲领中学为体西学为用的香水闺媛的芳泽?
>
> (Lin, 1994f: 18 -19. Chinese original.)
>
> Perhaps hast thou come to see the flat-chests, decorated with stars and crosses and Auspicious Corn! Or hast thou come to woo their daughters?
>
> Perhaps hast thou come to pay respects to long-bearded children, still playing with their honours and dignities as they had once played with their marbles? Or hast thou come to visit the elevated country bumpkins who have long outgrown their own importance, but not their own vulgarity?
>
> (Lin, 1935b: 220 -221. Lin Yutang's self-translation.)

The English version on the one hand simplifies the Chinese text by discarding such words as 痨病 (tuberculosis), 吃燕窝粥 (eat bird's nest soup), 善做讣闻的稳健青年 (mature young men good at writing epitaphs), 亲领中学为体西学为用的香水闺媛的芳泽 (to bathe in the perfume of daughters of the aristocratic scholars who advocate introduction of Western learning without fundamental changes to the ancient Chinese system of education), on the other hand it amplifies the Chinese text by translating 嘉禾章 into *stars and crosses and Auspicious Corn*.

He has tried to be idiomatic in both versions. The conventionalized metaphor 登天鸡犬 (chickens and dogs that ascend to heaven after their master becomes an immortal) is replaced by a new metaphor: "the elevated country bumpkins who have long outgrown their own importance, but not their own vulgarity."

Here, what counts is a teleology that directs each word to the total concept rather than close verbal correspondence. Whether a word in the Chinese version matches one in the English version is irrelevant. It is here with the translation of his own writing that Lin Yutang realizes his "total concept" ideal of translation.

A browse through his Chinese self-translation of the 11 chapters of *Between Tears and Laughter* will convince us that his Chinese is good enough for we are quite at ease with his Chinese text here. We do not get the same feeling as when we read his Chinese translations of Western literature, which are either too rigid or too unrestrained. We are at ease because he is at ease. He is at ease very much because he is translating himself. We can still find segmental matches between the two versions but he changes the text in a way that it is more acceptable to the Chinese reader:

> But if we take the historical perspective and view the development of human events, we are struck by a paradox which the science of human history so far has not been able to solve and the economic school of historians tend to ignore because they cannot make head or tail of it.
>
> (Lin, 1945: 11)
>
> 但是如果我们用历史的眼光来观察现世,我们便遇到一种难题,这是历史科学所无法解决而历史经济观一派所常欲避免的,因为这一派辨不出他是牛是马。
>
> (Lin, 1994j: 9)

The two versions are fairly close but the translator is very flexible in the treatment of some expressions. He translates *the development of human events* into 现世 and *are struck by* into 遇到. Particularly worth noting is the translation of *cannot make head or tail of it* — which contains an English idiom — into a perfectly acceptable Chinese metaphor 辨不出他是牛是马 (cannot tell whether it is an ox or horse). The following idiomatic translation is in the same vein:

> Yet, while we may be perfectly contented with the facts and figures in contemporary events and policies, such as the number of dive bombers and tanks with which we know we are going to defeat Hitler, we get curiously spiritual when we view human events of the past across a stretch of decades.
>
> (Lin, 1945: 11)
>
> 然而我们谈起目前的事势政策时,虽然只愿谈物质的数字;比如有多少架轰炸机坦克车可以击败希特勒,一旦谈到几十年的历史,便忽然变成唯心家。
>
> (Lin, 1994j: 10)

Only one perfectly familiarized with the idea in the original — the global total concept — can confidently handle local details of expression with real latitude. On the surface, none of these matches are perfect:

> be perfectly contented with: 只愿谈 (only want to discuss)
>
> in contemporary events and policies: 谈起目前的事势政策时 (when discussing current affairs and policies)
>
> the facts and figures: 物质的数字 (the physical numbers)

human events of the past across a stretch of decades: 几十年的历史 (history of decades)

get curiously spiritual 变成唯心家 (become spiritualists)

But they are perfect translations because they harmoniously fit in with the larger picture and contribute to the purpose of the larger expression.

III Lin Yutang's Strategic Shifts: A Comparative Study

1 Lin Yutang and Some Other Translators

Lin Yutang has won a name for himself as a great translator, but if we view a translation of his with one of another translator we cannot say that his is definitely superior. Meanwhile we cannot be sure that his translation is inferior. We cannot take a few words or sentences out of their context and declare that Lin Yutang is better or worse. As the "total concept" of a sentence or a text is the object of the translation, as long as this object is represented, the individual words or sentences themselves are trivial. What we can know for sure through an analysis of a text and its translation is the strategy or strategies a translator has followed. By virtue of comparison and contrast with versions by other translators, Lin Yutang's strategic shifts are further revealed.

Lin Yutang and Yang Xianyi: Similar Primary Strategy of Close Verbal Correspondence in the Chinese Translation of *Pygmalion*

The following is an excerpt from Bernard Shaw's play *Pygmalion* (dialogues from *Pygmalion* Act II) with translations by Lin Yutang① and Yang Xianyi② respectively, Lin Yutang's version (Lin, 1994d: 105 – 106) placed before Yang's (Yang, 1982: 41 –43):

① Translator's Note dated March 8, 1929.

② A revised edition. First published by the People's Literature Press in 1957.

HIGGINS. Well, I think that's the whole show. 黑董思：我想再没有了。(Lin)/息金斯：好啦，大概就这么多了。(Yang)

PICKERING. It's really amazing. I haven't taken half of it in, you know. 辟戈灵：真可赞叹。你知道，我还未听进去一半。(Lin)/辟克林：真了不起，了不起。你知道，我听懂了的还不到一半呢。(Yang)

HIGGINS. Would you like to go over any of it again? 黑董思：要不要再来一次？(Lin)/息金斯：那么，随便拿一部分再来一遍吗？(Yang)

PICKERING. No, thank you; not now. I'm quite done up for this morning. 辟戈灵：不要了，谢谢，现在不要。早晨的精神已经用完了。(Lin)/辟克林：不要了，谢谢，以后再说吧。这一早晨我已经够累了。(Yang)

HIGGINS. Tired of listening to sounds? 黑董思：听声音听倦了吧？(Lin)/息金斯：听这些发音有些腻了吧？(Yang)

PICKERING. Yes. It's a fearful strain. I rather fancied myself because I can pronounce twenty-four distinct vowel sounds; but your hundred and thirty beat me. I can't hear a bit of difference between most of them. 辟戈灵：是的。真吃力。我以为能发二十四种分明不乱的元音已经很了不得，但是你的一百三十种真使我望洋兴叹。这些大半的音我听不出一点的区别。(Lin)/辟克林：是呀，真费力。我自己念得出二十四个不同的元音，觉得已经不算坏了：可是你却能分别出一百三十个元音，比我高明多了。你这些发音，我多半都听不出分别来。(Yang)

HIGGINS. Oh, that comes with practice. You hear no difference at first; but you keep on listening, and presently you find they're all as different as A from B. What's the matter? 黑董思：这由练习慢慢得来。起初你听不见区别；但是还继续的听，不久就看见他们像 A 与 B 的大不相同。什么事？(Lin)/息金斯：这是练出来的。最初一点也听不出来；可是听久了，你会知道每个音都会有分别，就像 A 和 B 那样的不同。什么事？(Yang)

MRS. PEARCE. A young woman wants to see you, sir. 比尔斯太太：一位年轻女子要来见你。(Lin)/别斯太太：先生，有一个年轻女人要见你。(Yang)

HIGGINS. A young woman! What does she want? 黑董思：一位年轻女子！她有什么事？(Lin)/息金斯：年轻女人！她有什么事？(Yang)

There are slight differences between the two versions. Both employ transliteration for the translation of the names but each of the translators has developed a different system of transcription. In terms of semantic and verbal correspondence with the original, at times Lin deviates from the original while Yang does not. For instance, Lin's translation of *go over any of it again* is 再来一次 but Yang's translation is 随便拿一部分再来一遍. At other times, Lin is closer to the original while Yang deviates. For instance, Lin translates *I think* into 我想 but Yang's rendering is 大概; Lin translates *not now* into 现在不要

but Yang's rendering is 以后再说吧. As such differences only take place in some short segments, I would rather consider them a matter of diction. Neither of them attempts at drastic verbal changes. On the whole, both translators follow the original closely. Either Lin's 听声音听倦了吧 or Yang's 听这些发音有些腻了吧 is a close rendering of *Tired of listening to sounds*. The difference is accidental. Lin has happened to come across one word while Yang has hit upon another. In the translation of *A young woman! What does she want?* we do not really see any difference between Lin's "一位年轻女子！她有什么事?" and Yang's "年轻女人！她有什么事?" If there is any difference, at the time of translation Lin must have thought that 一位年轻女子 is good Chinese and Yang must have thought 年轻女人 is good Chinese. Meanwhile, it shall be pointed out that, although there is no strategic difference between the two translators in translating the same work, the aesthetic effect each version has upon the contemporary reader may not be the same. One gets the impression that Yan's version is more comfortable reading than Lin's. Lin's awkwardness here does not always come from his verbal loyalty to the original. 这由练习慢慢得来（Yang's concise colloquial rendering：这是练出来的）is the product of verbal loyalty whereas 像 A 与 B 的大不相同（Yang：就像 A 和 B 那样的不同），which uses the vernacular Chinese possessive case *de*（的），has been under the influence of the usage of the possessive case marker *zhi*（之）in classical Chinese literature.

The basic strategy of close verbal correspondence may be shifted to loose verbal correspondence any time, not only in the same text but also in later versions. In the 1945 edition of Lin's translation, we spot a number of significant changes：

郝先生：我想再也没有了。
毕柯灵：佩服之至。你知道，我一半还没有听进去。
郝先生：要不要再来一次?
毕柯灵：不要了，谢谢；现在不要。弄了这一个早半天，精神已经乏了。
郝先生：声音听得腻烦了吧?
毕柯灵：是的。真吃力。我二十四种元音能发得分明不乱的，自己以为很了不得了；但是你的一百三十种真叫我望洋兴叹。这些音有一大半我一点儿区别也听不出来。
郝先生：这要慢慢练习起来。起初你听不出有什么不同的地方；但是如果再继续的听下去，不久可就觉得他们有天壤之别了。有什么事?

皮太太：先生，有一个年轻女人要见你。

(Bernard, 1945. Trans. Lin Yutang: 43)

Certain verbal deviations make the meaning more transparent and the expression more idiomatic. For instance: 佩服之至 is a more accurate rendering of "It's really amazing" though literally it is further away from the original than 真可赞叹, and 不久可就觉得他们有天壤之别了 is more Chinese than 不久就看见他们像 A 与 B 的大不相同 in the rendering of "you find they're all as different as A from B." The longer rendering 弄了这一个早半天，精神已经乏了 is more intelligible than the brief rendering 早晨的精神已经用完了 for *I'm quite done up for this morning*. In general, changes are made to better comply with Chinese language norms. Interestingly in the later version Lin has also changed the Chinese transcription of the personal names in the play. He changes 辟克林 for Pickering to 毕柯灵 (which is not a big deal), 黑董思 for Higgins to 郝先生 (Mr. Hao, like a member of the Chinese Hao clan), and 别斯太太 for Mrs. Pearce to 皮太太 (Mrs. Pi, like a Chinese lady whose husband belongs to the Pi clan). Despite the increased level of looseness in the later version, the revisions that allow the expressions to be more flexible exactly show that Lin has followed a primary strategy of close verbal correspondence in his translation of the *Pygmalion*. In this case, loose verbal correspondence is but a secondary, alternative or supplementary strategy.

Lin Yutang and Zhu Guangqian[①]: Similar Primary Strategy of Close Verbal Correspondence in the Translation of Croce

Behind the primary strategy of close verbal correspondence and the secondary strategy of loose formal correspondence is always the pivotal concept of meaning. Whatever strategy is adopted, meaning must be unambiguously brought out. Lin is not different from Yang in his translation of *Pygmalion*, nor is he different from Zhu in his translation of excerpts from *Aesthetic as Science of Expression and General Linguistic*. In the preface to the first edition of his translation, Zhu (1947) says that he has followed two procedures in translating Croce: first, to translate "literally"; second, to polish the translation according

① Zhu's preface to the First Edition of his translation is dated February, 1947.

to Chinese language conventions in the absence of the original. A comparison of Lin's selected translation with the corresponding passages in Zhu's version shows that similar results have been achieved by both translators. The following is from a section headed "Practical Innocence of Art" in Douglas Ainslie's English version of Croce:

> The theme or content cannot, therefore, be practically or morally charged with epithets of praise or of blame. When critics of art remark that a theme is badly selected, in cases where that observation has a just foundation, it is a question of blaming, not the selection of the theme (which would be absurd), but the manner in which the artist has treated it. The expression has failed, owing to the contradictions which it contains. And when the same critics rebel against the theme or the content as being unworthy of art and blameworthy, in respect to works which they proclaim to be artistically perfect; if these expressions really are perfect, there is nothing to be done but to advise the critics to leave the artists in peace, for they cannot get inspiration, save from what has made an impression upon them. The critics should think rather of how they can effect changes in nature and in society, in order that those impressions may not exist. If ugliness were to vanish from the world, if universal virtue and felicity were established there, perhaps artists would no longer represent perverse or pessimistic sentiments, but sentiments that are calm, innocent, and joyous, like Arcadians of a real Arcady …
>
> (Croce, 1909: 84 –85)

Lin's translation in 1929:

> 所以题材或是内容不得从实际的或是伦理的观点有所褒贬。在艺术批评家说某种题材"选得不好"时,若非此语全无意义,便实际上并非訾议"题目的选错"(这便成一句荒谬话)乃是訾他处置排比这题目的方法,是訾议那不成功的表现,因为含有扞格不顺之处。倘使同此批评家对于一些艺术上认为无疵的作品,还要表示不满于其题目或其内容,斥为不合艺术;那末,如果其表现委实无疵,只好劝告那些批评家,别来干涉艺术家,因为艺术家所能受的神感,也只能凭着所得印象为限,只好请批评家去改造那环围艺术家的自然或社会,使他们不至于再得这种印象。一切丑恶能从世上消灭时,一个天下有道福乐的国度能建立时,艺术家也就无坏的与绝望的情感,可以表现,而自身安心乐业于升平世界,做太平天下的善民了。
>
> (Lin, 1994d: 227)

Zhu's translation, first edition in 1947, revised in 1956:

> 因此,题材或内容不能从实践的或道德的观点加以毁誉。艺术批评家们说某某题旨选择得不好时,如果那话有正当的根据,它所指责的不能是题旨的选择(这就会是荒谬的),只能是作者处理那题旨的方式,即内在矛盾所造成的表现的失败。

这些批评家们往往又说某些作品在艺术上是完美的，却谴责它们的题旨或内容不配为艺术，如果这些表现品真是完美的，就没有别的可说，只好请那些批评家们不要再搅扰艺术家们，因为艺术家们只能从曾经感动心灵的东西中取得灵感。批评家们最好注意去改变四周的自然与社会，使他们所认为可谴责的那些印象和心境不发生。如果丑恶可从世界中消灭，普遍的德行与幸福可以在这世界中奠定，艺术家们也许就不再表现反常的或悲观的感觉，而只表现平静的，纯洁的，愉快的感觉，成了真正理想国的理想人物。

(Croce, 1983: 61)

The two passages above closely resemble each other. This is the result of close adherence to the original. We cannot deny the structural and semantic similarity in

Lin: 所以题材或是内容不得从实际的或是伦理的观点有所褒贬
Zhu: 因此，题材或内容不能从实践的或道德的观点加以毁誉

nor can we say that the following are very much different from each other:

Lin: 艺术家也就无坏的与绝望的情感
Zhu: 艺术家们也许就不再表现反常的或悲观的感觉

The difference is usually an accidental preference of one word over another. It may also be a preference of one structure over another. Lin has opted to translate the English conditional clause headed by *if* into an adverbial clause of time, while Zhu prefers to translate the same conditional clause into a Chinese conditional clause headed by 如果 (if). Only occasionally does Lin ignore the verbal reality of the original and offer a paraphrase as in the translation for the last sentence of the paragraph.

Lin Yutang vs. Guo Moruo: Different Ways of Rendering the Spirit of the *Rubaiyat*

Some texts (such as poetry) allow more freedom for the translator to experiment with the language. As has been noted that Lin Yutang's translation of five quatrains of the *Rubaiyat* from English is an imitation in which there is loose verbal correspondence as well as close verbal correspondence and non-correspondence. There is no formula as to which part of a poem should be rendered close and which part loose or otherwise. Not committed to the letter, both Lin and Guo try to preserve the spirit of the poems. In the translation of the same quatrains, Guo also shifts between the different strategies, but where

Lin adheres to the original poem closely Guo does not necessarily do the same and where Lin deviates from the verbal expression Guo may do otherwise. As a result the two versions of the same quatrain look and sound very different. Here is a comparison of the three versions of Quatrains 7 and 15:

Quatrain 7, fourth edition of Fitzgerald:

> Come, fill the cup, and ① in the fire of Spring/② The Winter Garment of Repentance fling:/The Bird of Time has but a little way/To flutter — and the Bird is on the Wing.

Lin's translation:

> 来,①在这春日和风里斟个满大杯,把②岸然道貌的空架子一齐都丢开。时光的鸟已鼓翼前去了,而这鸟并没有很长的路可以飞。
>
> (Lin, 1994i: 20)

Guo's translation:

> 来呀,请来浮此一斛,/①在春阳之中脱去②忏悔的冬裳:/"时鸟"是飞不多时的——/鸟已在振翮翱翔。
>
> (Khayyam, 2003: 6)

Lin's version here is more distant from the source quatrain than Guo's with his use of 和风 (warm breeze) in ① and 岸然道貌的空架子 (the hollow air of hypocrisy) in ②.

Quatrain 15, fourth edition of Fitzgerald:

> And ③those who husbanded the Golden grain,/④And those who flung it to the winds like raindrop,/⑤Alike to no such aureate earth are turned/As, buried once, Men want dug up again.

Lin's translation:

> ③无论是那些守财如命吝啬的老太太,④或者是那些挥金似土慷慨的少奶奶,⑤都不能变成个甚么香土堆,瘗埋后还有人愿意挖他出来。
>
> (Lin, 1994i: 20)

Guo's translation:

> ③有的节谷如金,/④有的挥金如雨,/⑤玉女金童身归大梦,/墓又为人掘起。
>
> (Khayyam, 2003: 10)

Guo translates ③ *those who husbanded the Golden grain* into something like "some husbanded grains like gold." Lin translates it into "the miserly old ladies who take their possessions for their life." In the Lin version, the image is new but the description of misers is accurate. In the translation of ④ *And those who flung it to the winds like raindrop* Guo is closer than Lin to the source words but both adhere to the meaning of the source phrase. Guo's translation of ⑤ means literally "Jade maidens and golden boys go to the Big Dream (death) and their tombs are dug up" while Lin's adheres more closely to the English version①.

Lin Yutang and Huang Jiade: Looseness vs. Closeness in the Chinese Translation of *The Autobiography of a Super Tramp*

Lin's approach to *The Autobiography of a Super Tramp* in general can be categorized as loose verbal correspondence despite instances of close verbal correspondence and non-correspondence. Here is a selection from his translation:

> We were determined to be in the fashion, and to visit the various delightful watering-places on Long Island Sound. Of course it would be necessary to combine business with pleasure, and pursue our calling as beggars. With the exception of begging food, which would not be difficult, seeing that the boarding houses were full, and that large quantities of good stuff were being made, there was no reason why we should not get as much enjoyment out of life as the summer visitors. We would share with them the same sun and breeze; we could dip in the surf at our own pleasure, and during the heat of the day we could stretch our limbs in the green shade, or in the shadow of some large rock that overlooked the Sound. However, we could no longer stand the sultry heat of New York, where we had been for several days, during which time we had been groaning and gasping for air ...
>
> (Davies, 1963: 49)
>
> 长岛海峡,那也是天然的,充满了美景令人见而心欢的一个避暑胜地,我们羡慕着,当然也要学学时髦,去上一次。
>
> 但我们此去维持生活的方法,依旧是用乞讨来解决我们的面包。那里,食物方面自然不用担忧,因为来往的旅客占据满了每家旅馆的房间。精美的食料定能余剩给我们,那你们也许会享受到人生的乐趣,和一切旅行者同样。
>
> 和风,太阳,带给我们夏天的春意,在那里,我们还可以沐海水浴,躲在日光炎

① The comparison is complicated by Guo's failure to understand the last two lines of the quatrain. Here Guo has failed to understand the meaning and therefore cannot render them closely. Since the English poem itself is a translation from the Persian, I am not sure if we can criticize Guo's mistake.

炎的白天的绿荫之下,俯望着海峡那里的大石,打呵欠,伸懒腰,尽管悉听尊便!

然而,纽约,依然酷热得很。我们仅只小住几天,每天无不为没有新鲜和自由的空气的调剂,而在那里叹气和呻吟。

(Davies, 1986: 46)

It seems that Lin does not care about consistency of narrative details with the original. In this selection, only the underlined segments have some close counterparts in the translation. There are drastic changes in word order. The translation is by no means confined by English grammar. The translator has got a general idea of the sentence and produced that idea in Chinese using or not using linguistic information provided by the original. The result is a highly readable yet verbally unfaithful translation. Here, *some large rock that overlooked the Sound* is translated into Chinese as something like "we looked down at some large rock in the Sound"! This I suppose is close to the "licentious translation" which is criticized in his article "On Translation."

In contrast, Huang, who has read Lin's version①, is a close follower of the original and has established a close verbal correspondence between the translation and the original:

我仍决定要趁趁时髦,到长岛海峡那些怡情悦性的海边避暑胜地去游览。我们当然得兼顾事业和游乐,从事叫化工作。在那边要乞食是不难的,因为旅馆里都住满了人,精美的食品很多;除乞食工作之外,我们所享受的人生乐趣,一定可以和那些避暑的旅客一样多。我们和他们同享阳光与微风;我们可以随意作海水浴;在炎热的白天里,我们可以在青翠欲滴的浓荫里,或在俯望海峡的大石的隐影下,伸伸懒腰休息。然而,我们再也忍不住纽约的酷热;我们在那里小住数日,天天因找不到新鲜的空气而呻吟着,喘息着。

(Davies, 1940: 39)

Six Chapters of a Floating Life Translated by Lin Yutang vs. *Six Records of a Floating Life* Translated by Pratt and Chiang: The Effect of a Holistic Approach

Both versions② adhere to the original in both content and form. They do

① Lin's preface to *The Autobiography of a Super Tramp* is included in Huang's translation.

② The examples are from Lin Yutang's translation *Six Chapters of a Floating Life* (Shen. 1999: 67) and Pratt and Chiang's translation *Six Records of a Floating Life* (Shen, 1983: 47).

not strike us as very much different from each other. Most sentences in both versions have close verbal correspondence to the original sentences, like the following:

Then I laughed and said, "Will the lady teacher please stop a moment? I have a parable for explaining it, and she will understand at once." (Lin)/I laughed and said, 'Stop it, lady teacher. I have a comparison that will explain the problem.' (Pratt and Chiang) 余笑曰:"女先生且罢论,我有一言作譬,即了然矣。"

"The stork," I said, "can dance, but cannot plow, while the buffalo can plow, but cannot dance. That lies in the nature of things. (Lin)/ "A crane can dance but cannot plough, while an ox can plough but cannot dance. That is just the nature of things." (Pratt and Chiang) 鹤善舞而不能耕,牛善耕而不能舞,物性然也……"

Hearing this, Suyün struck me blow after blow with her fist in a rage, saying, "Who told you to smell it?" (Lin)/At this Su-yün could not be stopped from hitting me repeatedly. "Who told you to sniff around?" She shouted. (Pratt and Chiang) 素云不禁握拳连捶曰:"谁教汝狂嗅耶?"

However, sometimes Lin's version seemingly deviates from the original like in the translation of the following sentences:

You try it, then! (Lin)/What kind of an example are you going to give? (Pratt and Chiang) 君若何譬之?

You are making a fool of yourself by trying to teach the impossible to her. (Lin)/ Wouldn't it be a waste of time if you tried to teach each of them to play the other's game? (Pratt and Chiang) 先生欲反而教之,无乃劳乎?

In such instances, we cannot isolate the sentences from their respective contexts. *You try it, then!* is not a direct translation of 君若何譬之? but it makes a reference to the proceeding *I have a parable for explaining it*. Therefore such a deviation is the result of the translator's understanding of the text as a whole. Similarly, *trying to teach the impossible to her* is not a literally exact translation of 欲反而教之 and is based on the translator's inference rather than linguistic reality in the original while Pratt and Chiang's *to teach each of them to play the other's game* is more literal. Here, in the translation of *Six Chapters of a Floating Life*, Lin's idea of "total concept" is at work on the textual level although it is intended to account for sentence translation. It is the "total concept" that keeps the text focused and gives the translator occasional freedom in the representation of details.

2 Corrections or Revisions of Translations: Intuition in the Search for Exactness and Appropriateness of Expression

Some of Lin Yutang's translations (mostly English translations) are in fact his revisions of existing translations, which include *The Way and Its Power* translated by Arthur Waley, *Chuang Tzu* translated by Herbert A. Giles, and *The Conduct of Life*, Ku Hung-ming's translation of the *Zhongyong*. In the section headed "Borrowing Translations" of a previous chapter of this book, some of the revisions have been mentioned in passing as examples of borrowing. Here in this section, I would like to highlight the corrections and revisions using the same examples when necessary so as not to give my readers additional reading load.

A translator who builds his own translation on a more or less successful previous version is to be commended for two reasons. First, knowing the limitation of the enterprise of translating, he is humble enough to recognize the relative merits of the predecessor. Second, he is courageous enough to try to "correct" his predecessor as the translator's reputation is at risk if he makes a wrong correction: There is no single way of translating and there is no guarantee that the correction is any better than the original translation.

Lin Yutang and H. A. Giles in the Translation of *Chuang Tzu*[①]: Two Directions of Revision

Much of Giles is preserved in Lin's version. Putting the two texts together we can see exactly where changes are taking place. Some changes involve a new understanding on the part of the reviser, and some are concerned with the effect of expression in the target language.

Meaning-oriented, Lin has made the following corrections because he thinks that Giles' understanding is wrong or at least inexact. Most of his revisions show an obvious inclination toward close verbal correspondence while he works

---

① The examples to follow are from "Chuangtse, Mystic and Humorist" in *The Wisdom of China and India* (1942) by Lin Yutang and *Chuang Tzu*, translated by Herbert A. Giles, first published in 1889.

for semantic correspondence, e.g.,

a. I think one who knows how to govern the empire should not do so. (Lin)/Now I regard government of the empire from quite a different point of view. (Giles) 吾意善治天下者不然。(A new sentence is written. Lin is more literal.)

b. Birds and beasts multiplied; trees and shrubs thrived. (Lin)/Birds and beasts multiplied; trees and shrubs grew up. (Giles)禽兽成群,草木遂长。("thrived" is supposed to be more accurate than "grew up")

c. Who could know of the distinctions between gentlemen and common people? (Lin)/There were no distinctions of good and bad men. (Giles) 恶乎知君子小人哉 ("gentlemen and common" are more accurate than "good and bad men.")

d. At that time, there were no paths over mountains, no boats or bridges over waters. (Lin)/At that time, there were no roads over mountains, nor boats, nor bridges over water. (Giles) 当是时也,山无蹊隧,泽无舟梁 ("paths" is more accurate than "roads.")

e. Ceremonial halls and big dwellings are of no use to them. (Lin)/Palatial dwellings are of no use to them. (Giles) 虽有义台路寝,无所用之。(Apparently ceremonial halls and big dwellings is literally closer to the original.)

f. So he burned their hair and clipped them, and pared their hooves and branded them. He put halters around their necks and shackles around their legs and numbered them according to their stables. The result was that two or three in every ten died. (Lin)/So he branded them, and clipped them, and pared their hoofs, and put halters on them, tying them up by the head and shackling them by the feet, and disposing them in stables, with the results that two or three in every ten died. (Giles) 烧之,剔之,刻之,雒之,连之以羁,编之以皁栈,马之死者十二三矣。(Giles' three sentences are rewritten into one sentence. Lin's six actions more closely correspond to their counterparts in the original though it cannot be said with certainty whether *numbered them according to their stables* is really semantically closer to the original than Giles' *tying them up by the head and shackling them by the feet, and disposing them in stables.*)

g. I am good at managing horses. (Lin)/I understand the management of horses. (Giles) 我善治马 (The sentence is rewritten. Lin is verbally closer to the original.)

h. I am good at managing clay. (Lin)/I can do what I will with clay. (Giles) 我善治埴 (Lin is verbally closer to the original by rewriting the sentence.)

i. I am good at managing wood. (Lin)/I can do what I will with wood. (Giles) 我善治木 (Lin is verbally closer to the original by rewriting the sentence.)

In the above cases, Lin adheres verbally to the original where Giles does not, but other revisions are less concerned with the original. It is more about the expressiveness of the translation. They include checks on spelling, grammar and appropriateness so that the translation is more readable, comprehensible or acceptable.

The following are examples of his spelling and grammar checks:

j. Horses have hooves to carry them over frost and snow, and hair to protect them from wind and cold. (Lin)/Horses have hoofs to carry them over frost and snow; hair, to protect them from wind and cold. (Giles) 马,蹄可以用来践踏霜雪,毛可以用来抵御风寒

k. For the people have certain natural instincts — to weave and clothe themselves, to till the fields and feed themselves. (Lin)/The people have certain natural instincts: to weave and clothe themselves, to till and feed themselves. (Giles) 彼民有常性,织而衣,耕而食。

l. One day Polo (famous horse-trainer), appeared (Lin)/One day Poh Loh appeared, (Giles) 及至伯乐

m. But on what grounds can we think that the nature of clay and wood desires this application of compasses and square, and arc and line? (Lin)/But on what grounds can we think that the natures of clay and wood desire this application of compasses and square, of arc and line? (Giles) 夫埴木之性,岂欲中规矩鉤绳哉?

As Giles is an able writer in his native language, Lin cannot possibly find many serious language errors in his translation. What Lin does is to make a little adjustment so that the translation is more consistent with his own way of translating.

The concern with appropriateness has led to a reverse direction of revision: from close verbal correspondence to loose verbal correspondence.

n. Then he kept them hungry and thirsty, trotting them and galloping them, and taught them to run in formations, with the misery of the tasselled bridle in front and the fear of the knotted whip behind, until more than half of them died. (Lin)/Then he kept them hungry and thirsty, trotting them and galloping them, and grooming, and trimming, with the misery of the tasselled bridle before and the fear of the knotted whip behind, until more than half of them were dead. (Giles) 饥之,渴之,驰之,骤之,整之,齐之,前有橛饰之患,而后有鞭之威,而马之死者已过半矣。(*taught them to run in formations* does not literally correspond to the original phrase but it overcomes the awkwardness of *grooming, and trimming* which does not seem to semantically belong well with the rest of the sentence. Lin's sentence has a greater inner coherence.)

o. Nevertheless, every age extols Polo for his skill in training horses, and potters and carpenters for their skill with clay and wood. (Lin)/Nevertheless, every age extols Poh Loh for his skill in managing horses, and potters and carpenters for their skill with clay and wood. (Giles) 然且世世称之曰"伯乐善治马"而"陶、匠善治埴、木" (Interestingly, where Giles uses something else for 治, Lin persistently uses the word "manage" but when at last Giles is using "manage" Lin is using something else.)

p. They eat grass and drink water, and fling up their tails and gallop. (Lin)/They eat grass and drink water, and fling up their heels over the fields. (Giles) 龁草饮水,翘足而陆 (The word *gallop* contains the essence — meaning and image — of *fling up their heels over the fields* while the latter is a word-for-word translation.)

q. This is their common character, in which all share. Such instincts may be called "Heaven born." (Lin)/These are common to all humanity, and all are agreed thereon. Such instincts are called "Heaven-sent". (Giles) 是谓同德;一而不党,命曰天放 (Lin could not accept *and all are agreed upon* and omit it entirely.)

However, despite the differences we can point out between Lin's version and its antecedent and despite the conjectures we can make about Lin's textual strategy through comparison and contrast, it is not true that we can always spot a notable difference between his choice and that of his predecessor. Not all revisions can be measured in terms of distance from the original. Nor can we say a revision always makes a difference in the expressive power. All we can say about the following sentence pairs is that they reflect the idiosyncrasies of the translators: the sentences in each pair roughly mean the same and that they are almost equally intelligible. Two minds are not one, after all:

r. All things were produced each in its natural district. (Lin)/All things were produced, each for its own proper sphere. (Giles) 万物群生,连属其乡

s. Thus it was that birds and beasts could be led by the hand, and one could climb up and peep into the magpie's nest. (Lin)/The former might be led by the hand; you could climb up and peep into the raven's nest. (Giles) 是故禽兽可系羁而游,鸟鹊之巢可攀援而窥

t. (For in the days of perfect nature,) man lived together with birds and beasts, and there was no distinction of their kind. (Lin)/For then man dwelt with birds and beasts, and all creation was one. (Giles) (夫至德之世,) 同与禽兽居,族与万物并

Lin Yutang and Ku Hung-ming in the Translation of *The Doctrine of the Mean*: Conservatism in the Revision of a "Perfect" Translation

Ku Hung-ming (Ku Hungming, Gu Hongming) is one of the brilliant translators that command the admiration of Lin Yutang. Lin has not attempted a new version of *The Doctrine of the Mean*. Instead, he makes some minor adjustments of Ku's text. The changes that he makes are particularly revealing about his strategy in approaching Chinese sacred texts. The strategy is close verbal correspondence in spite of his claim that his method is *paraphrase*. He thus speaks of his revision of Ku:

> … I have however found it necessary to add, delete and substitute phrases or lines, bringing about, I believe, a closer adherence to the original, and have naturally changed certain spellings of Chinese names to make them uniform with the rest of the book.
>
> (Lin, 1938: 102)

The following are some of his substitutions, additions and deletions in detail.

Substitution:

Where Ku deviates far from the original, Lin replaces the deviations with his closer solutions. This practice is evident throughout the text:

> 天命之谓性,率性之谓道,修道之谓教:
>
> The ordinance of God is what we call the law of our being. To fulfil the law of our being is what we call the moral law. The moral law when reduced to a system is what we call religion.
>
> (Ku, 1928: 14)
>
> What is God-given is what we call human nature. To fulfil the law of our human nature is what we call the moral law. The cultivation of the moral law is what we call culture.
>
> (Lin, 1938: 104)
>
> 隐恶而扬善:
>
> He looked upon evil merely as something negative; and he recognized only what was good as having a positive existence.
>
> (Ku, 1928: 18)

He ignored the bad (words?) and broadcast the good. (Lin, 1938: 112)

> 自诚明,谓之性;自明诚,谓之教。诚则明矣,明则诚矣:
>
> The intelligence which comes from the direct apprehension of truth is intuition. The apprehension of truth which comes from the exercise of intelligence is the result of education. Where there is truth, there is intelligence; where there is intelligence, there is truth.
>
> (Ku, 1928: 44, 45)
>
> To arrive at understanding from being one's true self is called nature, and to arrive at being one's true self from understanding is called culture. He who is his true self has thereby understanding, and he who has understanding finds thereby his true self.
>
> (Lin, 1938: 123)
>
> 道之不行也,我知之矣……

I know now why there is no real moral life.

(Ku, 1928: 16)

I know now why the moral life is not practiced.

(Lin, 1938: 105)

明乎郊社之礼、禘尝之义,治国其如示诸掌乎。

If one only understood the meaning of the sacrifices to Heaven and Earth, and the significance of the services in ancestral worship, it would be the easiest thing to govern a nation.

(Ku, 1928: 43)

If one only understood the meaning of the sacrifices to Heaven and Earth, and the significance of the services in ancestral worship in summer and autumn, it would be as easy to govern a nation as to point a finger at the palm.

(Lin, 1938: 115)

However, it shall be noted that not all substitutions involve profound semantic change. In the following example, only some structural changes take place. Such changes do not alter the meaning of the sentence.

(中庸其至矣乎!) 民鲜能久矣!

People are seldom capable of it for long.

(Ku, 1928: 16)

For a long time, people have seldom been capable of it.

(Lin, 1938: 105)

Besides, while we appreciate Lin's effort to improve on existing translations, we shall be aware that his corrections or revisions are not always justified. This involves disparate understanding of the original on the part of the two translators. For instance, for the following excerpt, the two translators present us with different translations:

在下位不获乎上,民不可得而治矣;获乎上有道:不信乎朋友,不获乎上矣;信乎朋友有道:不顺乎亲,不信乎朋友矣;顺乎亲有道:反诸身不诚,不顺乎亲矣;诚身有道:不明乎善,不诚乎身矣。

If those in authority have not the confidence of those under them, government of the people is an impossibility. There is only one way to gain confidence for one's authority. If a man is not trusted by his friends, he will not gain the confidence for his authority. There is only one way to be trusted by one's friends. If a man does not command the obedience of the members of his family, he will not be trusted by his friends. There is only one way to command the obedience of the members of one's family. If a man, looking into his own heart, is not true to himself, he will not command the obedience of the members of his family. There is only one way for a man to be true to himself. If he does not know what is good, a man cannot be true to himself.

(Ku, 1928: 36, 37)

If the people in inferior positions do not have confidence in those above them, government of the people is an impossibility. There is only one way to gain confidence for one's authority: if a man is not trusted by his friends, he will not have confidence in those above him. There is only one way to be trusted by one's friends: if a man is not affectionate toward his parents, he will not be trusted by his friends. There is only one way to be affectionate toward one's parents: if a man, looking into his own heart, is not true to himself, he will not be affectionate toward his parents. There is only one way for a man to be true to himself. If he does not know what is good, a man cannot be true to himself.

(Lin, 1938: 121)

In one sentence, Lin must have thought that Ku's interpretation of the original is wrong or otherwise unacceptable:

If those in authority have not the confidence of those under them, government of the people is an impossibility.

(Ku, 1928: 36)

Lin tries to correct him:

If the people in inferior positions do not have confidence in those above them, government of the people is an impossibility.

(Lin, 1938: 121)

Unfortunately, Lin's correction makes no difference semantically. The common interpretation by Chinese scholars is:

If the people in inferior positions do not have *the* confidence *of* those above them, it is impossible for them to get the authority for the government of people. ①

In another sentence, where Ku does not make the meaning quite clear, Lin makes a wrong correction:

---

① See a modern Chinese interpretation based on classic sources in Yang, Hong & Wang Gang. 1997. *Zhongyong with Modern Chinese Translation and Annotations*. Lan Zhou: Gansu Minzu Press: 51. [杨洪、王刚注译. 1997.《中庸》. 兰州: 甘肃民族出版社: 51.]

If a man is not trusted by his friends, he will not gain the confidence for his authority. (Ku)

... if a man is not trusted by his friends, he will not have confidence in those above him. (Lin)

whereas the standard interpretation by modern Chinese scholars is

There is a method to gain the confidence of one's superiors: if a man is not trusted by his friends, he will not gain the confidence of those above him.

To err is human. Even the most confident translator is vulnerable to errors.

Addition:

On other occasions, Lin may add something to Ku's translation so that the exact meaning in the original may be better brought out:

明乎郊社之礼、禘尝之义,治国其如示诸掌乎。

If one only understood the meaning of the sacrifices to Heaven and Earth, and the significance of the services in ancestral worship, it would be the easiest thing to govern a nation.

(Ku, 1928: 43)

If one only understood the meaning of the sacrifices to Heaven and Earth, and the significance of the services in ancestral worship in summer and autumn, it would be as easy to govern a nation as to point a finger at the palm.

(Lin, 1938: 115)

是故君子戒慎乎其所不睹,恐惧乎其所不闻。

Wherefore it is that the moral man watches diligently over what his eyes cannot see and is in fear and awe of what his ears cannot hear.

(Ku, 1928: 14)

Wherefore it is that the moral man (or the superior man) watches diligently over what his eyes cannot see and is in fear and awe of what his ears cannot hear.

(Lin, 1938: 104)

喜怒哀乐之未发,谓之中;发而皆中节,谓之和。中也者,天下之大本也;和也者,天下之达道也。

When the passions, such as joy, anger, grief, and pleasure, have not awakened, that is our true self, or moral being. When these passions awaken and each and all attain due measure and degree, that is the moral order. Our true self or moral being is the great reality (lit. great root) of existence, and moral order is the universal law in the world.

(Ku, 1928: 15)

When the passions, such as joy, anger, grief, and pleasure, have not awakened, that is our *central* self, or moral being (*chung*). When these passions awaken and each and all attain due measure and degree, that is *harmony*, or the moral order (*ho*). Our central self or moral being is the great basis of existence, and *harmony* or moral order is the universal law in the world.

(Lin, 1938: 104)

君子中庸，小人反中庸。

The life of the moral man is an exemplification of the universal moral order. The life of the vulgar person, on the other hand, is a contradiction of the universal moral order.

(Ku, 1928: 15)

The life of the moral man is an exemplification of the universal moral order (*chungyung*, usually translated as "the Mean"). The life of the vulgar person, on the other hand, is a contradiction of the universal moral order.

(Lin, 1938: 121)

Deletion:

Lin's deletions are not to bring closer verbal correspondence between the translation and its original. Rather, they serve to bring clarity to the translation. A major deletion is the removal of much of Chapter XXVIII of the *The Doctrine of the Mean*, the rest of the chapter incorporated into his Chapter XXIX, because in his opinion, this is a "bad chapter."

The following deletion takes place because there seems to be overlapping in Ku's translation:

言前定则不跲，事前定则不困，行前定则不疚，道前定则不穷。

When what is to be said is previously determined, there will be no breakdown. When what is to be done is previously determined, there will be no difficulty in carrying it out. When a line of conduct is previously determined, there will be no occasion for vexation. When general principles are previously determined, there will be no perplexity to know what to do.

(Ku, 1928: 36)

When what is to be said is previously determined, there will be no difficulty in carrying it out. When a line of conduct is previously determined, there will be no occasion for vexation. When general principles are previously determined, there will be no perplexity to know what to do.

(Lin, 1938: 121)

In Ku's translation, Lin thinks that "When what is to be done is previously determined" and "When a line of conduct is previously determined" mean basically the same thing. Unable to find a satisfactory close solution, he has decided to remove the redundancy by deleting the repetition. A close translation can be found in James Legge's version. ①

Self-Revisions: Looking for the Exact Word

We cannot say that Lin's translations are perfect but we can say that over the years he developed a perfect seriousness toward translating, never completely satisfied with his own translations, constantly making improvements as new editions were published. In accordance with his theory of translation, his self-improvements are made in two directions: to go closer to the original author and to go closer to the reader. The two directions are often contradictory but he has done his best to strike a balance between them. He proof-reads in order to be faithful to the author and edits the translation to be responsible to the reader.

As has been mentioned, his translation of *The Book of Tao* is based on the work of Arthur Waley and other translators. It should also be noted that he has subjected his own translation to revisions. When an early edition as in *The Wisdom of China and India* (1942) and a later edition as in *The Wisdom of Laotse* (1948) are compared, profuse revisions in the latter version can be spotted.

A chief aim of his revision is to make the translation as close to the original as possible. He has checked his translation against the original to make sure that he does not betray it. The following table consists of typical instances of his effort to shorten the distance between the translation and its Chinese original:

---

① James Legge's close rendition: "If what is to be spoken be previously determined, there will be no stumbling. If affairs be previously determined, there will be no difficulty with them. If one's actions have been previously determined, there will be no sorrow in connection with them. If principles of conduct have been previously determined, the practice of them will be inexhaustible."

Table 6 Lin Yutang's Self-Revision of Laotse to Be Closer to the Original

From the Chinese original (Chapter numbers are in brackets.)	From "Laotse, the Book of Tao" in *The Wisdom of China and India* (1942)	From *The Wisdom of Laotse* (1948)
常有,欲以观其徼。(1)	Oftentimes, one regards life with passion, In order to see its manifest results.	Oftentimes, one regards life with passion, In order to see its manifest forms
常使民无知无欲。(3)	So that the people may be purified of their thoughts and desires.	So that the people may be innocent of knowledge and desires.
湛兮,似或存。(4)	Yet crystal clear like still water it seems to remain.	Yet dark like deep water it seems to remain.
非以其无私邪?故能成其私。(7)	Is it not because he does not live for self That his self achieves perfection?	Is it not because he does not live for self That his self is realized?
致虚极,守静笃。(16)	Attain the utmost in Humility, Hold firm to the basis of Quietude.	Attain the utmost in Passivity, Hold firm to the basis of Quietude.
绝仁弃义,民复孝慈;(19)	Banish "love," discard "justice," And the people shall recover love of their kin;	Banish "humanity," discard "justice," And the people shall recover love of their kin;
众人熙熙,如享太牢,(20)	The people of the world are merry-making, As if eating of the sacrificial offerings,	The people of the world are merry-making, As if partaking of the sacrificial feasts,

(to be continued)

From the Chinese original (Chapter numbers are in brackets.)	From "Laotse, the Book of Tao" in *The Wisdom of China and India* (1942)	From *The Wisdom of Laotse* (1948)
孔德之容，惟道是从。(21)	The marks of great Virtue Follow alone from the Tao.	The marks of great Character Follow alone from the Tao. (Such substitution also takes place in Chapters 23, 38, 54, 55 etc.)
不自矜，故长。(22)	He does not pride himself, And is therefore the ruler among men.	He does not pride himself, And is therefore the chief among men.
B. 复归天下于朴。 C. 朴散(则为器)，(28)	D. And returns again to pristine simplicity. E. Break up this pristine simplicity	A. And returns again to the natural integrity of uncarved wood. B. Break up this carved wood
(朴散)则为器(28)	And it is shaped into tools	And it is shaped into vessel
夫兵者，不祥之器，(31)	Of all things, soldiers are weapons of evil, Hated by men.	Of all things, soldiers are instruments of evil, Hated by men.
夫亦将知止，知止可以不殆。(32)	It were well one knew where to stop for repose. He who knows where to stop for repose May from danger be exempt.	It were well one knew where to stop. He who knows where to stop May be exempt from danger
侯王若能守之(37)	If kings and barons can keep the Tao	If princes and dukes can keep the Tao
而王公以为称。(42)	Yet the kings and dukes call themselves by such names.	Yet the princes and dukes call themselves by such names.

(to be continued)

From the Chinese original (Chapter numbers are in brackets.)	From "Laotse, the Book of Tao" in *The Wisdom of China and India* (1942)	From *The Wisdom of Laotse* (1948)
故失道而后德,失德而后仁。(38)	After Tao is lost, then (arises the doctrine of) kindness, After kindness is lost, then (arises the doctrine of) justice.	After Tao is lost, then (arises the doctrine of) humanity, After humanity is lost, then (arises the doctrine of) justice.
出生入死。 生之徒,十有三; 死之徒,十有三;(50)	Out of life, death enters. The organs of life are thirteen; The organs of death are (also) thirteen. ①	Out of life, death enters. The companions (organs) of life are thirteen; The companions (organs) of death are (also) thirteen.
是为习常。(52)	This is to steal the Absolute.	This is to rest in the Absolute.
夫两不相伤, 故德交归焉。(60)	When both do not do each other harm, Virtue (power) flows towards them.	When both do not do each other harm, The original character is restored. ②

① This part has proved to be a great challenge to *Laotse* translators. Unfortunately despite his effort to be exact Lin's translation is almost unintelligible. It seems that he too like many others has failed to identify the relationships between the Chinese characters. According to popular Chinese interpretations, a reasonable translation should be something like "Coming out is called birth. Entering (the earth) is called death. Three of the ten paths lead to life. Another three of the ten paths lead to death."

② In the latter version, Lin generally translates *de* (德) into "character," but decides to preserve the word "virtue" as in "This is the Mystic Virtue" (Chapter X) or to use another word as "humanity" in Chapter 38. In the Chinese language there is no spacing between words, so it is sometimes confusing as to which characters make a word. The two versions show Lin's uncertainty in deciding whether 故德 consists of one word or two. If it is one word, it means "original character," if two, it means "therefore, character ..."

On the other hand, revisions are made so that the translation is as close to the reader as possible. The translation must be presented according to the linguistic conventions of the target language. This includes a correctness or appropriateness check within the translation with little reference to the original. Such revisions involve spelling, capitalization, grammar, the mood, or acceptability of a word (or an expression) and the like. Among others, the following revisions are basically of this nature:

Table 7 Lin Yutang's Self-Revision of *Laotse* to Be Closer to the Reader

Chinese Original (Chapter numbers are in brackets.)	"Laotse, the Book of Tao" in *The Wisdom of China and India* (1942)	*The Wisdom of Laotse* (1948)
天门开阖(10)	In opening and shutting the Gates of Heaven	In opening and shutting the Gate of Heaven
名已既有(32)	Since names there were,	Since there were names,
(知止)可以不殆(32)	May from danger be exempt.	May be exempt from danger.
故天无以清,将恐裂 地无以宁,将恐发;神无以灵,将恐歇;谷无以盈,将恐竭;万物无以生,将恐灭; 侯王无以贞,将恐蹶。 (39)	Without charity, the Heavens might shake, Without stability, the Earth might quake, Without spiritual power, the gods might crumble, Without being filled, the valleys might crack, Without the life-giving power, all things might perish, Without the ennobling power, the princes and dukes might stumble.	Without charity, the Heavens would shake, Without stability, the Earth would quake, Without spiritual power, the gods would crumble, Without being filled, the valleys would crack, Without the life-giving power, all things would perish, Without the ennobling power, the princes and dukes would stumble.

(to be continued)

Chinese Original (Chapter numbers are in brackets.)	"Laotse, the Book of Tao" in *The Wisdom of China and India* (1942)	*The Wisdom of Laotse* (1948)
上士问道,勤而行之(41)	When the highest type of men hear the Tao (truth), They practice it diligently.	When the highest type of men hear the Tao (truth), They try hard to live in accordance with it,
仓甚虚(53)	And the granaries are very low.	And the (people's) granaries are very low.
厌饮食(53)	Surfeit with good food and drinks,	Surfeited with good food and drinks,
人多利器,国家滋昏(57)	The more sharp weapons there are, The more prevailing chaos there is in the state.	The more sharp weapons there are, The greater the chaos in the state.
以道莅天下,其鬼不神(60)	Who rules the world in accord with Tao would find that the spirits lose their power.	Who rules the world in accord with Tao Shall find that the spirits lose their power.
其脆易泮, 其微易散。(64)	That which is brittle (like ice) is easy to melt; That which is minute is easy to scatter.	That which is brittle (like ice) easily melts; That which is minute easily scatters.
古之善为道者,非以明民(65)	The Ancients who knew how to follow the Tao Aimed not to enlighten the people,	The ancients who knew how to follow the Tao Aimed not to enlighten the people,
常知稽式,是谓玄德(65)	And to know always the Ancient Standard Is called the Mystic Virtue.	And to know always the ancient standard Is called the Mystic Virtue.

The two orientations are the two sides of the same coin. Without capturing the accurate meaning, there cannot be effective expression. Without effective expression we cannot be sure that meaning is understood accurately.

Lin's perfect seriousness in translation is best represented by *Six Chapters of a Floating Life*. Before serialized publication in the *Tien-hsia Monthly*, he had made over ten revisions. After its publication he continued to make improvements and had it published in book form. The postscript to the book was dated January 1929. The 1999 edition by the Foreign Language Teaching and Research Press in Beijing is based on the 1929 version. However, that is not the end of his revisions. When the 1929 version is compared with a still later version in *The Wisdom of China and India* (1942), considerable effort to make new improvements is spotted. While he was still proof-reading against the original, effort was also directed to improving the expressiveness, or the fluency of his translation.

The following are typical instances of his moving closer to the original in the later version:

Table 8 Lin Yutang's Self-Revision of *Six Chapters of a Floating Life* to Be Closer to the Original

Original	*Six Chapters of a Floating Life* (1929 edition, republished in 1999)	*The Wisdom of China and India* (1942)
秋侵人影瘦,霜染菊花肥	Touched by autumn, one's figure grows slender, Soaked in frost, the chrysanthemum blooms full.	Soaked in autumn, one's figure becomes thin, Touched by frost, the chrysanthemum becomes fat.
喜同戍人得赦	I felt like a garrison prisoner receiving his pardon.	I felt like an exiled prisoner receiving his pardon.
无师之作	I have had no one to teach me poetry	I have had no teacher in poetry
归来完姻时,原订随侍到馆	Now, when I came home for the wedding, it had been agreed that as soon as the ceremonies were over, I should go back at once to my father's place in order to resume my studies.	Now, when I came home for the wedding, it had been agreed that I could go back any time.

(to be continued)

Original	*Six Chapters of a Floating Life* (1929 edition, republished in 1999)	*The Wisdom of China and India* (1942)
有一种落花流水之趣	His lines come naturally like dropping petals and flowing waters	His lines come naturally like falling flowers and flowing water

At the same time, some revisions take place without much reference to the original. The translator may simply edit his earlier version to make sure that his translation is more friendly to the English language reader. The following instances consist of a few grammar checks, a spelling check, one removal of unnecessary information, one error correction and one addition of clarifying information.

Table 9 Lin Yutang's Self-Revision of *Six Chapters of a Floating Life* to Be Closer to the Reader

Original	*Six Chapters of a Floating Life* (1929 edition, republished in 1999)	*The Wisdom of China and India* (1942)
有一种落花流水之趣	His lines come naturally like dropping petals and flowing waters	His lines come naturally like falling flowers and flowing water (grammar check)
若为儿择妇,非淑姊不娶。	If you were to choose a girl for me, I won't marry any one except Cousin Sù.	If you choose a girl for me, I won't marry any one except cousin Su. (grammar check; spelling check)
芸与余同齿而长余十月,自幼姊弟相呼,故仍呼之曰淑姊。	Yün was the same age as myself, but ten months older, and as we had been accustomed to calling each other "elder sister" and "younger brother" from childhood, I continued to call her "Sister Su."	Yün was of the same age as myself, but ten months older, and as we had been accustomed to calling each other "elder sister" and "younger brother" from childhood, I continued to call her "Sister Su." (grammar check)
询其故。	... and I asked her the reason why.	... and I asked her the reason. (grammar check)

(to be continued)

Original	*Six Chapters of a Floating Life* (1929 edition, republished in 1999)	*The Wisdom of China and India* (1942)
鸿案相庄廿有三年,年愈久而情愈密。	And so we remained courteous to each other for twenty-three years of our married life like Liang Hung and Meng Kuang [of the East Han Dynasty], and the longer we stayed together, the more passionately attached we became to each other.	And so we remained courteous to each other for twenty-three years of our married life like Liang Hung and Meng Kuang of old, and the longer we stayed together, the more passionately attached we became to each other. (removal of unnecessary information)
是年七夕,芸设香烛瓜果,同拜天孙于我取轩中。	On the seventh night of the seventh moon of that year, Yün prepared incense, candles and some melons and other fruits, so that we might together worship the Grandson of Heaven in the Hall called "After My Heart."	On the seventh night of the seventh moon of that year [1780], Yün prepared incense, candles and some melons and fruits, so that we might together worship the Grandson of Heaven in the Hall called "After My Heart." (addition of clarifying information, correction of error)

Evidently Lin Yutang tries to be as close to the reader as possible.

IV Making Sense of Sign with Sensitivity

Thus we can summarize Lin Yutang's process of translation with 3 S's: sign, sense and sensitivity, corresponding respectively to the aesthetic concepts of content, form and spiritual activity of the artist. In discussions of translations, we speak of *letter and spirit*, *form and content*, *utterance and meaning*, *medium and message*, *signifier and signified*, and *language and thought*, et cetera. In general terms, *letter*, *form*, *utterance*, *medium*, *signifier* and *language* belong to the same category of *sign* as the linguistic, and *spirit*, *content*, *meaning*, *message*, and *thought* belong to the category of *sense* as spiritual fact. A unit of written expression, from a word to a text, contains two basic elements: sense and sign, or meaning and its representation. To bring the two elements together requires a third element, the translator's sensitivity.

In translation, sense or the spiritual fact can be transferred but the sign or the linguistic has to be entirely new. A successful translation transfers the former and transforms the latter. It is with the linguistic that an average translator frequently finds himself not at ease. A translation is, in a manner of speaking, another text. Each version is unique in its own right. Writing is a spirit that holds words together. In a similar way, translation is also a spirit that holds words together. That spirit is the translator's genius or sensitivity. Lin's own theory of translation addresses all three aspects of text formation: the transfer of sense, the construction of sign, and the translator's genius. Having had a look at the ways — the strategic shifts — that Lin Yutang constructs a text in translation, we now can conclude that to him translation is about making sense of sign with sensitivity in a textual unity.

Lin's continuous strategic shifts are quite revealing about translation. There is no set way to translate a word, an expression or a text into another. A stable, non-volatile perfect match therefore cannot be established between the original and the translation. In other words, an enduring perfect translation is not possible. A translation is not an exact equivalent of its original. It is a provisional solution to the revealing of the truth housed by the original. It approximates the truth via its resemblances to its original, of which it is never an exact copy. As manifestation of truth, it is not truth itself but points to the truth or leads to the truth. Translation is transition.

Now that a translation is transition to truth behind a text, that translating is a flux of change and a dynamic process and that perfect non-volatile translation is not possible, what can at best be done is to provide some adequacy in the transfer of meaning and some readability. There can be no ending criticizing any translator for his occasional failings to transfer content with appropriate form.

Therefore, a translation always requires reader tolerance and cooperation, or a temporary suspension of disbelief. A translation should be read for its merit, flashes of the translator's genius that shed light on the intended truth, not for its demerits, the awkwardness of expression that has been brought about by the limitation of translation. No translator daunted by harsh criticisms would have delighted in his own work.

The greatest merit of Lin's translations lies not in the products themselves, but the perfectionist attitude in the process of translating. Translations cannot be perfect, but the translator can translate with perfect seriousness, always striving for the better.

CHAPTER Five

Manipulating Translation: the Author-Translator Interpreted

As has been shown in Chapter Three, translation to Lin Yutang is an act of self-expression and one of his ways to intervene in the world. This entails manipulation of translation in both matter and manner. In terms of matter, nearly all his translations, either Chinese or English, either from the old or from the new, fit in with his self-expression. In terms of manner, translations may be tailored in whatever way he deems to be appropriate for his expression.

I Manipulating Translation for Self-Representation

1 Lin Yutang's Authorial Self-Representation through Translations

Lin's translator identity is an important part of his authorial self, of the Lin Yutang that has been known to the world through his texts. In trying to make sense of his life, Lin has found in translating a convenient instrument.

His way of translating is of a distinctive kind. He exercises perfect control over his translations as if he is the master, getting heard his own voices instead of being the mouthpiece of the original authors. As Robinson (2001) notes, traditionally the translator is often a spirit-channeler, one who lets spirits (any author, social agents or transcendental spirits) speak through herself. While Robinson focuses on one aspect of translatorship, there is another aspect to it:

the translator is also an autonomous self working on his world. If we can justify Robinson's terminology and regard Lin Yutang the translator as a spirit-channeler, he is also channeling his own spirit, for he is the "I," the subject, the doer of his translations.

The subject is in the making, for his identity is partly decided by what he does and how he does it. Lin's authorial identity is partly shaped by his translations. Lin Yutang the person is not any different in anatomical terms from other persons and his life remains very much a mystery despite the biographical information we have. In a manner of speaking the physical person does not count. What concerns us is the Lin Yutang that we see in the texts, the spiritual image he presents to us through the sum total of those texts.

The importance of translating for the shaping of Lin's authorial identity is marked by the great volume and time span of his work. It is also marked by the thematic consistency of his translations with his general themes of expression. The shaping has taken place as a process of negotiation between his self and his non-self (the world). In his lifetime, the world exerted its influence through various channels: family, country folks, the church, the missionary school, St. Johns, his foreign contacts, the institutions he served, and particularly Chinese and foreign books, to name just a few. As he grew older and as he continued to receive influences from the world, he reacted to the influences by writing, translating and performing other acts of expression. Translation was one of his ways intended to influence the world. Interestingly, the texts, which were outside the author-translator's self, once translated, again became part of the objective world, which had been shaping the identity of the author-translator.

Consistent with his belief in the expressionist aesthetics of Croce and the creative criticism of Spingarn, Lin has very much treated translating as an activity of artistic expression in which we can find the unity of his genius and taste. His genius is represented by his translations as works of art to negotiate human experience and the same genius has made him a cross-cultural critic through his translations.

2 The Realization of Artistic Genius and Translation as a Tool for Cultural Negotiation

Negotiation and Community

People are different. Languages are different. East and West are different. Past and present are different. Yet we are one world and past and present constitute a continuity of time. In the world of differences, negotiation is often a necessity. The idea of negotiation has been extended from its primary definition of trying to reach an agreement by sitting face to face at the table to any effort to find a sort of agreement or settlement. Scholars have opted for its metaphorical sense in the study of quite a number of wide-ranging issues①. Translation scholars have also noticed the similarities between translation and negotiation (Pym, 2000; Eco, 2003). The negotiation analogy has been also applied to the study of cultures and identities (Caughey, 2006). In the study of Lin, Qian Jun is concerned with how he negotiates modernity between East and West (Qian, 1996), and Diran Sohigian studies the interaction between Lin's life and his times without explicitly using the metaphor (Sohigian, 1991). The analogical use of the word *negotiate* basically follows the primary sense of *negotiate* as is found in the dictionary:

> negotiate:
> [no obj.] to try to reach an agreement or compromise by discussion with others: *his government's willingness to negotiate.*

---

① For example: Nippert-Eng, Christena E. *Home and Work: Negotiating Boundaries through Everyday Life.* Chicago, IL: University of Chicago Press, 1996; Cummins, Jim. *Negotiating Identities: Education for Empowerment in a Diverse Society.* Ontario, CA: California Association for Bilingual Education, 1996; Finch, Janet, and Jennifer Mason. *Negotiating Family Responsibilities.* London; New York: Tavistock/Routledge, 1993; Robin, Arthur L., and Sharon L. Foster. *Negotiating Parent-Adolescent Conflict: A Behavioral-Family Systems Approach.* The Guilford Family Therapy Series. New York: Guilford Press, 1989; Emmel, Barbara, Paula Resch, and Deborah Tenney. *Argument Revisited, Argument Redefined: Negotiating Meaning in the Composition Classroom.* Thousand Oaks, Calif.: Sage Publications, 1996.

[with obj.] obtain or bring about by negotiating: *he negotiated a new contract with the sellers.*

[with obj.] find a way over or through (an obstacle or difficult path) : *there was a puddle to be negotiated ...*

(Pearsall, 1998: 1240 –1241)

One important decision the translator has to make is what is translatable and what not. Some texts are untranslatable. Others are partially translatable. Even the most translatable texts may have elements that are not translatable. Any translation in order to be readable or to make some sense at all must be more or less made relevant to the target reader experience. Aware of this, Lin stresses the importance of reader psychology as a major consideration in making translations. Thus the translator becomes a linguistic negotiator. He negotiates between the two languages and the two linguistic communities. In making a translation, as can be gathered from his translations, Lin must have borne in mind the following though he has never explicitly stated the same:

Culturally:

There are things in common between the East and the West.

The isolated worlds — the Eastern World and the Western World — can become one world by increased understanding between peoples; translation increases the common ground.

Some of the ills or weaknesses of one culture may be remedied through the importation of texts from another culture.

Some differences between the two cultures should be respected and therefore a translation has to compromise somewhere for maximum acceptance.

Linguistically:

Anything translatable must have information or content.

In transferring information or content, the verbiage has to be reconstructed to adapt to the norms of the target language.

In the transfer of content and form, which often do not go side by side, compromises have to be made based on considerations of target reader acceptability and the mission of the source text.

The translator negotiates. This has been noticed by translation scholars. What the translator negotiates according to Lawrence Venuti is "the linguistic and cultural differences of the foreign text" (Venuti, 2000: 468). English and

Chinese are two diametrically different linguistic systems in phonetics, morphology and syntax. The two languages mark out two communities which are in broad terms also two cultural systems. Thus each community has a dual nature: it is at once linguistic and cultural. In literature, they are inseparable, for culture is encoded in language. However, as the two communities come into contact, such inseparability comes into question. Part of the cultural message encoded in the Chinese language can be transferred into the English language and vice versa. It seems that cultural message and its medium are often separable. Where translations can be done, the message and the medium are separable and where translations are impossible, they are inseparable. The primary function of translation is to arrive at understanding by overcoming the differences.

Benjamin says, "Translation is a mode. (2000: 16)" In certain works, there is an inherent quality: translatability. The fact that something is translated and understood shows that it has in its nature an innate potential to be intelligible across linguistic communities. Translating is transplanting the potential where a textual realization has not been found. Different cultures have different characteristics, but the differences are not as great as they seem. The character of each culture centering on one language is the natural development of the experience of that linguistic community. Each culture has its own particularities, which tend to be mistaken for differences. Even if some of the particularities are differences, as long as they can be told in another language to another community, they form part of the shared human cultural experience. There is no Shakespeare in China, nor is there Shaw, Emerson or Thoreau. This does not mean that they are really different in nature. Rather, the difference is superficial or phenomenal. The fact that they can touch and move Chinese hearts and the hearts of speakers of other languages means that they as products of Western experience have a universal appeal. There is no Confucius in the English-speaking world, nor Laotse (Lao Zu) or Cao Xueqin, but through translation such authors have established a presence in the English-speaking world. Likewise, they have entered other communities. Sometimes a writing in one language may contain an idea that is not expressed in the other but if it can be expressed in the other language the original writing contains a potential to be textually materialized in the other language. The fact that a reader in English as a foreign language can understand Russian and Japanese literature in English translation illustrates how translation can uplift a literary work from its particular place of origin and original local significance.

Therefore, neither transfer of cultural differences or elimination of them is the primary concern of the translator. The translator negotiates the differences and helps establish a cultural equilibrium between the communicating linguistic communities. The translator uplifts. He elevates individual or local experience to a higher level, bringing particularity all the way up to universality. Thus, the translator by the translation of a single text goes beyond the two communicating communities to establish a third community around the translation and its original, a community that transcends linguistic and experiential differences. This is especially true when a commissioned or self-commissioned translator proficient in two languages translates in both directions of the language pair. By translating various texts in both directions, the translator is building a utopia-like community around the originals and their translations. Human experience is heterogeneous and translations bring about a kind of equilibrium between the cultural centers.

Lin does not translate differences for differences' sake. He is on the one hand increasing common ground between the East and the West by elevating isolated experience to common experience like what has been mentioned above, and on the other hand, tries to match Chinese culture as an important part of Eastern culture with Western culture and directly points out their similarities. One case in point is the selective translation of New Criticism writers such as Spingarn and Croce and Chinese writers of the *xingling* school such as Yuan Zhonglang. In fact, he identifies them with each other and calls both schools the School of Expression.

Lin Yutang's Cosmopolitanism and Negotiated Utopia

Lin showed signs of a revolutionary in the 1920s, but he did not develop into one. Instead he became a thinker who took on his shoulders the responsibility of criticizing and constructing China's intellectual value system. He wanted a revolution against the old social and moral order but was never a revolutionary as might have been expected by Hu Feng and others (Shi, 2005). In the 1930s and beyond, as he increasingly wrote and translated in English, his vision was gradually globalized. He was talking to the Chinese about Westerners and to the latter about the former, his attention focused on mutual understanding between peoples for the construction of an ideal human value system, a utopia which is not exactly his mission to execute but is supposed to bind Chinese and English communities with shared values. Over time, he has created a larger umbrella community, which we can conceptualize but not see.

As a two-way translator and with his volumes of translations in Chinese and English, and what is more as a self-conscious translator, Lin has built a community around the texts he has translated. To understand the nature of the community, we can examine it in three dimensions: the moral, the physical and the aesthetic corresponding respectively to traditional Chinese aesthetic concepts of *yi* (the moral), *zhi* (the physical) and *wen* (the aesthetic) as advocated by Zhang Xuecheng. The three dimensions respectively address three questions: (1) Why have the translations been done? (2) What translations are there? (3) How are the translations made?

In line with his general ethics, his translations have a moral end. This is reflected in his choice of themes. They serve either to establish a rational world order or to nourish the individual soul. The English translation of the Taoist and Confucian classics, the Chinese translation of the feminist *Hypatia*, and *Pygmalion* against the middle class mentality all display Lin's social conscience and his conception of a better world. *Six Chapters of a Floating Life* — the story of the simple yet idyllic home life of an ordinary Chinese scholar and his wife, his translations of vignettes from Chinese antiquity, and many other translations show his concern for the individual. All these translations with their originals constitute a new community or a moral world, a utopia. Lin himself is at the center of this third community, for it is built from materials he has chosen and processed according to his vision. The essence of the matter is "common sense," which is one of his favorite words and a key word of his works. Lin's life is devoted to the expansion of common ground with common sense. When we say that a text is translatable we never mean that it is 100% translatable. The part of the text that is translatable as Benjamin has noted is nothing but information (Benjamin, 2000). Translation therefore primarily involves the sharing of information. It is a way of communicating common sense and the different outgrowths of common sense in different linguistic communities. On the other hand, the language a linguistic community uses is relative to its own experience. One language community develops a different system of categories and concepts from another. The same world is mirrored in different ways in different languages. A great deal of a people's thought is bound up with its language. Each language in its writing of texts and delivery of speeches directly draws on its own repository of linguistic devices. Therefore, unavoidably, the very commonsense of humanity or the universality of human nature lies in the variety and difference of its manifestations. In order to reach common ground, differences are negotiated, differences which are at once cultural and linguistic. As a two-way translator, Lin is not a cultural ambassador as conceived by some Chinese scholars (e.g., Gao, 2004; Dong, 2004). The word ambassador is downgrading, for an ambassador represents his government and hides himself. In more exact words, he is a cultural mediator or negotiator, taking stock of both sides and carefully defining common ground.

A second dimension is the physical. This refers to the representational content of the translator's work. An idea of justice or truth does not make a translator as it does not make an artist. There must be a physical object. The translations are the physical substantialization of the translator's idea. Lin's moral community or utopia has an existence in these physical "objects." Speaking of Chinese wisdom, it is always preferable to illustrate with passages from the Chinese classics than to be merely engaged in pedagogical explanations. The Chinese way of life is better seen in stories by people who have lived it than in a third person narrative. The physical dimension of the third community involves choice of matter and structure of presentation. Lin's choice of matter is based on how interesting the matter is rather than merely on its moral significance. The works he has chosen are intriguing in their own right before they are translated, as *Six Chapters of a Floating Life* has interested Chinese minds and the writings of Jastrow have nourished American minds. By translating both ways between the two languages, Lin establishes a utopia above the divisions of East and West. As this virtual community increases and, because the community or utopia has a physical existence in texts, we know it is going to effect changes in the real world communities. The structure of presentation involves the treatment of the matter so that translations are coherent and work together to support the translator's cause. Various strategies — conventional and unconventional — are followed to make his translations meaningful. These strategies include traditional text-to-text transfer and unconventionalities as revealed in Chapter Three of this book.

A third dimension of the utopia is aesthetic. This involves the form or manner of his presentation. In line with his "common sense" is his use of the familiar style, which not only characterizes his writings but also the bulk of his translations. To make the translation close to reader experience and to give the translation a high readability is always his concern. In terms of the aesthetic form in translation, he distinguishes between "inner form" and "outer form" after the Su Tung-porian distinction between the constant form (*changxing*) and the inner spirit (*changli*) of Chinese painting. Philosophically, Lin favors the Taoist and Confucianist common-sense philosophy; aesthetically he glorifies a blending of Chinese and Western theories of self-expression. His emphasis of feeling is Crocean in nature, and his translation of what he likes corresponds to the Chinese school of self-expression with which he identifies himself. Nabokov objects to the imposition of new form to Pushkin's poetry. Lin applies new form (rhyming) to the poems he translates.

A holistic view of Lin's third community must incorporate these three dimensions. Isolated, each dimension may run the risk of appearing inessential and insignificant.

Negotiating Cultural Differences: Translating the Far Away and the Long Ago

Lin Yutang is considered to have "devoted his lifetime to the theory and practice of integrating Chinese and Western cultures" (Ye, 1991: 99). As his Chinese and English translations grew, they increasingly showed signs of cosmopolitanism in the translator, who embraced both the East and the West, both historical heritage and modern intellectual frontiers. A careful study of the translator's texts reveals that they are selected not so at random as claimed by the translator. Though different in nature, each translation has some degree of relevance to the target language culture. For the East, he has translated modern texts from the West, while for the West, he has translated texts from the Chinese tradition of literature. The far away and long ago are mingled in a crucible to generate his utopian ideals of human existence.

Despite his familiarity with Western classics as shown in *My Country and My People*, *The Importance of Living* and *On the Wisdom of America*, when translating from English to Chinese, he is evidently interested in Western literature of his own time. Almost all of his translations from the English deal with concerns of the modern. *Hypatia, or Woman and Knowledge* is the feminist work of a British woman author who rebels against male domination by advocating free love and free sex for women. *The Diary of a Communist Schoolboy* by a Russian author tells a story of new education as taking place in a Russian school. The translation of a critical biography of Henrik Ibsen and his love letters as well as *Pygmalion* by Bernard Shaw introduces new drama to his readers. The translation of Benedetto Croce, J. E. Spingarn, Oscar Wilde, E. Dowden and Van Wyck Brooks introduces New Criticism to his Chinese readers. *Keeping Mentally Fit*, a book on popular psychology, represents a kind of new scholarship from the West. *The Autobiography of a Super Tramp* represents new experience in modern England and America. He also communicates to Chinese readers international sympathy for the Chinese Nationalist revolution by translating Arthur Ransome's *The Chinese Puzzle* into Chinese.

As a translator of Chinese literature, he has shown a growing interest in the translation of Chinese tradition as found in Chinese literature of antiquity, canonical and marginal alike. Over time he has made selective translations of classics of Chinese thought as well as vignettes and stories from various historical sources. His selective translations of ancient Chinese philosophy appear in *The Wisdom of China and India*, *The Wisdom of Laotse*, and *The Wisdom of Confucius*. His other English translations include works by authors of various standing. They are often intended to provide spiritual nourishment for the reader's soul. The majority of such translations are found in *The Importance of Understanding*, which consists of his English translations of Chinese vignettes and passages from major or minor Chinese authors. What deserves a passing mention is his translation of a few Chinese authors of his time such as Lu Xun, Lao She, Lao Xiang, Xie Bing-ying (Ping-ing) and Yao Ying. Together these modern Chinese authors constitute a very small portion of all his English translations, but such translations show his concerns as a modern Chinese and serve to communicate the spirit of the rejuvenating ancient country to the outside world.

Procedures of Negotiation: Use of Linear and Non-Linear Methods

In order to reach a solution the translator-negotiator experiments with his methods of negotiating. He tries one tentative strategy after another in approaching different texts. Whatever strategy serves his purpose is unscrupulously adopted. Sometimes he follows a linear method and creates a one-on-one parallel in the target language. Sometimes his approach is nonlinear.

The Chinese translation of *The Diary of a Communist Schoolboy* is evidently a symmetrical textual realization of the English translation of the Russian novel, and "On My Library" is symmetrical with its Chinese original. A translator translates and the translation corresponds to its original or source text. Such is our usual conception of translation. Lin is no doubt capable of such linear translation. In his effort to negotiate however such a linear method is insufficient. In order for his negotiation to be effective, he has to go out of the usual way to incorporate some nonlinear methods.

His supra-textual unconventionality — the use of nonlinear methods — challenges the prototypical conception of translation in more ways than one:

(1) A translation does not have to offer a text-to-text equivalence in content and form, and may have new functionality in the translator's system of expression. From time to time, a translation cannot adequately express Lin's own idea. In such cases, he would hybridize the translation with his own writing and other translations. Sometimes a translation speaks more powerfully when it appears in an anthology. He tries to drive home a profound understanding of the world by translating fragments of human experience. Such fragmentary translations, organized in anthologies, showcase his literary ideal of self-expression and his worldview that the East and the West compliment each other and shall harmoniously coexist.

(2) A translator does not have to translate. He may borrow translations. Translations by other translators may be used when it is befitting. In *The Wisdom of China and India*, the India part consists mainly of works by other translators from Hindu or Chinese sources, and the China part borrows many translations from other translators. When the translations by Ku Hung-ming, James Legge, Cao Fu and others are adequate for his purpose he borrows them without bothering to attempt new versions.

(3) A translation does not serve a single purpose. It is simply raw material which can be re-used on different occasions for different purposes. At times, the same translation may be used to explain a certain point of view and at other

times it contributes to the understanding of another motif. The repeated use of *Six Chapters of a Floating Life* and "The Mortal Thoughts of a Nun," for example, demonstrates this point.

(4) Neither in content nor in form is a translation bound to resemble its source text. Dramatic rewriting is permitted for self-expression. Lin sometimes crosses the border between translation and creative writing by rewriting Chinese stories in English. Extreme cases are found in *Miss Tu* (*Du Shiniang*) and *Famous Chinese Stories*, wherein original plots are kept (sometimes distorted) and the story is rewritten in English with added narrative details. The rewriting is often so substantial that they no longer mean the same thing as they have meant to Chinese readers. Lin does not claim to have translated them. He has retold them. They are new stories, ones that are both Chinese and Western, or rather, neither Chinese nor Western. A precise definition would be that they are Lin Yutang stories, representing Lin Yutang's vision of a possible human existence.

Negotiation Procedures: Crossing Linguistic Differences

Given the great differences between Chinese and English in their encoding of the world, and since correspondence between the two languages is a complicated picture, Lin denounces any single streamlining method in translating. In his tentative textual maneuvers, he has learned to shift between various strategies of translating, literally rising to the occasion.

Chapter Four has illustrated how Lin makes strategic shifts along the translation continuum. Therefore, if someone says that Lin is a literalist he is probably right, but only in certain texts or certain portions of a text; if someone says that Lin is a liberalist, he is both right and wrong; if someone says that Lin is in the middle between a literalist and a liberalist, that understanding is again partial. A close reading of Lin's translations in juxtaposition with their originals shows the complexity of his translation strategies. When we take his translations as a whole rather than individual texts, no single translation strategy applies. The strategy of the translator must be viewed as dynamic, changing from moment to moment. Through the juxtaposition of Lin's translations with their originals or his translations with versions by other translators, we discover that semantic correspondence being a kind of ideal the translator is forever making strategic shifts along a verbal-semantic translation continuum and his translation often settles somewhere on it:

On one end of the continuum is *metaphrase*, on the other *imitation*, and in the middle *paraphrase*. In general, the transfer of meaning is a rather undisputed objective of translation. The problem is what verbal strategies to adopt in order to transfer meaning.

From earlier discussion of Lin Yutang's translations in Chapter Four, we find him searching for semantic correspondence along this continuum, moving from close verbal correspondence to loose verbal correspondence and even to formal non-correspondence. This is a tentative process for solution-finding. Based on his estimation both direct and oblique methods are used for optimum transfer of meaning. The strategic shifts are his ways of negotiating linguistic differences in order to convey the message. His continued revisions of some of his translations are additional indicators of the negotiation process.

No one can negotiate cultural differences without overcoming the language barrier. As the years went by, Lin increasingly felt the importance of the role of a good dictionary in the cultural exchange between the two largest linguistic communities. His world knowledge, linguistic knowledge and translation experience finally enabled him to compile the *Chinese-English Dictionary of Modern Usage*. It is a Chinese-English dictionary with an English-Chinese index. He has checked every entry and provided the English translation for it (Chen, 1974). The dictionary provides not only definitions for the Chinese words and phrases but also various contexts for the same word and how a word is translated in its different contexts.

3 Artistic Taste and Translation as a Tool for Cultural Criticism

Translation in a Critical Context

Straddling the cultural border between China and the West, Lin is an avowed cultural critic. The cultural critic in him has given the translator a distinctive voice. In other words, his translations also represent his identity as a cultural critic.

With a little genius, an ordinary translator may turn out good translations of some individual works simply by knowing well two languages and having access to good dictionaries and references. Behind Lin's translations is a broad cross-cultural vision. The translator has been at the same time a celebrated cultural critic with his contributions to the English language magazines such as *China Critic*① and to the Chinese language magazines such as *Analects Fortnightly* (*lunyu*). Besides, a large number of his books are or contain cultural criticism, such as *My Country and My People, The Importance of Living, Between Tears and Laughter, On the Wisdom of America*. From his vantage point, he makes sweeping criticism of Chinese culture and Western particularly American culture. In his view, the construction of a new culture cannot be done without cultural criticism. In "The Task of Modern Criticism"②, he says:

> The old culture will not go of itself. Neither will a new culture automatically come into being. Both the going of the old and the birth of the new depend on our intellectual power of criticism.
>
> (Lin, 1994c: 123. Translated from the Chinese.)

He is aware of his critical vantage point and is quite proud of it. Unlike an ordinary translator, he has a special vision. With his Chinese roots and his diligence in reading Chinese literature, his American-style education in the missionary schools and college, later American and European education, especially with his extensive reading in English and possibly in German and French too, he has a much larger vision than the individual works he has translated. When we align his translations with his writings of cultural criticism, we perceive their integrity as a whole. They well belong with each other. Translation for him, like his critical writings, is an instrument to share his vision of the world.

As a language professional, he is not of a piece with ordinary translators because he is also a critic. Nor is he of a piece with many if not most monolingual critics because of his bilingual proficiency. With his expert command of both Chinese and English, he does not rely on secondhand and

---

① Under two collections: *The Little Critic, Essays, Satires and Sketches on China (First Series: 1930 –1932)*, 1935. *The Little Critic, Essays, Satires and Sketches on China (First Series: 1930 –1932)*, 1935.

② "论现代批评的职务."

dated resources for his criticism. On top of his mastery of Chinese and English, he has been an avid and efficient reader in both languages, and thus has developed an in-depth understanding of the two cultures. Naturally Western culture has become his frame of reference for his criticism of Chinese culture, which in turn is also a frame of reference for his criticism of Western culture. On a higher plane, the two frames make a new frame. It will take more genius of the monolingual critic to reach the same level.

For his translations alone he may be justifiably called a cultural critic, because in them he has displayed an understanding of the social, political, historical, and artistic contexts and significance of the texts and has developed his own system of cultural values for change toward the better. The translator has assumed the role of a cultural critic or the cultural critic has found its expression in the translator. There may be quite a few Chinese translators who have attained prominence by their profuse and meticulous translations imbued with their personal genius before and after him and among his contemporaries. In the past century or so, translation has been the profession of countless Chinese individuals and a side occupation of innumerable Chinese scholars. The translator's Who's Whos and monographs on Chinese translators offer us long lists of major and minor Chinese translators. By far the greater number of them translate from English to Chinese and a few are known for their English translations of Chinese literature or translating both ways. On the surface, Lin Yutang is but one translator of the hordes of translators in the century which includes his lifetime and beyond. When his translations are allied, they make a unique landscape. There is a particular significance to his translations as a whole. They are more than translations. They are also works of cultural criticism. By translating on a broad canvas — few Chinese translators have surpassed him in diversity of genres, the range of topics and the deftness to handle both directions of the language pair (Chinese/English) — he is delineating the strengths and weaknesses of both Chinese and Western cultures.

Lin the translator-negotiator and Lin the translator-critic are one. There is no way to separate the two. The very process of negotiating is a process of criticizing. Like the negotiator, the critic devotes his attention to both content and form. The choice of one composition rather than another and the decision to translate something in part or in full, to rewrite a text or to process it whatever way he finds handy are a kind of criticism of both the receiving culture and the culture that houses the source texts. He gives the target culture what needs to be known to overcome ignorance or narrow-mindedness. He exports from the source culture what is worthy of wider publicity. In the shifts of manner, he preserves what is good and discards what is wrong or irrelevant.

The Cultural Critic in the Form of a Translator

Unhappy with the current state of affairs domestic and international, Lin seeks help from the remote in space and in time.

The aim of Lin's criticism is to construct a better world and his method to do so is to deconstruct the present world by translating, importing from one culture to another.

In so doing, he is combating cultural borders between the East and the West. He thus introduces his *The Wisdom of China and India*.

> Today the East and the West must meet. It frightens one to read in the morning papers that Wendell Willkie was in Chungking one Friday and back in America the following Monday, over the week-end, as it were. It was almost like magic. No matter what will be the type of world cooperation after the war, we are sure that the East and the West will be living closely together, and dependent on each other. Somehow after the breaking-up of the nineteenth-century political world, a new world must be forged out of the elements of Anglo-Saxon, Russian and Oriental cultures. The "Wisdom of China" is an effort to unravel some of the mysteries of the Oriental, and specifically the Chinese point of view — some of the basic ways of looking at things as revealed in native Chinese literature and philosophy.
>
> (Lin, 1942: 567)

On the surface, he is translating differences, Chinese culture as a different culture which is "a human, rationalistic, and easily understandable type of culture" (ibid: 567), and Chinese thought as vastly different from Western thought "in style and method and in values and objectives" (ibid: 567), but at heart he has a deep conviction in the universality of essential human values and says that "what touches the human heart in one country touches all" (Lin, 1998b: 1). He wants the differences to become shared human knowledge through translation.

The very act of translating Chinese philosophy which displays distrust of systematic philosophy is a negation of Western philosophy, "a logically built and cogently reasoned philosophy of knowledge or of reality or of the universe (Lin, 1942: 568)" because he thinks what the world really wants is a philosophy of living like that of the Chinese. He deplores that "the world has gone to pieces as a direct result of scientific materialism invading our literature and thought (ibid: 574)," and thinks that Chinese humanism provides the cure. His other English translations, mainly of scattered sources on Chinese life, the human experience as recorded by the Chinese, are intended to provide nourishment for the soul as they have profoundly influenced the translator himself. The Chinese vignettes, selected passages from major and minor authors in Chinese history, and a complete translation of the novelette *Six Chapters of a Floating Life* (*Fu Sheng Liu Ji*) give the Western reader a good feel of Chinese life as the translator sees it.

His Chinese translations, though less well organized than his English translations, contribute to the deconstruction of the Chinese status quo. *Hypatia, or Woman and Knowledge* by Dora Russell, a feminist treatise which advocates free love is heresy to the traditional Chinese society. His translation of Bernard Shaw's *Pygmalion*, which is an attack on middle-class morality, is designed to enlighten the clogged minds of many of his countrymen (Lin, 1994d: 85). The translation of Brandes' critical biography of Ibsen the revolutionary poet and dramatist is also meant to enlighten the Chinese people. The translation of *Keeping Mentally Fit* is intended to lift Chinese youth in the early decades of the twentieth century out of gloom, worries, anxieties and depression brought about by the times they were in. *Autobiography of a Super Tramp*, the personal account of a British man's experience in America and Britain and a shocking challenge to the mock seriousness of established morality, tells the new Western experience and embodies the admirable free spirit of the individual. The translation is not just for the entertainment of Chinese readers. It involves a high level of recognition of the value of the novel and its relevance to the Chinese. Through the translation of *The Chinese Puzzle*, a British journalist's account and analysis of the Chinese Nationalist Revolution, he wants the Chinese to know the common interests between the Chinese and the British that the revolution may bring about. His English translation of Ping-ing's diaries communicates the throbbing of the Chinese hearts in the new era to the West.

The educational innovation in *Diary of a Communist Schoolboy* by a Russian author is what has been experimented with in China as part of the world trend.

Mention needs to be made of the dual nature of the translator's choice of matter and manner. As has been noted earlier, the translator's choice of matter and manner is a process of negotiating between the cultures. The same process is also critical. The choice of one essay, story, play, author or one type of writing instead of another, the very preference is a matter of critical taste.

Lin's translation of Chinese philosophy is intended to introduce to Western readers a different philosophy so that they will not be too superstitious about their own. His translation comes after his criticism of the intellectual world which according to him "is definitely going to pieces, because our traditional values are gone (Lin, 1942: 570)." His translation forms a part of his criticism and offers a cure:

> China's peculiar contribution to philosophy is therefore the distrust of systematic philosophy. I confess this must distress many college sophomores who are so anxious to have systems that have no loopholes in them and are strongly entrenched against all possible attacks. They want to be able to say, either that criminals are born and not made, or else that criminals are made and not born, and they want to *prove*① it. The Chinese reply is that there is no such air-tight system on earth, and has never been any. Such systems do not exist except in the minds of the deluded, logical dunderheads.
>
> (ibid: 569)

Lin thinks that "the present disintegration of knowledge and collapse of values call for a restoration of certain human values" (Lin, 1942: 572) but the approach, the technique, the philosophical basis for the study of any kind of human values aren't there. His solution is Confucianism or what he terms Chinese humanism. Chinese humanism (Confucianism) "concentrates on certain human values" and follows a different approach (Lin, 1942: 571). In his view, it excludes both physics and metaphysics, and concentrates on the values of human relationships. He points out that the Confucian final test for any civilization "is whether it produces good sons, good brothers, good husbands, good friends and good individuals who have a delicate sensibility and are most anxious to avoid hurting others' feelings." (ibid: 572) For this purpose he has

---

① Lin's original italic.

translated in part or in full some of the important Confucian classics. Because he is not translating for translation's sake, when an existing translation is good enough for his purpose of criticism and construction, he simply borrows them.

Lin attributes the disintegration of knowledge to scientific materialism:

> It can be proved that the world has gone to pieces as a direct result of scientific materialism invading our literature and thought. The professors of the humanities are reduced to the position of finding mechanistic laws governing human activities, and the more rigorous the "natural laws" can be proved to be, and the more freedom of the will is proved to be a chimera, the greater is the professor's intellectual delight ...
>
> (Lin, 1942: 574).

His criticism is creative. While deploring the shattering of human knowledge, he points out that the East and the West must build a new world together:

> Our conception of the nature of man has been falsified, debased. The bottom has been knocked out of our human universe; the structure cannot hold; something must break. Out of the shattered fragments of modern knowledge a new world must be built, and the East and West① must build it together.
>
> (Lin, 1942: 576)

However, by Chinese philosophy, Lin does not mean Confucianism alone. He has an equal fervor for the introduction of Taoist texts to the West. He says, "... for the immediate problems of this contentious modern world, it is more important to read Laotse than to read Confucius." (ibid: 576) Both Confucianism and Taoism are well represented in *The Wisdom of China and India*. While his translations of Confucian texts constitute one volume (*The Wisdom of Confucius*), his translations of Taoist texts constitute another (*The Wisdom of Laotse*).

Like his choice of matter, his choice of manner is also of a dual nature. It is at once constructive and critical. In order to negotiate his utopia, he often goes out of the translator's usual way: he borrows a translation when it is sufficient for his purpose such as in *The Wisdom of China and India*; he joins his translations and creative writings into one for the purpose of effective criticism

---

① Should be "the West." This is one of Lin's occasional pen slips.

and construction of his utopia such as in the proverbial *My Country and My People*, *The Importance of Living*, *The Life and Times of Su Tungpo*; his translations often appear in anthologies with themes like "the wisdom of China," "the New Criticism," "Chinese Theory of Art", et cetera; he often adapts a piece or totally rewrites it such as in *Famous Chinese Short Stories*; the repeated use of previous translations such as *Six Chapters of a Floating Life* is also characteristic of Lin Yutang.

In my previous discussion of the translator-negotiator and the translator-critic, I have never been able to effectively separate the two. In Lin Yutang we find the unity of genius and taste. His genius materializes in the cultural negotiator and his taste in the cultural critic. If it can be said that the negotiator is for common ground between the cultures, the critic exposes the differences with an eye to make corrections. Both the negotiator and the critic are working toward the same end. As a cultural negotiator he is conscious of his textual creations as works of art and as a cultural critic he is conscious of the context and the making of his works.

By transporting both ways between the East and the West, Lin conceptualizes a better new world, incorporating the strengths of both cultures and overcoming the weaknesses. He is a member of this new world or his textual utopia. This is evidenced by his self-identification in the translator's notes and introductions to his translations. He displays a spirit of cosmopolitanism by identifying himself with both Chinese readers and readers of his English translations.

Not only does he identify with Chinese readers in the preface to his Chinese translation of *The Autobiography of a Super Tramp*, he but also thinks of himself one of his Western readers when translating for the English audience. He frequently speaks of "we" and "our," considering himself the like of his English language readers:

> Our international world is rapidly coming to the end of an era. So is our modern intellectual world. The world of ideas is definitely going to pieces, because our traditional values are gone. That brings us to the second difference between Oriental and Occidental philosophy; the difference in approach and values.
>
> (Lin, 1942: 570)

Maneuvering in Contradictions

If one is perplexed by Lin's world in translations there shall be no wonder. In *Memoirs of an Octogenarian* he describes himself as "a bundle of contradictions." He loves contradictions. He thus says of himself:

> ... He loves to see safety parade busses kill somebody, and once went a long way to a temple in Western Hill near Peiping to see a eunuch's sons. Described① himself as a pagan, while at heart a Christian. Now devoted to literature, but always thinks it a mistake that he did not enroll in the School of Science when he was a college freshman. Loves China and criticizes her more frankly and honestly than any other Chinese ... Admires the west intensely, but is contemptuous of the western educational psychologists. Once called himself a "realistic idealist" and "a warm-hearted cynic." Loves whimsical writers and writers with a fine fancy, but equally loves realistic common sense ... .
>
> (Lin, 1975: 1 –2)

Here Lin has noticed the contradictions of life. What he has not said is that as a translator, he is also "a bundle of contradictions." He has longed to be autonomous but has never been completely independent of patronage. His translations are both fragmentary and systematic. He has translated marginal and canonical literature alike. As his life is characterized by contradictions, so is his work as a translator.

1 Autonomy through Patronage Networks

Throughout his work as a translator, Lin has been driven by a desire for self-expression. Translation for him is an active process of self-representation. He has carried his self-will to great lengths in the selection of materials. He has

① This ungrammaticality is characteristic of Lin Yutang's old-age English in *Memoirs*. Other mistakes in this excerpt include "Now devoted ... but always thinks ... ," "Loves China and criticizes ... ," "Admires ... but is contemptuous ... ", and "Loves whimsical writers ... but equally loves ... ."

persistently translated according to his likes, not to be talked into translating unless he has a genuine interest. *The Importance of Understanding*, *The Wisdom of China and India*, *The Wisdom of Confucius*, *The Wisdom of Laotse*, translations of Shaw and New Criticism writers are all instances of his autonomy over his translating.

He has frequently projected himself into his translations. Translation to him is not a casual pastime. It is to be manipulated for the definition of his ideal world.

Not only does he explicate his purpose of translation in prefaces and introductions to his translations, in the translations he sponsors he makes it clear as well. In 1936, he wrote for the first issue of the *Hsi-feng* magazine, part of whose mission was to publish Chinese translations from the Western press:

> … Attention to the translation of Western press dates back to Lin Zexu and Wei Moshen. The translations we see today are too highbrow. They are either literary classics or works of politics and economics. Life, society and family in the West are ignored and disregarded. Should this trend continue, how can literature be popular and how can magazines be read by a wider public? They simply become the game of the literati who read each other. Our comrades, not knowing what Western literature is, enjoy talking about the joys and woes of westerners, the change of their tradition, their domestic life and the ills of their society. We think that this is the right way to have an intimate knowledge of the true face of Western culture …
>
> (Lin, 2004: 188) ①

Conscious of what he was doing as a translator he had his own agenda. Once Lu Xun tried to influence him only to be disappointed:

> Yutang has been an old friend of mine. I should treat him in a way befitting a friend. Before *This Human World* was founded, the *Analects Monthly* was becoming rather nonsensical. I wrote to advise him to give it up. I was not asking him to die as a revolutionary. I suggested that he translate some English masterpieces. Given his proficiency in English, his translations will be good not only for today but also for the

① Translated from the Chinese. "The Shortcomings of Chinese Magazines — On the Commencement of the *Hsi-feng* Magazine." *The Cosmic Wind* XIV (April 1, 1936). In Lin, Yutang. (2004. *The Best Lin Yutang Esssays*. Beijing: Jiuzhou: 188. [林语堂. (2004.《林语堂散文经典全编》. 北京：九州出版社：188.]

> future. He replied that he would do so in his old age. Until then did I realize that my advice to Yutang was an old man's rubbish. I am sure that I gave the advice out of kindness. I would like to see him useful and immortal in China. It is not my intention to silence him. It is welcome if he can be more progressive but I do not see such a possibility. As I do not impose myself on others, there is nothing more to say.
>
> In recent publications such as the *Analects Monthly*, Yutang, indignant as ever, indulges himself in trivia, out of which it is not in my power to pull him. As to Mr. Tao and Mr. Xu, they are to Lin as Yan Zi and Zeng Zi to Confucius. As the disciples are not to be compared with the master, nothing can be thought of to help.
>
> (Lu Xun, 2004: 145 –146. Translated from the Chinese.)

Lin's translation was not isolated from his times. It was his reaction to the time and space where he found himself. He translated what he thought the world needed. When translating literature from English, his interest was in Chinese translation of new literature instead of classic literature from Europe and America, knowing that it was not urgent for him to translate English masterpieces because many other people had been doing it. He was more concerned with the immediate problem: Chinese writers were too bookish and China needed writings as familiar as life.

Meanwhile, he knew that he had an advantage and could do something different. His productive competence in English gave him an advantage so that he could speak to a world audience by writing and translating in English. His personal preference for English might have come from an intelligent awareness of a comparative advantage on the part of a linguistic artist. In an age of translation boom in China, people entered the business in droves regardless of their qualification. One book, as soon as it was discovered to be of some value commercial or otherwise, often appeared in different versions by different publishers. There were not so many Chinese whose English was good enough to enable them to translate the other way. The market demand in America and elsewhere for Chinese literature made it possible for him to release his energies. And there he was, a brilliant presence on the international book market with his English writings and translations.

Nonetheless, Lin's autonomy is not unlimited. He has to work through patronage networks both in China and in the West. He has been on the one hand bound by his Chinese background and on the other hand guided by the tastes of Westerners.

To Westerners, he appears to be an interpreter of Chinese culture. That is precisely what the West expects him to be and he consciously collaborates with the expectation of Westerners. When English language readers enjoy the wisdom of Confucius and Laotse and admire the Chinese art of living, probably most of them have no idea what a bitter critic Lin has been to the Chinese. In "The Spirit of Chinese Culture," a lecture he gave at Oxford University in 1932, he interpreted the spirit of Chinese culture as the spirit of humanism, saying that Chinese humanism "implies, first, a just conception of the true ends of human life, secondly, a complete devotion to these ends, and thirdly, the attainment of these ends by the spirit of human reasonableness, or the Doctrine of the Golden Mean, which you may also call the Religion of Common Sense." (Lin, 1935b: 7) Later the speech was translated into Chinese and published in the first volume of the *Shenbao Monthly*. In his brief introduction, he admits that the lecture is "in the main a flattery of Oriental Civilization." In fact, he is an out-and-out critic of Chinese culture. He thinks that the timid and sterile national character of the Chinese needs to be reformed by the more aggressive spirit of the West. But as soon as he sets foot on foreign soil, he begins to defend what he attacks at home. In his own words and in my translation, he "almost downgrades into a diplomat" (Lin, 1994c: 139). He says, "Were I born a European, I would have loved the beautiful lady in a Chinese painting, but the feeling changes when I come back to China. I begin to realize that the Oriental beauty is pockmarked. When you see from afar, she has a good figure, but when you come close, she is such an awful sight ... (Lin, 1994c: 140. My translation.)" He deplores China's backwardness in government, economy, industry and academics and condemns its indulgence in civil wars in front of foreign invasion. He wants Chinese readers to dwell more on the weaknesses of Chinese culture and not to be conceited as inheritors of Oriental culture.

Since the publication of *My Country and My People* in the U. S., Lin's authorial identity took a drastic turn. He was known to the world as "an interpreter of China" and that identity brought him fame and fortune. According to the biography by his daughter (Lin, 2002), he received handsome income for his publications in English, $36,000 in 1938, $42,000 in 1939 and $46,800 in 1940, great sums in those days. This in part accounts for his transformation from the angry young man in China to the smiling Chinese philosopher speaking in maxims in America. In his early days of an author and translator, the warlord government had very weak control over publications. He formed close relationships with Leftist writers such as Lu Xun and Yu Dafu, and his pen was fiery, but very shortly he was blacklisted by the Peiping government for arrest. His early Chinese translations in general were meant to reform the national character. Then gradually his revolutionary ardor subsided as revolution was such a bloody cause. To escape censorship, he became a humorist writing familiar essays occasionally making sarcastic comments. He "thanked" Chiang Kai-shek's KMT government for being more strict with the press than the Peiping warlord government because he could not speak directly and was able to perfect his art of writing. Confronted with oppression Lu Xun was only more indignant and relentless and consolidated his authorial identity as an intellectual icon of Chinese revolution, and some of the country's other intellectuals chose to be running dogs of the warlord government. Lin chose a third way. Eventually, he found an outlet in the international book market that suited him perfectly and he voluntarily went into an intellectual exile in the West. For the most part of his life in the West, outspoken as he was, he was conforming to the tastes of Western readers. In America, censorship was more cultural than political. The immigrant Chinese writer Eileen Chang (Zhang Ailing) was said to have once received a plot and outline for a novel from the publisher. Lao She's tragic ending of *Luotuo Xiangzi* translated as *The Rickshaw Boy* was completely rewritten by the translator into a happy ending, and the translation received critical acclaim. Lin has been known to change his texts on the advice of his editors and publishers.① *The Importance of Living*, according to *Linyutang Zhuan* (*Biography of Lin Yutang*) by Taiyi Lin, is an afterthought of the publisher after the success of *My Country and My People*, because Americans loved the final chapter of the bestseller. So publisher and

① More details on patron influence on the English writings or translations of Lin Yutang, Lao She, and Chang Ailing can be found in Yin, Xiao-huang. "Worlds of Difference: Lin Yutang, Lao She, and the Significance of Chinese-Language Writing in America." in Sollors, Werner. *Multilingual America: Transnationalism, Ethnicity, and the Languages of American Literature*. New York: New York University Press, 1998: 176 –185.

author collaborated to make it one more book! Not only do these two books contain large portions of translations, but also most of Lin's English translations fit in or can be organized to belong somewhere with the two books. His English translations in *The Wisdom of Laotse*, *The Wisdom of Confucius*, *The Wisdom of China and India*, and *The Importance of Understanding* are thematized to make good supplementary reading for his first two bestsellers. What is more, in *Miss Tu* and *Famous Chinese Short Stories*, even storylines are altered so that they can be enjoyed by Western readers. Life for Lin anyway was not without difficulties. Living expenses were high in New York. As inventor of the Mingkuai Chinese typewriter he almost went broke and his savings in the Bank of China evaporated overnight. Both he and his wife had extended families to take care of. He had to constantly publish.

Westerners just do not take what Lin wants to give. He has to give what they want to take. In a letter to Tao Kangde, another Chinese journalist, he says that he never intended to write *The Importance of Living*. What he wanted to do was to translate from the Chinese five or six books that represent the Chinese art of living and the spirit of Chinese culture, but his publisher John Walsh thought *The Importance of Living* should be written first. Many Americans were fascinated by the last chapter of *My Country and My People* under the title of "The Importance of Living." Lin's description of the high-mindedness of Chinese poets, how they loaf and enjoy leisure fascinated the go-getting American people. The publisher wanted Lin to give the busy Americans a timely cure. He followed Walsh's advice and he made it. Upon completion of the manuscript he made revisions according to suggestions by Pearl S. Buck and John Walsh. Fortunately such a carefully planned book was chosen by the Book-of-the-Month Club as a special recommendation for December 1937, which guaranteed the book's prospect as a bestseller. Lin anyway did not give up his translation project. In his subsequent years overseas, as he continued to turn out volumes after volumes of English prose and fiction, he managed somehow to translate/edit a few volumes from the Chinese: *The Wisdom of Confucius*, *The Wisdom of China and India*, *The Wisdom of Laotse*, *Widow, Nun and Courtesan: Three Novelettes from the Chinese*, *Famous Chinese Short Stories*, *The Importance of Understanding: Translations from the Chinese* and *The Chinese Theory of Art: Translations from the Masters of Chinese Art*. One thing needs to be noted. Maybe translation for him was never as lucrative as original writing. As far as we know, for *The Wisdom of Confucius* in the Modern Library series, the Random House only paid him US $600 once and for all (Lin, 2002: 150). Because he would like to do the work, he did not seem to care much about the pay in this instance.

2 Systematicity through Fragmentation

An important feature of Lin Yutang's translations is their fragmentation. In both the West and China, translators have been known for translating a single author or a single work complete, or a series of carefully chosen authors or volumes such as Dryden's English translation of Virgil, Pope's English translation of Homer, Martin Luther's German translation of the *New Testament*, James Legge's English translation of Chinese classics, Arthur Waley's English translation of Chinese classics, Fitzgerald's English translation of *The Rubaiyat*, Yan Fu's Chinese translation of Adam Smith, Zhu Shenghao's Chinese translation of Shakespeare, Fu Lei's Chinese translation of Balzac, Roman Roland and other French authors, Ye Junjian's Chinese translation of Hans Christian Andersen, Xuan Zang's Chinese translation of Buddhist sutras from the Sanskrit. Such translations give readers a sense of wholeness of some sort, for the texts are rendered intact. This is the conventional way of translating. In most cases, the original is the immortal God and the translator is trying to grasp a piece of that immortality through their meticulous work. In the translation of a few works from English to Chinese or the other way around, such as the Chinese translation of *The Autobiography of a Super Tramp*, *The Diary of a Communist Schoolboy*, *The Chinese Puzzle*, and *Pygmalion*, and in his English translation of *Six Chapters of a Floating Life*, Lin seems to be conventional. On second thoughts he is not a conventional translator. These translations are invariably small volumes and they are of different authorship, different genres and different times. What is more, the bulk of Lin's translations consists of either short pieces, or selections from longer works. The small volumes, the short pieces and the excerpts, from a diversity of sources, are but fleet fragments of Chinese or Western life. Unlike the conventional translator, Lin does not in the least seem to be working for a share of any author's immortality. He does not seem to be worried that his translations are but casual, temporal and transitional texts.

Behind the fragments we can perceive a kind of systematicity. In terms of scope, with or without an intention, Lin's translations over time have grown into a somewhat systematic expression, which is first of all a natural outgrowth of his personal interest and the result of his "casual dipping" in reading and casual translating. He is not so much devoted to a particular author or a particular work as he is to his conception of the world. On a broad canvas, his translations deal with various aspects of human existence. Love and hate, life and death, individual and society, man and nature, philosophy and life, history and fiction ... there is hardly any topic left untouched.

In terms of topology of his translations, they belong very well with each other to constitute his vision of the world. However diverse his Chinese translations are, they are coherent and constitute a larger unit of expression, whose characteristic is "translating the new": *Hypatia*, *or Woman and Knowledge* speaks for women's rights, including free love and free sex; *Yibusheng Pingzhuan* (*A Critical Biography of Ibsen*) is about the life of a revolutionary poet and playwright; *Pygmalion* is an attack on middle-class hypocrisy; through his Chinese translation of the essays of J. E. Spingarn, E. Dowden, Van Wyck Brooks, and excerpts from *Wilde: Intentions* and Croce's *Aesthetic as Science of Expression and General Linguistic* Lin is better able to state his idea of art: art is self-expression and shall be free of all rules. There is a common thread linking these fragments: these translations reflect the translator's "progressive" position. If we can say that his Chinese translations appear very much fragmentary, his English translations appear more so. He has translated a few small volumes which include *Laotse* (*the Book of Tao*), *Six Chapters of a Floating Life*, *The Travels of Mingliaotze* and *The Epigrams of Chang Chao*. Each volume is so small that it can hardly stand alone as a book. Even in a bilingual edition the size of each volume does not become impressive. The rest of his English translations are short stories or novelettes, poetry, essays, et cetera from scattered sources. One book alone, *The Importance of Understanding: Translations from the Chinese*, contains 107 fragments (sections) in a space of 494 pages. However, the fragments in English assemble and are assembled to fit into the Lin Yutang system of expression or constitute a unit of expression in their own right, which I categorized under "English Translations: Translating the Old" in Chapter

Three. There is an inner link and an outer link between the fragments. First, they are the outgrowths of Lin's personal preferences and second, the translator has often consciously given the translations an organization. Here we need to refer to an earlier discussion of how translation is found as expression in the Lin Yutang system of self-expression. As Lin has not strictly followed a map in making his translations and themes emerge over time after more translations are done, it is interesting to see how fragments grow to cluster around themes and themes cluster to form a thematic hierarchy of expression. Here is how the themes emerge and converge in his translations:

(1) In his Chinese translations, we can roughly establish the following formula:

Feminism + Revolution + New Education + New Drama + New Criticism + New Thought + New Scholarship + New Experience + ... = the New/Modern from the West①

(2) In his English Translations, a rough formula is found as below:

a Story of Chinese Life (in Old China) + the Wisdom of China + Classic Chinese Literature of the Soul + Traditional Chinese Art + Chinese Language + Voices of New China (Progress) + ... = Chinese Tradition and Aspiration for Change②

(3) Finally, his Chinese translations and English translations combine to form his expression in translation:

---

① Feminism: *Hypatia, or Woman and Knowledge*; revolution: *The Chinese Puzzle*; new education: *The Diary of a Communist Schoolboy*; new drama: Ibsen and Shaw. New Criticism: Benedetto Croce, J. E. Spingarn, Oscar Wilde, E. Dowden and Van Wyck Brooks; New Thought: *Training for Efficiency* and *Every Man a King* by Orison Swett Marden and *A Plan for Self-Management* by Lord, Everett William; new scholarship: *Keeping Mentally Fit*; new experience: *The Autobiography of a Super Tramp.*

② Chinese Modernity (Progress): *Letters of a Chinese Amazon*, etc.; a Story of Chinese Life: *Six Chapters of a Floating Life* (1935); the wisdom of China: *Laotse, the Book of Tao, Chuangtse, the Mystic*, Selections from the *Liki*, etc.; classic Chinese literature of the soul: *The Importance of Understanding* (1960); Chinese art: *Theories of Chinese Art: from the Masters of Chinese Art*; the Chinese language translated: *Modern Chinese-English Dictionary of Current Usage* (1972).

the New/Modern from the West + Chinese Tradition and Aspiration for Change = a Harmonious New World of Tradition and Progress Built by the East and the West Together

3 Universality and Eternity through Marginality and Temporality

Two important features of Yutang's translations are cosmopolitanism and timelessness. It is his exploration of universal and eternal motifs that has won him worldwide readership. An important element of his appeal lies in his "common sense," common sense across space and time. With such a conviction, he has translated some gems of Chinese literature, ranging from the canonical Confucian and Taoist classics to the marginal literature in Chinese history such as the ditties and "The Mortal Thoughts of a Nun" in *My Country and My People*, and the epigrams of Chang Chao, from literature of antiquity to the diary of a contemporary girl soldier. According to him, Confucianism is a humanistic philosophy in which common sense looms large, and Taoism is a world-wise "roguish" philosophy. They largely constitute the wisdom of the Chinese. His favorite literature is literature from the heart and therefore his English translations are intended to provide nourishment for the soul. His Chinese translations basically serve the same purpose. Through his translations, either from Chinese to English or otherwise, he attempts to communicate universal human values and tries to increase understanding between the East and the West. His immersion in both Eastern and Western cultures has provided him with a unique vision that is lacking in many other translators.

Such cosmopolitanism and timelessness start with his exploitation of his own peripheral status. When critics ironically say that Lin is good at talking about the Chinese to foreigners and about the foreign to the Chinese, which is equal to saying that he is opportunistic and not deep, he takes it to be a compliment. It is there that his very strength lies. He has developed his identity by striding the cultural border. His very identity as author-translator is based on his marginal status, from which he has gradually established a ubiquitous and lasting authorial presence.

His is an awkward position. To the Chinese he is an expatriate, to the Americans he is a Chinese, a guest. People on either side may not take him seriously. English readers love him because he is a lovable Chinese. Chinese readers love him much because of his immense popularity overseas. On either side of the bridge is a fortress, which he approaches from without. He is admitted, and there are banquets and jovial conversations but there may always be a tinge of suspicion hovering overhead. This is someone that does not really belong. Thus deplorably, due to his detachment and displacement, Lin has in a manner of speaking become a version of Don Quixote. His phenomenal success with his writings and translations does not change much the structure of world politics as is his ambition. In an age of mass consumption, his books are, like other products, consumed by a segment of the market.

Nonetheless, the important thing is that he *is* there, making a difference with his texts. Despite the confinement of the peripheral status, he has done a great job as a translator in the sharing of human knowledge. The wide circulation of his translations does undeniably contribute to increased understanding between the peoples and add to variety of our cultural feast. That marginal status gives him great convenience to move about, for he can always choose to identify with both sides or not to be affiliated with either side of the bridge.

The truth about human life is eternal but texts only record momentary fragments of truth. What Yutang celebrates is beautiful life itself, not the texts about it. He does honor articulate authors but does not worship texts themselves however well written they are. His translations like his literary creations are intended to serve his time as he views it. As long as he does his best, it does not worry him that they may not be perfect. He knows that they are not replacements of original texts, but transitions to the original, or to be more exact, introductions to eternal truth as he sees it.

Appendix I

Books Attributed to Lin Yutang

Non-fiction: 19

1. *Jian Fu Ji*《翦拂集》(*Beixin*, 1928)
2. *Da Huang Ji*《大荒集》(*shenghuo*, 1934)
3. *Xing Su Ji*《我的话上册(行素集)》(*shidai*, 1934)
4. *Pi Jing Ji*《我的话下册(披荆集)》(*shidai*, 1936)
5. *Wu Suo Bu Tan Yi Ji*《无所不谈一集》(*wenxing*, 1965)
6. *Wu Suo Bu Tan Er Ji*《无所不谈二集》(*wenxing*, 1967)
7. *Wu Suo Bu Tan He Ji*《无所不谈合集》(*wenxing*, 1974)
8. *My Country and My People* (Reynal & Hitchcock, 1935)
9. *The Importance of Living* (Reynal & Hitchcock, 1937)
10. *The Chinese Way of Life* (World Publishing, 1959)
11. *From Pagan to Christianity* (World Publishing, 1959)
12. *Imperial Peking: Seven Centuries of China* (Crown Publishers, 1960)
13. *Between Tears and Laughter* (John Day, 1943)
14. *The Vigil of a Nation* (John Day, 1944)
15. *On the Wisdom of America*(John Day, 1950)
16. *The Little Critic: Essays, Satires and Sketches on China, First Series*: 1930 – 1932 (Commercial Press, 1935)
17. *The Little Critic: Essays, Satires and Sketches on China, Second Series*: 1933 –1935 (The commercial Press, 1935)
18. *With Love and Irony* (John Day, 1940)
19. *The Pleasures of a Nonconformist* (World Publishing, 1962)

Textbooks: 11

1. *Kaiming English Reader*《开明英文读本》(3 volumes, *Kaiming*, 1930)
2. *English Literature Reader* (my translation of the Chinese title)《英文文学读本》(2 volumes, Kaiming, 1930)
3. *Kaiming English Grammar*《开明英文文法》(2 volumes, Kaiming, 1930)

4. *Kaiming English Teaching Notes* (my translation of the Chinese title)《开明英文讲义》(3 volumes, in collaboration with Zhang Yougu, Commercial Press, 1935)
5. *Readings in Modern Journalistic Prose* (Commercial Press, 1931)

Academic research: 4

1. *Papers in Linguistics* (my translation of the Chinese title)《语言学论丛》(Kaiming, 1933)
2. *A History of the Press and Public Opinion in China* (*biefa yanghang*, 1936)
3. *Ping Xin Lun Gao e*《平心论高鹗》(*Wenxing*, 1966)
4. *Index of Characters in the Hongloumeng* (my translation of the Chinese title)《红楼梦人名索引》(Hwa-Kang, 1976)

Fiction: 9

1. *Moment in Peking* (John Day, 1939)
2. *A Leaf in the Storm* (John Day, 1940)
3. *Chinatown Family* (John Day, 1948)
4. *The Vermilion Gate* (John Day, 1953)
5. *Looking Beyond* (Prentice Hall, 1955)
6. *The Secret Name* (Farrar, Straus and Cudahy, 1958)
7. *The Red Peony* (World Publishing, 1961)
8. *Juniper Loa* (World Publishing, 1963)
9. *The Flight of the Innocents* (G. P. Putnam's Sons, 1964)

Biographies: 3

1. *The Gay Genius: The Life and Times of Su Tungpo* (John Day, 1947)
2. *Lady Wu* (World Publishing, 1957)
3. *Memoirs of an Octogenarian.* (Mei Ya Publications, 1975)

Translations: 29

1. *Letters of a Chinese Amazon and Wartime Essays* (Kaiming, 1930)
2. *Confucius Saw Nancy and Essays about Nothing* (Commercial Press, 1935)
3. *The Wisdom of Confucius*(Random House, 1938)
4. *The Wisdom of China and India*(Random House, 1942)
5. *The Wisdom of Laotse* (Random House, 1948)
6. *Widow, Nun and Courtesan: Three Novelettes from the Chinese Translated and Adapted by Lin Yutang*(John Day, 1951)
7. *Famous Chinese Short Stories, Retold by Lin Yutang*(John Day, 1952)
8. *A Nun of Taishan (a Novelette) and Other Translations* (Commercial Press, 1936)
9. *Six Chapters of a Floating Life* (Hsi-feng, 1939)
10. *Ancient Vignettes from the Chinese Translated by the Have-Not-Done Studio*①《有不为斋古文

① My English translation of the Chinese title.

小品》(bilingual)(Hsi-feng, 1940)

11. *The Travels of Mingliaotse*《冥寥子游》(bilingual)(Hsi-feng, 1940)
12. *Widow Chuan* (William Heinemann., 1952)
13. *The Wisdom of China* (M. Joseph, 1949)
14. *Chuangtse*: *Translated by Lin Yutang* (World Books, 1957)
15. *The Importance of Understanding: Translations from the Chinese* (World Publishing, 1960)
16. *The Chinese Theory of Art: Translations from the Masters of Chinese Art* (G. P. Putnam Sons, 1967)
17. *Nüzi Yu Zhishi*,《女子与知识》, Chinese translation of *Hypatia*, *or Woman and Knowledge* by Dora Russell) (*Beixin*, 1929)
18. *Guomin Geming Waiji*《国民革命外纪》, Chinese translation of *The Chinese Puzzle* by Arthur Ransome (under the pseudonym of *Shinong* 石农, *Beixin*, 1929)
19. *Xin'e Xuesheng Riji*《新俄学生日记》, Chinese translation of (*The Diary of a Communist Schoolboy* by Ognyov, Nikolai, translated into English by Werth, Alexander, 1928 (in collaboration with Zhang Yousong, Chunchao Books Company, 1929)
20. *Mai Hua Nü*《卖花女》, Chinese translation of *Pygmalion* by Bernard Shaw. (Kaiming, 1929)
21. *Xin de Wen Ping*《新的文评》(*Beixin*, 1930)
22. *Zengyang Xunlian Ni Ziji*《怎样训练你自己》, Chinese translation of *A Plan for Self-Management* by Everett William Lord(Dongfang, 1939)
23. *Cheng Gong Zhi Lu*《成功之路》, Chinese translation of Orison Swett Marden's *Training for Efficiency*, and *Every Man a King* (*Zhongguo Zazhi Gongsi*, October, 1939; might have been falsely attributed to Lin Yutang, see 4.2.1.7.)
24. *Yibusheng Pingzhuan Jiqi Qingshu*《易卜生评传及其情书》, Chinese translation of Brandes' essay on Henrik Ibsen and Ibsen's love letters (Chunchao Books Company, 1929)
25. *Panghuang Piaobozhe*《彷徨飘泊者》, Chinese translation of *Autobiography of a Super Tramp* by W. H. Davies (Shuofeng, 1941)
26. *Rensheng Richang Xinli Zhinan*《人生日常心理指南》, Chinese translation of *Keeping Mentally Fit — A Guide to Everyday Psychology* by Joseph Jastrow (first edition unknown, Shaanxi Normal University Press, 2004)
27. *Ti Xiao Jie Fei*《啼笑皆非》, Chinese translation of his own English book *Between tears and Laughter*. About half of the book has been by Lin Yutang himself. (Commercial Press, 1945).

1 bilingual dictionary:

Chinese-English Dictionary of Modern Usage (The Chinese University of Hong Kong, 1972).

Appendix II

Lin Yutang Translation Timeline

1924

Translated the word *humor* into *youmo* (幽默) in "Call for Translation of an Essay and for Humor." *Chenbao Literary Supplement*, May 23, 1924.

More on *youmo* in "Miscellaneous Remarks on Humor," *Chenbao Literary Supplement*, May 9, 1924.

"Proposal for the Standardization of Proper Names in Translation," May 21, 1924.

1925

Translation of *Sylvesterabend* (New Year Eve) published in the 11th issue of the *Yusi* magazine, Jan. 26, 1925. Source language and author not specified.

"Good Advice for the Literary Guru," *Yusi* No. 31, June 15, 1925.

1926

Translation of five quatrains of Edward Fitzgerald's translation of the *Rubaiyat* of Omar Khayyam, the *Yusi* magazine, No. 66, June 15, 1926.

"In Reply to a Criticism of the Translation of Omar Kayyam" published in the *Yusi* Magazine, No. 68, March 1, 1926.

1927

Jan. 1, 1927. "译尼采《走过去》," translation of "On Passing-By" by Friedrich Nietzsche, as benediction upon Lu Xun's departure from Amoy University.

March to September, 1927. Secretary in the Foreign Ministry of the Nationalist government in Hankow (Hanko). Met Durham S. F. Chen and the two were planning to translate the complete works of Dr. Sun Yat-sen into English. The plan was aborted as their stay in Hanko was cut short. Met Xie Bingying (Hsieh Ping-ying) a girl cadet from the Wuchang Military Academy and translated her letters from the front and excerpts from her war diary, known as "Letters of a Chinese Amazon."

Moved to Shanghai to become a freelance author and translator.

Chief English language editor at the Shanghai-based Academia Sinica.

1928

"Thomas Hardy on Life, Death and God," the Yusi magazine, No. 11, Volume 4, March 12, 1928.

"Zarathustra and the Jester," a self-translation of *Satianshi yu Dongfangshuo* (萨天师与东方朔), *Yusi*, Volume 4, No. 33, 1928, original issue of *China Critic* not found, collected in *The Little Critic: Essays, Satires and Sketches on China (First Series: 1930 – 1932)*. Shanghai: The Commercial Press, Limited, 1935.

1929

Chinese translation from English of Nikolai Ognyov's *The Diary of a Communist Schoolboy* (《新俄学生日记》). In collaboration with Zhang Yousong. Published in June, 1929 by the Shanghai Chunchao Books Company.

Chinese translation of *The Chinese Puzzle* (1927) by Arthur Ramsome. Shanghai: Beixin Books Company. July, 1929. Under the pseudonym of Shi Nong (石农).

Chinese translation of Mrs. Bertrand Russell's *Hypatia, or Woman and Knowledge* published under the name of 林玉堂 by the Shanghai-based Beixin Publishing Company, 1929.

"Introduction" to *The New Criticism*, a collection of translations to be published shortly. No. 30, Volume 5.

Chinese translation of *Pygmalion* by Bernard Shaw, published by Kaiming Bookstore, Shanghai, 1929. Reprinted in July, November, 1931. The Translator's Note is dated March 8, 1929.

Translation of excerpts from *Aesthetic as the Science of Expression and General Linguistic* by Benedetto Croce, the *Yusi* magazine, No. 36, Volume 5, November 10, 1929.

Publication of *Yibusheng Pingzhuan*, Chinse translation of G. Brandes's critical study of Ibsen and some love letters of Ibsen, Shanghai: Chunchao Books Company, 1929.

1930

Publication of *Xin de Wen Ping* (*New Criticism*), selective Chinese translation of essays in New Criticism, published by Beixin, 1930. Essays include J. E. Spingarn's Creative Criticism: Essays on the Unity of Genius and Taste, Benedetto Croce's Aesthetic as the Science of Expression and General Linguistic, J. E. Spingarn's "Seven Arts and Seven Fallacies" (my back-translation of the Chinese title), Oscar Wilde's "The Critic as Artist" from *Intentions* (with Translator's introduction), "French Criticism" by E. Dowden, and "The Critic and Young America" by Van Wyck Brooks.

Letters of a Chinese Amazon and War-Time Essays. Shanghai: The Commercial Press Limited, 1930. Translation of Hsieh Ping-ing's war diaries published together with Lin's own war-time essays.

1932

"Three Jokes about Translation" (翻译趣谈三则). *Analects Forthnightly*. No. 1. September 16, 1932.

"A Discussion of *youmo*" (关于"幽默"的讨论). *Analects Fortnightly*, No. 3, Oct. 6, 1932.

"'A Discussion of *youmo* and *yumiao*" ("幽默"与"语妙"之讨论) (Attached: A Reply to Qing Ya on the Chinese Translation of the Word *Humor*), *Analects Fortnighly*, No. 3, Oct. 16, 1932.

1933

"On Translation," preface to Wu Shutian's book *On Translation*, which was published in Jan., 1937.

On "Humor" ("论'幽默'"), *Analects Fortnighly*, No. 33, 34, 35.

Two articles of the same content almost published simultaneously in both Chinese and English: "让娘儿们干一下吧!" *Shenbao*, August, 1933. "The Little Critic: Should Women Rule the World?" *The China Critic*, VI (August 17, 1933), 814 -815.

1934

"*Shanghai Zhi Ge*" (上海之歌), *Xing Su Ji*, 1934. Probably a Chinese translation of an earlier essay written in English: "A Hymn to Shanghai," *The Little Critic*, *Essays*, *Satires and Sketches on China* (*First Series*: 1930 -1932). Shanghai: The Commercial Press, Limited, 1935. The English was also republished later as "Hymn to Shanghai." *The Atlantic Monthly*, CLVII, (January, 1936), 109 -110.

Two articles of the same content almost published simultaneously in both Chinese and English: "The Little Critic: On Bertrand Russell's Divorce", *The China Critic*, VII (September 6, 1934), 885 -886. "*Luosu Lihun*" (罗素离婚), *This Human World*, No. 11, September 5, 1934.

"On Ku Hung-ming" (辜鸿铭论), Chinese translation of George Brandes' study of Ku Hung-ming. This Human World, No. 12, September 20, 1934.

"A Modern Translation of the Declaration of Independence" (今译《美国独立宣言》), translation of the American Declaration of Independence in Pekingese colloquial. *Analects Fortnightly*, No. 54, December 1, 1934.

Two articles of the same content almost published simultaneously in both Chinese and English: "The Little Critic: A Lecture Without an Audience — A Wedding Speech," *The China Critic*, VII (October 11, 1934), 1002 -1003. "一篇没有听众的演讲——婚礼致词," *Analects Fortnighly*, No. 53, 1934 年 11 月 16 日.

Translation of Yao Ying's essay "On My Library." "The Little Critic: On My Library," *The China Critic*, VII (June 28, 1934), 617 -618.

"The Little Critic: A Chinese Aesop," *The China Critic*, VII (September 13, 1934), 907 -908.

"*Zhongguo Wenhua Zhi Jingshen*" (中国文化之精神), *Da Huang Ji*, 1934. Chinese translation of an English lecture earlier delivered at Oxford University. "The Spirit of Chinese Culture," *The China Critic*, V (June 30, 1932), 651 -654.

Either the Chinese or the English is a self-translation: "*Hunjia Yu Nüzi Zhiye*" (婚嫁与女子职业), *Xing Su Ji*, 1934. "Marriage and Careers for Women," *The Little Critic*,

Essays, Satires and Sketches on China (*First Series*: 1930 –1932) ,1935.

Either the Chinese or the English is a self-translation: "*Lun Zhengzhi Bing*" (论政治病). *Xing Su Ji*. 1934. *The Little Critic*: *On Political Sickness*. *The China Critic*, V (June 16, 1932), 600 –601.

"*Jiading Wo Shi Tufei*" (假定我是土匪), *Analects Fortnighly*, No. 44, July 1, 1934, a self-translation of "If I Were a Bandit," *The Little Critic, Essays, Satires and Sketches on China (First Series: 1930 –1932)*. Shanghai: The Commercial Press, Limited, 1935.

"*Tan Yanlun Ziyou*" (谈言论自由), *Xing Su Ji*, 1934, a self-translation of "The Little Critic: On Freedom of Speech," *The China Critic*, VI (March 9, 1933), 264 –265.

Either the Chinese or the English is a self-translation: "*si mandaren*" (思满大人), *Xing Su Ji*, 1934. "The Little Critic: The Lost Mandarin," *The China Critic*, V (November 17, 1932), 1219 –1220. Also included in Asia, XXXIV (June, 1934), 366 –367.

"*Wode Jieyan*" (我的戒烟), *Xing Su Ji*, 1934, a self-translation of "My Last Rebellion Against Lady Nicotine," *The Little Critic, Essays, Satires and Sketches on China (First Series: 1930 –1932)*. Shanghai: The Commercial Press, Limited, 1935.

"*Wo Zenyang Mai Yashua*" (我怎样买牙刷), *Xing Su Ji*, 1934, a self-translation of "The Little Critic: How I Bought a Toothbrush", *The China Critic*, V (August 18, 1932), 850 –851.

"The Little Critic: Unconscious Chinese Humor," *The China Critic*, VII (November 22, 1934), 1148.

"The Little Critic: A Cock-Fight in Old China," *The China Critic*, VII (November 22, 1934), 1148.

1935

"Postscript to the" Western Humor "Special Issue of *Analects Fortnightly*" (跋《西洋幽默专号》). *Analects Fortnightly*, No. 56, January 1, 1935.

"The Little Critic: The Humor of Mencius," *The China Critic*, VIII (January 3, 1935), 17 –18. This was considered a translation by Lin Yutang himself and was collected in *A Nun of Taishan* (*a Novelette*) *and Other Translations*. Shanghai: The Commercial Press, Limited, 1936.

"The Little Critic: The Humor of Liehtse," *The China Critic*, VIII (January 17, 1935), 65 –66. This was considered a translation by Lin Yutang himself.

"The Little Critic: A Chinese Galli-Curei (by Liu Eh)," *The China Critic*, IX (April 18, 1935), 62 –63.

"The Little Critic: The Epigrams of Chang Ch'ao, translated by Lin Yutang," *The China Critic*, IX (April 25, 1935), 86 –87.

"The Little Critic: A Chinese Ventriloquist, translated by Lin Yutang," *The China Critic*, IX (May 16, 1935), 158.

"The Little Critic: The Donkey That Paid Its Debt," The *China Critic*, IX (May 30,

1935), 205 -208.

Chinese translation of *The Autobiography of a Super Tramp* by W. H. Davies was completed in July, 1935. The book was later published in March 1941 by the Shanghai-based Shuofeng Bookstore (朔风书店).

"The Little Critic: T'ang P'ip'a, translated by Lin Yutang," The *China Critic*, IX (June 13, 1935), 255 -256.

One of the two versions of the same article is a self-translation: "*lun woshou*" (论握手), *Analects Fortnightly*, No. 72, September 16, 1935. "On Shaking Hands," *The China Critic*, X (August 22, 1935), 180 -181.

"Preface to '*Six Chapters of a Floating Life*,' A Novel by Shen Fu." *T'ien Hsia Monthly*, I (August, 1935), 72 -75.

"Six Chapters of a Floating Life A Novel by Shen Fu. Chapter I. Translated by Lin Yutang," *T'ien Hsia Monthly*, I (August, 1935), 76 -101.

"The Little Critic: 'Taiping'Christianity," *The China Critic*, X (September 26, 1935), 301 -302.

"Six Chapters of a Floating Life A Novel by Shen Fu. Chapter II. Translated by Lin Yutang," *T'ien Hsia Monthly*, I (September, 1935), 208 -222.

"The Little Critic: The Humor of Su Tungp'o," *The China Critic*, XI (October 3, 1935), 15 -17.

"The Little Critic: Chinese Dog-Stories," *The China Critic*, XI (October 17, 1935), 64 -65.

"Six Chapters of a Floating Life A Novel by Shen Fu. Chapter III. Translated by Lin Yutang," *T'ien Hsia Monthly*, I (October, 1935), 316 -340.

"The Little Critic: Some Chinese Jokes I Like," *The China Critic*, XI (November 21, 1935), 180 -182.

"Six Chapters of a Floating Life A Novel by Shen Fu. Chapter IV. Translated by Lin Yutang," *T'ien Hsia Monthly*, I (November, 1935), 425 -467.

"On the Differences between Chinese and English" (写中西文之别), *The Cosmic Wind*. No. 6, December 1, 1935.

My Country and My People. New York: Reynal & Hitchcock, Inc., 1935. (A John Day Book) Large portions of the book are translations.

1936

"*lian yu fazhi*" (脸与法制), *Pi Jing Ji*, 1936, a self-translation of "The Little Critic: What Is Face?" The China Critic, IV (April 16, 1931), 372 -373.

"The Little Critic: Chinese Satiric Humor" (a translation), *The China Critic*, XII (January 9, 1936), 36 -38.

"The Little Critic: 'Oh, Break Not My Willow-Trees!'" (a translation), *The China Critic*, XII (January 30, 1936), 108 -110.

"The Little Critic: On Charm in Women" (a translation), *The China Critic*, XII (March 5, 1936), 231 -233.
"The Little Critic: T'ao Yuanming's 'Ode to Beauty'translated by Lin Yutang," *The China Critic*, XII (March 26, 1936), 300 -301.
"The Little Critic: Preface to 'A Nun of Taishan'," *The China Critic*, XIV (September 3, 1936), 231 -232.
"*Lundun de Qigai*"(伦敦的乞丐), *Pi Jing Ji*, 1936. A self-translation of "The Beggars of London," *The Little Critic, Essays, Satires and Sketches on China (Second Series: 1930 - 1932)*. Shanghai: The Commercial Press, Limited, 1935.
Confucius Saw Nancy and Essays about Nothing. Shanghai: The Commercial Press, Limited, 1936. *Confucius Saw Nancy* is a self-translation of "子见南子", a tragicomedy published in Benliu Volume 1, No. 6, 1928.
A Nun of Taishan and Other Translations. Shanghai: The Commercial Press, Limited, 1936. Translations in this collection include:
A Nun of Taishan (Liu Eh) (刘鹗：老残游记) (with a preface by Lin Yutang)
Talking Pictures, (Lao Sheh) (老舍：有声电影)
Ah Chuan Goes to School! (Lao Hsiang) (老向：村儿辍学记)
Salt, Sweat and Tears (Lao Hsiang) (老向：吾民其为毛人乎)
On My Library (Yao Ying) (姚颖：我的书报安置法)
Unconscious Chinese Humour
The Humour of Feng Yuhsiang
The Humour of Mencius
The Humour of Liehtse
The Humour of Su Tungp'o
A Chinese Aesop
Chinese Satiric Humour
Some Chinese Jokes That I Like
The Donkey That Paid Its Debt
"Taiping" Christianity
Three Sketches of Sounds:
A Chinese Galli-Curei (Liu Eh)
A Chinese Ventriloquist (Lin Ts'ehuan)
T'ang P'ip'a (Wang Yuting)
On Charm in Women (Li Liweng) (李渔：说韵)
Ode to Beauty (T'ao Yuanming) (陶潜：闲情赋)
Homeward Bound I Go! (T'ao Yuanming) (陶潜：归去来辞)
The Epigrams of Chang Ch'ao (张潮：幽梦影)
Ah Chen's Death (Shen Chunlieh) (沈君烈：哭震女文)

A Cock-Fight in Old China (Yuan Chunglang) (袁宏道：山居斗鸡记)

Chinese Dog-Stories (Wang Yen) (王言：圣师录)

"*Lun Tang Zai Chuang Shang*" (论躺在床上), *The Cosmic Wind*, No. 9, January 16, 1936, a self-translation of "The Little Critic: On Lying in Bed," *The China Critic*, XI (November 7, 1935), 134 – 136.

"Postscript to the April Fools Day Editorial of the *Zilinxibao* Newspaper" (跋众愚节《字林西报》社论), *Analects Fortnighly*, No. 16, 1936. The postscript contains two poem translations.

"*Zhongguo Jiu You Chouchong Fou?*" (中国究有臭虫否?), *Pi Jing Ji*, 1936, a self-translation of "The Little Critic: Do Bed-Bugs Exist in China?" *The China Critic*, IV (February 19, 1931), 179 – 180.

1937

"Letter to Yu Dafu on the Translation of *Moment in Peking*" ((给郁达夫的信—关于《瞬息京华》), *The Cosmic Wind*, No. 49, October 16, 1937.

"The Vagabond Scholar, by T'u Lung, translated by Lin Yutang," *Asia*, XXXVII (November, 1937), 761 – 764.

The Importance of Living, Raynal & Hitchcock, Inc., 1937; — Toronto: McClelland & Stewart, Ltd., 1937; — Toronto: Longmans, Green & Co., 1937. This is a John Day book which includes large portions of translations from the Chinese such as from the "*Vase Flowers*" of Yuan Chunglang, the *Epigrams of Chang Chao*, *The Travels of Mingliaotse*, etc.

1938

The Wisdom of Confucius. Edited and translated with an introduction and notes by Lin Yutang. New York: The Modern Library, Random House, 1938; — London: Hamish Hamilton Ltd., 1938.

1939

September. New York City. His daughters, Adet Lin and Anor Lin completed the translation of Hsieh Ping-ing's autobiography and more war diaries. Lin Yutang spent about a week revising the translation. The translation was later published as *The Girl Rebel* (1940).

A bilingual edition of Lin Yutang's translation of *Six Chapters of a Floating Life* was published in May, 1939 by the Shanghai-based *Xi Feng She*.

Chinese translation of *A Plan for Self-Management* (《怎样训练你自己》) by Everett William Lord was publsihed by the Shanghai-based Dongfang Books Company (东方图书公司) in 1939, reprinted in 1940.

1940

April 5, Los Angles. Wrote a preface to *The Girl Rebel* (《女兵自传》), his daughters' translation of Hsieh Ping-ing's autobiography and war diaries.

Publication of *Yibusheng Pingzhuan Jiqi Qingshu* (《易卜生评传及其情书》, a translation of G. Brandes's critical study of Henrik Ibsen and Ibsen's love letters, published by the Shanghai-based Dadong Books Company (大东书局), 1940.

A bilingual edition of *Ancient Vignettes from the Chinese Translated by the Have-Not-Done Studio* (《有不为斋古文小品》), published by the Hsi-feng She, 1940. The book includes 11 selections by Tao Yuanming, Wang Xizhi, Jin Shengtan, Li Liweng and Chen Meigong, et al.

A bilingual edition of *The Travels of Mingliaotse* (《冥寥子游》), published by the Hsi-feng She, 1940.

With Love and Irony. New York: The John Day Company. 1940. Illustrated by Kurt Wiese. This book contains some of Lin's self-translations from the Chinese.

1942

"Laotse Speaks to Us Today, translation and comment by Lin Yutang," *Asia*, XLII (November, 1942), 619 -621.

"The Epigrams of Lusin, translation and comment by Lin Yutang," *Asia*, XLII (December, 1942), 687 -689.

The Wisdom of China and India. New York, Random House, 1942. The book is an anthology of translations by other translators and by Lin Yutang himself.

1943

Tales and Parables of Old China. Translated by Lin Yutang. San Francisco. The Book Club of California, 1943. The text is reproduced from *The Wisdom of China and India*.

1945

The Chinese edition of *Between Tears and Laughter* was published by the Commercial Press in Chongqing, January, 1945, undergoing several reprints in the same year. Lin translated 11 of the chapters and the other chapers were translated by Xu Chengbin (徐诚斌).

Lin's self-translations from the English include

1. A Confession 前序第一
2. Karma 业缘篇第二
3. The Emergence of Asia 时变篇第三
4. The Suicide of Greece 述古篇第四
5. Churchill and Pericles 证今篇第五
6. World War III 果报篇第六
7. The "White Man's Burden" 排物篇第七
8. "Government by Music" 明乐篇第八
9. Mathematics and Peace 卜算篇第九
10. Defense of Courtesy 明理篇第十
11. Europeanization of the World 欧化篇第十一

1948

"*Introduction*," to *All Men Are Brothers* [Shui Hu Chuan]. Translated from the Chinese by Pearl S. Buck. New York: The Limited Editions Club, 1948.

The Wisdom of Laotse. Edited and Translated with an Introduction and Notes by Lin Yutang. New York: Random House, Inc., 1948. — New York: Random House, 1948; — Westport, Conn.: Greenwood, 1948.

1950

Miss Tu 杜十娘. London: William Heinemann Ltd., 1950. Based on an old popular Chinese legend, Tu Shih-Niang Nu Ch'En Pai Pao Hsiang, which appeared in the Ching Shi T'Ung Yen, collected by Feng Menglung.

1951

Widow, Nun and Courtesan 寡婦、妾與歌妓: *Three Novelettes from the Chinese Translated and Adapted by Lin Yutang*. New York: The John Day Company, 1951. — Toronto: Longmans, Green & Co., 1951. — N. Y: John Day, 1951.

1952

Famous Chinese Short Stories: Retold by Lin Yutang. New York: The John Day Company, 1952. — London: William Heinemann Ltd., 1952.

This book includes the following stories:

1. Curly-Beard 虬髯客传
2. The White Monkey 白猿传
3. The Stranger's Note 无名信
4. The Jade Goddess 碾玉观音
5. Chastity 贞节坊
6. Passion 莺莺传
7. Chienniang 离魂记
8. Madame D. 狄氏
9. Jealousy 西山一窟鬼
10. Jojo 小谢
11. Cinderella 叶限
12. The Cricket Boy 促织
13. The Poet's Club 东阳夜怪录
14. The Bookworm 书痴
15. The Wolf of Chungshan 中山狼传
16. A lodging for the Night 李卫公靖
17. The Man Who Became a Fish 薛伟
18. The Tiger 张逢
19. Matrimony Inn 定婚店
20. The Drunkard's Dream 南柯太守传

Widow Chuan: *Retold by Lin Yutang*, *Based on Chuan Jia Chun*, *by Lao Hsiang*. London: William Heinemann Ltd., 1952.

1957

Chuangtse: Translated by Lin Yutang. Taipei, World Book C., 1957.

1960

The Importance of Understanding: Translations from the Chinese. Cleveland: The World Publishing Company, 1960. This is an anthology of Lin's own translations except for two Buddhist sutras.

The anthology includes:

1. "A Chinese Fantasia: The Song of Life." A group of poems by different Chinese poets of different ages, bearing on the central theme, The Song of Life. 咏怀集·集古
2. "Quiet Dream Shadows" Chang Chao 幽梦影·张潮
3. What Can I Do about It? Chin Shengtan 西厢记序·金圣叹
4. Friendly Chats Chin Shengtan 水浒传序·金圣叹
5. Dreams, Interesting and Otherwise Shih Chenlin 西青散记序·史震林
6. Beginning of Knowledge and of Sorrow Shih Chenlin 华阳散祸亭·史震林
7. The Seven Remedies Chang Chao 七疗·张潮
8. The Past and Future Wang Shichih 兰亭集序·王羲之
9. The Universe a Lodging House Li Po 春在宴桃李·李白
10. Human Contradictions Wang Kaiyun 秋醒词序·王开运
11. The Wear and Tear of Life Chuangtse 齐物论一节·庄周
12. The Butterfly's Dream Chuangtse 蝶梦·庄周
13. The Ambition-Mind and the Profit-Mind Shi Chenlin 论心·史震林
14. On Zest in Life Yuan Chunglang 叙陈正甫会心集·袁中郎
15. On Love Chou Chuan 英雄气短说
16. The Mortal Thoughts of a Nun Anonymous 尼姑思凡
17. The Death of a Queen Pan ku 李夫人临死托武帝·班固
18. To a Beauty Tao Yuanming 闲情赋·陶潜
19. In Memory of a Woman Shen Fu 浮生六记二节·沈复
20. In Memory of a Child Shen Chunlieh 哭震女文·沈君烈
21. A Great Love Letter Tsui Inging 莺莺札·元稹
22. Taiyu Predicting Her Own Death Tsao Shuehchin 黛玉葬花诗·曹沾
23. Forlorn Li Yi-An 秋情声声慢·李清照
24. The Story of a Collection of Antiques Li Yi-An 金石录后序·李清照
25. Spring Fever Lin Yutang 春愁·林语堂
26. Summer Heat Yao Ying 源暑·姚颖
27. Harvest Moon on West Lake Chang Tai 西湖七月半·张岱

28. How I Celebrated New Year's Eve　Lin Yutang 记除夕・林语堂
29. An Invitation from a Mountain Resident　Wang Wei 山中 裴秀才 书・王维
30. The Stone Bell Mountain　Su Tungpo 石钟山记・苏轼
31. The Peach Colony　Tao Yuanming 桃花源记・陶潜
32. The River of Folly　Liu Tsungyuan 愚溪诗序・柳宗元
33. The North Peak of Lushan　Po Chuyi 庐山草堂・白居易
34. The Half-and-Half Song　Li Mi-An 半半歌・李密庵
35. On Going Around　Anonymous 曲城说・佚名
36. How to Relax　Chang Nai 息机说・张鼐
37. Moments with Su Tungpo　Su Tungpo 志林书札选・苏轼
38. On Wealth and Commerce　Szema Chien 货殖传节・司马迁
39. Is There Retribution?　Szema Chien 伯夷叔齐传节・司马迁
40. How to Be Happy though Rich　Li Liweng 富人行乐法・李渔
41. How to Be Happy though Poor　Li Liweng 穷人行乐法・李渔
42. The Origin of Foot-Binding　Yu Huai 妇人鞋补救考・余怀
43. A Woman's Body　Anonymous 杂事秘幸・佚名
44. Professional Matchmakers　Chang Tai 扬州瘦马・张岱
45. On Charm in Women　Li Liweng 说韵・李渔
46. A Family Letter　Tseng Kuofan 家书・曾国藩
47. The Home Garden　Chen Chiju 园宅・陈继儒
48. Cut Flowers and Vases　Chang Tehchien 瓶花谱・张德谦
49. How to Enjoy Birds　Cheng Panchiao 养鸟・郑燮
50. The Origin and Preparation of Tea　Lu Yu 茶经注补・陈鉴附茶考(茶经唐・陆羽原著)
51. The Nine-Blessings Couch　Ting Shiungfei 九喜榻・丁雄飞
52. The Arts of Sleeping, Walking, Sitting, and Standing　Li Liweng 随时即景就事行乐之法四节・李渔
53. Hints to Hosts and Guests　Shen Chungying 觞政・清沈中楹
54. Fashions in Cuisine　Anonymous 三风十行记食・佚名
55. Eggplant Terrine　Tsao Shuehchin 风姐说茄子鲞・曹沾
56. From an Artist's Notebook　Li Jih-Hua《紫桃轩杂缀》选・明代文学家、画家嘉兴李日华 附历代简表
57. Communion with Nature　Lu Kueimeng 书李贺小传后・陆龟蒙
    A Note on Chinese Names 附名字号释
58. Rhythmic Vitality and Verisimilitude. A collection of various important artists' opinions on the first law of rhythmic vitality, enunciated by Shieh Ho, which has remained the keystone and inviolable principle of Chinese painting throughout the ages. 气韵与形似・集古

59. Painting the Inner Law of Things Su Tungpo 论画理·苏轼
60. A Painting of Five Hundred Lohans Tsin 五百罗汉图·佚名
61. Sound Mimicry Lin Tsehuan 秋声诗序·林嗣环
62. Beautiful Singing Liu Ao 大明湖说书·刘鹗
63. The Sound of the Pipa on the Water Po Chuyi 琵琶行·白居易
64. Tungpo on the Art of Writing Su Tungpo 与友人论文书选·苏轼
65. The Familiar Style Lin Yutang 说小品文·林语堂
66. Literature and Complexion Shih Chenlin 说散记文·史震林
67. The Discovery of Self Chang Tai 琅环诗集序·张岱
68. The Moral Censor Shih Chenlin 计算叟·史震林
69. Little Half Catty Huang Choushing 小半斤谣·黄周星
70. The Never-Never Land Huang Choushing 梦檀城选·黄周星
71. What the Donkey Said Li Fuyen 驴言·李复言
72. Some Dog Stories Wang Yen 圣师录·王言
73. Sound Movies Shu Shehyu 有声电影·舒舍予
74. Tales with Morals Chiang Chinchih 雪涛小书·江进之
75. The Wit of the Ancients 古代幽默
76. The Person Spoken to Han Fei 说难·韩非
77. The Art of Persuasion 讽谏·战国策
78. Parables of Chuangtse Chuangtse 寓言·庄周
79. Parables of Liehtse Liehtse 寓言·列子
80. The Old Man at the Fort Liu An 塞翁失马·淮南子
81. Something to Weep About Mencius 齐人章·孟轲
82. Truth Is Harder to See Than the Sun Su Tungpo 日喻·苏轼
83. The Ferryman's Wisdom Chou Yung 小港渡者·周容
84. The Beggar's Philosophy Yuan Chieh 丐论·元结
85. On City Noises Sha Changpai 市声·沙张白
86. The Emperor's Friend Fan Ye 严子陵转·范晔
87. Letter Declining Marriage to a Princess Anonymous 让妻表·佚名
88. Letter on the Secret of Getting Along Tsung Chen 报刘一丈书·宗臣
89. Letter Severing Friendship Chi Kang 与山巨源绝交书·嵇康
90. Mi Fei, the Eccentric Genius Chen Chiju 米襄阳志林序·陈继儒
91. Why I Became a Monk Li Chuowu 豫约二节·李贽
92. The Tao of God and the Tao of Man Chuangse 大宗师节选·庄周
93. The Even Tenor of Our Life Chuangtse 马蹄·庄周
94. Against Wars of Aggression Motse 非攻·墨翟
95. The Sages and Ourselves Mencius 圣人与我同类·孟轲
96. Farmers Are Best Cheng Panchiao 农夫第一·郑燮

97. Kingship　Huang Tsungshi 原君 · 黄宗羲
98. On the Importance of Partiality　Kung Tsechen 论私 · 龚自珍
99. Do Ghosts Exist?　Wang Chung 论鬼 · 王充
100. A Thought on Immortality　Chang Shihyuan 自主说 · 张士元
101. Selection from the Lankavatra Sutra 楞伽经选
102. Selection from the Surangama Sutra 首楞严经选
103. Thoughts and Epigrams 隽语清言
104. The Book of a Cynic　Shu Shuehmou 归有园尘谈 · 徐学谟
105. Wish I Had Heard It from an Elder　Chen Chiju 安得长者言 · 陈继儒
106. Talk with a Monk　Chen Chiju 岩栖幽事 · 陈继儒
107. Proverbs 俗谚

1967

The Chinese Theory of Art: Translations from the Masters of Chinese Art. New York: G. P. Putnam's Sons, 1967.

—. London, United Kingdom: Heinemann, 1967.

1972

Chinese-English Dictionary of Modern Usage. Chinese University of Hong Kong, distributed by McGraw-Hill, New York, 1972.

1974

"On the Translation of Poetry"（论译诗）, *Wu Suo Bu Tan He Ji*, 1974.

"English Translation of Two Shingshiangtse Poems of Su Tung-p'o"（译东坡《行香子》二首）, *Wu Suo Bu Tan He Ji*, 1974.

"English Translation of Eight *Leyinci* Poems"（译《乐隐词》八首）, *Wu Suo Bu Tan He Ji*, 1974.

"An English Translation of 'Taiyu Predicting Her Own Death'"（英译黛玉《葬花诗》）, *Wu Suo Bu Tan He Ji*, 1974.

"An English Translation of 'The Mortal Thoughts of a Nun'"（《尼姑思凡》英译）, *Wu Suo Bu Tan He Ji*, 1974.

Lin Yutang's Letter to the Editors of the Ziyoubao Newspaper（"林语堂给《自由报》编者函"）, *Wu Suo Bu Tan He Ji*, 1974.

"Appreciation of The Red Chamber Dream." *Renditions: A Chinese-English Translation Magazine*, 2 (1974), pp. 23－30.

"*Ji Nongli Yuandan*"（记农历元旦）, *Wu Suo Bu Tan He Ji*, 1974. The Chinese version of "How I Celebrated the New Year's Eve," *The Little Critic, Essays, Satires and Sketches on China (Second Series: 1930－1932)*. Shanghai: The Commercial Press, Limited, 1935.

Bibliography

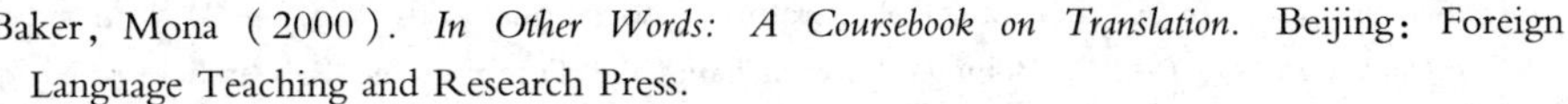

Baker, Mona (2000). *In Other Words: A Coursebook on Translation*. Beijing: Foreign Language Teaching and Research Press.

Benjamin, Walter (2000). The Task of the Translator, an introduction to the translation of Baudelaire's *Tableaux Parisiens*. In Venuti, L. *The Translation Studies Reader*. London & New York: Routledge.

Brandes, Georg (1929). *Henrik Ibsen: A Critical Study and His Love Letters*. Trans. Lin Yutang. Shanghai: Chunchao Books Company. [布兰地司 (1929).《易卜生评传及其情书》. 林语堂译. 上海: 春潮书局.]

Brandes, Georg (1940). *Henrik Ibsen: A Critical Study and His Love Letters*. Trans. Lin Yutang. Shanghai: Chunchao Books Company. [布兰地司 (1940).《易卜生评传及其情书》. 林语堂译. 上海: 大东书局.]

Catford, J. C. (1965). *A Linguistic Theory of Translation*. London, Oxford University Press.

Caughey, John L. (2006) *Negotiating Cultures and Identities: Life History Issues, Methods, and Readings*. Lincoln: University of Nebraska Press.

Chan, Leo Tak-hung (2004). *Twentieth-Century Chinese Translation Theory: Modes, Issues and Debates*. Amsterdam/Philadelphia: John Benjamins.

Chan, Wing-tsit (1940, Dec.). Lin Yutang, Translator, *THE WISDOM OF CONFUCIUS* (Review of the book *The Wisdom of Confucius*), *Pacific Affairs*, 13:4, 483.

Cao, Fu (1943). *Motivational Philosophy* and Beyond (Preface). In *Ren Sheng Xing Qu*. Shanghai: Guangting Publishing House. [曹孚 (1943). 从《励志哲学》说起 (代序),《人生兴趣》. 上海:光亭出版社.]

Chen, Durham S. F. (1974, October 21). Dr. Lin Yutang as I Know Him: Some Random Recollections (Chinese version). *Huaxue Monthly*, No. 34. In Zhu, Chuanyu (Ed.). *Lin Yutang: Biographical Documents (Photocopied)*. Taipei: Tianyi Publishing House. [陈石孚. 我所认识的林语堂先生——一些片断的回忆.《华学》月刊第三十四期,"中华民国"六十三年十月二十一日. 载朱传誉编《林语堂传记资料影印本》(1981). 台北: 天一出版社.]

Chen, Fukang (2000). *A History of Translation Theory in China*. Shanghai: Shanghai Foreign Language Education Press. [陈福康 (2000).《中国译学理论史稿》. 上海外语教育出版社.]

Chen, Jie (2002). *A Modern Translation of Chinese Classics with Annotations: The Book of Poetry*. Guangzhou: Huacheng Press. [陈节注译 (2002).《新注今译中国古典名著 诗经》. 广

州：花城出版社.］

Chen, Rongdong (1997). A Translation Theory That Should Not Be Ignored-Lin Yutang's Theory of Translation in "On Translation". *China Translators Journal* (04). ［陈荣东 (1997). 一篇不该忽视的译论——从《论翻译》一文看林语堂的翻译思想.《中国翻译》(04).］

Chen, Xiying (1929). On Translation. *Xinyue*, No. 4, Vol 2. In The Editorial Board of *Translation Newsletter* of the China Translators Association (Eds.) (1984) *Articles on Translation (1894 –1948)*. Beijing: Foreign Language Teaching and Research Press. ［陈西滢 (1929). 论翻译. 原载《新月》1929 年第 2 卷第 4 号. 载中国翻译工作者协会《翻译通讯》编辑部编《翻译研究论文集(1894—1948)》(1984). 北京：外语教学与研究出版社.］

Cheng, Fangwu (1984). On the Translation of Poetry. The Editorial Board of *Translation Newsletter* of the China Translators Association (Eds.) (1984). *Articles on Translation (1894 – 1948)*. Beijing: Foreign Language Teaching and Research Press. ［成仿伍 (1984). 论译诗. 载中国翻译工作者协会《翻译通讯》编辑部编.《翻译研究论文集(1894—1948)》(202). 北京：外语教学与研究出版社.］

Chu, Dongwei (2005). The Union of the Writer and the Translator — A Case Study of *My Country and My People*. *Kaifeng University Journal* (04), 69 –72. ［褚东伟 (2005). 作家与译家的统一——对林语堂《吾国与吾民》"英文原著"的个案研究.《开封大学学报》(04), 69—72.］

Chuang, Tzu (1889). Chuang Tzu (Translated by Herbert A. Giles). Edited by Galileo Library hosted by Michael Presky in 1995. Retrieved from Galileo Library: http://www.galileolibrary.com

Confucius (1997). *The Analects*. Trans. Arthur Waley. Beijing: Foreign Language Teaching and Research Press.

Croce, Benedetto (1909). *Aesthetic as Science of Expression and General Linguistic*. Trans. Douglas Ainslie. London: Macmillan.

Croce, Benedetto (1983). *Aesthetic as Science of Expression and General Linguistic and Guide to Aesthetics*. Trans. Zhu Guangqian. Foreign Literature Press. ［克罗齐 (1983). 朱光潜译.《美学原理美学纲要》. 北京：外国文学出版社.］

Davies, W. H. (1940). *The Autobiography of a Super Tramp*. Trans. Huang Jiade. Shanghai: Xifeng. ［戴维斯 (1940). 黄嘉德译.《流浪者自传》. 上海西风社.］

— (1941). *The Autobiography of a Super Tramp*. Trans. Lin Yutang. Shanghai: Shuofeng. ［戴维斯 (1941). 林语堂.《彷徨漂泊者》. 上海：朔风书店.］

— (1963). *The Autobiography of a Super Tramp*. London: Brown, Watson.

— (1986). *The Autobiography of a Super Tramp* (Lin Yutang Masterpieces Vol. 14). Trans. Lin Yutang. Taipei: Jinlan Cutural Press. ［Davies, W. H. 著 (1986).《林语堂经典名著 14 彷徨漂泊者》. 林语堂译. 台北：金兰文化出版社.］

Dong, Hui (2004). Translation as a Fine Art — An Appreciation of Lin Yutang's Translation of Classic Chinese Poetry. *Journal of Xi'an Foreign Languages University* (01), 52 -54. [董晖(2004). 使翻译成为美术之一种——林语堂英译中国古典诗词赏析.《西安外国语学院学报》(01), 52—54.]

Dryden, John (1992). On Translation. In Schulte, R. and J. Biguenet. *Theories of Translation: an Anthology of Essays from Dryden to Derrida* (pp. 17 -31). Chicago, University of Chicago Press.

Eco, Umberto (2003). *Mouse or Rat? Translation as Negotiation*. London: Weidenfeld & Nicolson.

Foucault, Michel (1969). What Is an Author? (the text of a lecture presented to the Societé Francais de philosophie on 22 February, 1969). In Adams H. (Ed.) (2006). *Critical Theory since Plato*. Third Edition. Beijing: Peking University Press.

Guo, Moruo (1923). A Discussion of the Methods of Literary Translation. In The Editorial Board of *Translation Newsletter* of the China Translators Association (Eds.) (1984) *Articles on Translation (1894 -1948)*. Beijing: Foreign Language Teaching and Research Press. [郭沫若 (1923). 译文学书方法的讨论. 载中国翻译工作者协会《翻译通讯》编辑部编《翻译研究论文集(1894—1948)》(1984),北京:外语教学与研究出版社.]

Guo, Zhuzhang (1999). *Studies on Famous Translators*. Wuhan: Hubei Education Press. [郭著章 (1999).《翻译名家研究》. 武汉: 湖北教育出版社.]

He, Lin (1940). On Translation. In *Jinri Pinglun*, No. 9, Vol. 4, 1940. In The Editorial Board of *Translation Newsletter* of the China Translators Association (Eds.) (1984). *Articles on Translation (1894 -1948)*. Beijing: Foreign Language Teaching and Research Press. [贺麟 (1940). 论翻译. 选自《今日评论》1940 年第 4 卷第 9 期.《翻译研究论文集(1894—1948)》(1984). 北京: 外语教学与研究出版社.]

Hsieh, Ping-ing & Lin Yutang (1930). *Letters of a Chinese Amazon and War-Time Essays*. Shanghai: The Commercial Press Limited.

Hsieh, Ping-ing (1974). Blessings from Far Away, written on September 9, 1974, first published in *Huagang Xuebao* (09), 21 -27. In Zhu, Chuanyu (Ed.) (1981). *Lin Yutang: Biographical Documents (Photocopied)*. Taipei: Tianyi Publishing House. [谢冰莹(1974). 遥远的祝福,写于 1974 年 9 月 9 日,《华冈学报》(09): 21—27. 载朱传誉(主编)(1981).《林语堂传记资料影印本》. 台北: 天一出版社.]

Hsieh, Ping-ing (1999). Diaries in the Army. In Cheng, Dan (Ed.). *Representative Works of Hsieh Ping-ing*. Beijing: Huaxia Press. [谢冰莹 (1999). 从军日记. 程丹编选 (1999).《谢冰莹代表作》. 北京: 华夏出版社.]

Hu, Feng (1935). On Lin Yutang (originally published in 1935). In Zitong (Ed.) (2003). *Seventy Years of Comments on Lin Yutang* (241 ~ 260). Beijing: China Huaqiao Press. [胡风 (1935). 林语堂论. 载子通编 (2003).《林语堂评说七十年》(241—260). 北京: 中国华侨出版社.]

Hu, Kaibao (2005). *The Historical Texts of English-Chinese Lexicography and the Modernization of the Chinese Language*. Shanghai: Shanghai Yiwen Press. [胡开宝著 (2005).《英汉词典历史文本与汉语现代化进程》. 上海译文出版社.]

Hu, Yilu (1984). On the Translation of Names. In The Editorial Board of *Translation Newsletter* of the China Translators Association (Ed.). *Articles on Translation (1894 – 1948)*. Beijing: Foreign Language Teaching and Research Press. [胡以鲁 (1984). 论译名. 载中国翻译工作者协会《翻译通讯》编辑部编.《翻译研究论文集(1894—1948)》. 北京:外语教学与研究出版社.]

Jastrow, Joseph (1928). *Keeping Mentally Fit — a Guide to Everyday Psychology*. New York: Garden City.

Jastrow, Joseph (2004). *Keeping Mentally Fit — A Guide to Everyday Psychology* by Joseph Jastrow. Trans. Lin Yutang. Xi'an: Shaanxi Normal University Press. [Jastrow (2004). 林语堂译. 人生日常心理指南》. 西安:陕西师范大学出版社.]

Khayyam, Omar (2003). *Rubaiyat (Bilingual and Illustrated)*. Trans. Guo Moruo. First published in 1930 by the Creation Society. Beijing: China Social Sciences Press. [莪默·伽亚谟著 (2003).《鲁拜集 英汉对照插图珍藏》. 爱德华·菲茨杰拉德英译，郭沫若汉译. 1930 创造社出版. 中国社会科学出版社.]

Ku, Hung-ming (1928). *The Conduct of Life, or The Universal Order of Confucius*. London: John Murray (First edition: 1906).

Lao Tzu (1998). *Tao Te Ching*. Trans. Arthur Waley. Beijing: Foreign Language Teaching and Research Press.

Lao Zi (1998). *Lao Zi*. Trans. Sun Yongchang. Guangzhou: Huacheng Press. [老子 (1998). 孙雍长注译. 老子. 广州:花城出版社.]

The Shih King, or Book of Poetry (2001). Trans. James Legge. Retrieved from Blackmask Online (http://www.blackmask.com)

Liang, Shiqiu (1928). Translation. First published in *Xinyue*, No. 10, Vol. 1, 1928. In The Editorial Board of *Translation Newsletter* of the China Translators Association (Ed.) (1984). *Articles on Translation (1894 – 1948)*. Beijing: Foreign Language Teaching and Research Press: 133 – 134. [梁实秋. (1928). 翻译. 原载《新月》1928 年第 1 卷第 10 号. 载中国翻译工作者协会《翻译通讯》编辑部 (1984).《翻译研究论文集(1894—1948)》. 北京: 外语教学与研究出版社:133—134.]

Lin, Taiyi (2002). *Biography of Lin Yutang*. Xi'an: Shanxi Normal University Press. [林太乙 (2002).《林语堂传》. 西安: 陕西师范大学出版社.]

Lin, Yutang (1924). Call for the Translation of an Essay and for Humor. *Chenbao Supplement* 05 – 23. [林语堂 (1924). 征译散文并提倡幽默.《晨报副刊》. 05—23.]

— (1930). *New Criticism*. Shanghai: Beixin Books Company. [林语堂 (1930).《新的文评》. 上海: 北新书局.]

— (1931). *Readings in Modern Journalistic Prose*. Shanghai, Commercial Press.

— (1933). *Papers in Linguistics*. Shanghai: Kaiming Bookstore. [林语堂 (1933).《语言学论丛》. 上海: 开明书店.]

— (1934a). *Da Huang Ji*. Shanghai: Shenghuo Bookstore. [林语堂 (1934a).《大荒集》. 上海:生活书店.]

— (1934b). *Xing Su Ji*. Shanghai: Shidai Books Company. [林语堂 (1934b).《行素集》. 上海: 时代图书公司.]

— (1935a). *My Country and My People*. New York: Reynal & Hitchcock.

— (1935b). *The Little Critic: Essays, Satires and Sketches on China, First Series: 1930 –1932*. Shanghai: The Commercial Press.

— (1935c). *The Little Critic; Essays, Satire and Sketches on China (Second Series: 1933 – 1935)*. Shanghai, China: The Commercial Press.

— (1936). *A Nun of Taishan (a Novelette) and Other Translations*. Shanghai, China: The Commercial Press.

— (1937). *The Importance of Living*. New York: Reynal & Hitchcock

— (1938). *The Wisdom of Confucius*. New York: The Modern Library (Random House).

— (1939). *Moment in Peking. A Novel of Contemporary Chinese Life*. New York: John Day.

— (1940). *With Love and Irony*. New York: John Day.

— (1941). *A Leaf in the Storm, a Novel of War-Swept China*. New York: John Da

— (1942). *The Wisdom of China and India*. New York, Random House.

— (1943). *Between Tears and Laughter*. New York: John Day.

— (1945). *Between Tears and Laughter*. London: Dorothy Crisp & Co.

— (1947). *The Gay Genius: the Life and Times of Su Tungpo*. New York: John Day.

— (1948). *The Wisdom of China*. London: Michael Joseph.

— (1950). *On the Wisdom of America*. New York: The John Day Company.

— (1952). *Famous Chinese Short Stories: Retold by Lin Yutang*. New York: The John Day Company.

— (1953). *The Vermilion Gate, a Novel of a Far Land*. New York: John Day.

— (1955). *Looking Beyond*. New York: Prentice-Hall.

— (1959a). *From Pagan to Christian*. Cleveland: World Pub. Co.

— (1959b). *The Chinese Way of Life*. Cleveland: World Pub. Co.

— (1960). *The Importance of Understanding, Translated from the Chinese by Lin Yutang*. 1 ed. New York: World Publishing.

— (1961a). *Imperial Peking: Seven Centuries of China*. New York: Crown.

— (1961b). *The Red Peony*. Cleveland: World Publishing.

— (1962). *The Pleasures of a Nonconformist*. Cleveland: World Publishing.

— (1964). *The Flight of the Innocents*. New York: Putnam.

— (1967). *The Chinese Theory of Art: Translations from the Masters of Chinese Art*. London, Heinemann.

—(1969). *The Chinese Theory of Art: Translations from the Masters of Chinese Art*. London: Panther Books.

—(1972). *Chinese-English Dictionary of Modern Usage*. Hong Kong: The Chinese University of Hong Kong Press. [林语堂.(1972).《林语堂当代汉英词典》. 香港:中文大学出版社.]

—(1974). *Wu Suo Bu Tan He Ji*. Taipei: Kaiming Bookstore. [林语堂.(1974).《无所不谈合集》. 台北:开明书店.]

—(1975). *Memoirs of an Octogenarian*. Taipei & New York: Mei Ya Publications.

—(1994a). *Shi Yi Ji (2)*. Complete Masterpieces of Lin Yutang. Vol 18. Changchun: Northeast Normal University Press. [林语堂(1994a).《林语堂名著全集第十八卷 拾遗集(下)》. 长春:东北师范大学出版社.]

—(1994b). *Papers in Linguistics*. Complete Masterpieces of Lin Yutang. Vol. 19. Changchun: Northeast Normal University Press. [林语堂.(1994b).《林语堂名著全集第十九卷 语言学论丛》. 长春,东北师范大学出版社.]

—(1994c. *Jian Fu Ji, Da Huang Ji*. Complete Masterpieces of Lin Yutang. Vol. 13. Changchun: Northeast Normal University Press. [林语堂.(1994c).《林语堂名著全集第十三卷 翦拂集 大荒集. 长春:东北师范大学出版社.》

—(1994d). *Hypatia, Henrik Ibsen: a Critical Study, Pygmalion, New Criticism*. Complete Masterpieces of Lin Yutang. Vol. 27. Changchun: Northeast Normal University Press. [林语堂.(1994d.《林语堂名著全集第二十七卷 女子与知识、易卜生评传、卖花女、新的文评》. 长春:东北师范大学出版社.]

—(1994e). *Xing Su Ji, Pi Jing Ji*. Complete Masterpieces of Lin Yutang. Vol. 14. Changchun: Northeast Normal University Press. [林语堂.(1994e).《林语堂名著全集第十四卷 行素集 披荆集》. 长春:东北师范大学出版社.]

—(1994f). *The Vermilion Gate*. Complete Masterpieces of Lin Yutang. Vol. 5. Changchun: Northeast Normal University Press. [林语堂.(1994f).《林语堂名著全集第五卷 朱门》. 长春:东北师范大学出版社.]

—(1994g). *Autobiographical Sketch of Lin Yutang, From Pagan to Christianity, Memoirs of an Octogenarian*. Complete Masterpieces of Lin Yutang. Vol. 10. Changchun: Northeast Normal University Press. [林语堂.(1994g).《林语堂名著全集第十卷 林语堂自传、从异教徒到基督徒、八十自叙》. 长春:东北师范大学出版社.]

—(1994h). *Wu Suo Bu Tan He Ji*. Complete Masterpieces of Lin Yutang. Vol. 16. Changchun: Northeast Normal University Press. [林语堂.(1994h).《林语堂名著全集第十六卷 无所不谈合集》. 长春:东北师范大学出版社. 长春:东北师范大学出版社.]

—(1994i). *Shi Yi Ji (1)*. Complete Masterpieces of Lin Yutang. Vol. 17. Changchun: Northeast Normal University Press. [林语堂.(1994i).《林语堂名著全集第十七卷 拾遗集(上)》. 长春:东北师范大学出版社.]

— (1994j). *Between Tears and Laughter.* Trans. Xu Chengbin and Lin Yutang. Complete Masterpieces of Lin Yutang. Vol. 23. Changchun: Northeast Normal University Press. [林语堂. (1994j). 徐诚斌、林语堂译.《林语堂名著全集第二十三卷 啼笑皆非》. 长春: 东北师范大学出版社.]

— (1998a). *My Country and My People.* Beijing: Foreign Language Teaching and Research Press.

— (1998b). *The Importance of Living.* Beijing: Foreign Language Teaching and Research Press.

— (2004). *The Best Lin Yutang Esssays.* Beijing: Jiuzhou. [林语堂 (2004).《林语堂散文经典全编》. 北京: 九州出版社.]

Lu Xun (1998). Thinking Once Before Acting. In Wang, Dehou (Ed.). *The Complete Edition of Lu Xun's Works (1): Essays.* Hangzhou: *Zhejiang Wenyi.* [鲁迅 (1998). 一思而行. 王得后编.《鲁迅作品全编:杂文卷 (下册)》. 杭州: 浙江文艺出版社: 374—375.]

— (2004). *Letters on Arts and Literature (2).* The Lu Xun Anthology. Vol. 24. Harbin: Heilongjian People's Press. [鲁迅 (2004).《鲁迅文集第 24 卷 文艺书简 (下册)》. 哈尔滨: 黑龙江人民出版社.]

Lin Yutang House, The. Chronological List of Lin Yutang's Works. http://www.linyutang.org.tw/lin4.html [林语堂作品年表,林语堂故居:http://www.linyutang.org.tw/lin4.html]

Ma, Jishen (1981). Coffee, Lin Yutang and Dictionaries. November, 1979. In Zhu, Chuanyu (Ed.). *Lin Yutang: Biographical Documents (Photocopied).* Taipei: Tianyi Publishing House. [马骥伸 (1981). 咖啡 · 林语堂 · 辞典. 民国 68 (1979) 年 11 月. 载朱传誉(主编).《林语堂传记资料影印本》. 台北: 天一出版社.]

Ma, Zuyi (1998). *A Brief History of Translation in China (Before the May 4 Movement).* Second Edition. Beijing: China Translation & Publishing Corporation. [马祖毅 (1998).《中国翻译简史:"五四"以前部分 (增订版)》. 中国对外翻译出版公司.]

Marlowe, M. (2004). *Against the Theory of "Dynamic Equivalence"* (Revised, April 2004). Bible Research, Internet Resources for Students of Scripture. http://www.bible-researcher.com/dynamic-equivalence.html

Morgan, Margery M. (1983). GEORGE BERNARD SHAW. British Writers Vol. 6. British Council: Pages 101 - 132. Retrieved from Literature Resource Center: http://galenet.galegroup.com

Munday, J. (2001). *Introducing Translation Studies: Theories and Applications.* London, Routledge.

Newmark, Peter (2001). *Approaches to Translation.* Shanghai: Shanghai Foreign Language Education Press.

Newmark, Peter (1993). *Paragraphs on Translation.* UK, USA & Australia: Multilingual

Matters.

Ognyov, Nikolai (1929a). *The Diary of a Communist Schoolboy (a Novelette)*. Trans. Lin Yutang and Zhang Yousong. Shanghai: Chunchao Books Company. [俄国奥格约夫原著. (1929a).《新俄学生日记(中篇小说)》. 林语堂、张友松合译. 上海: 春潮书局初版.]

— (1929b). *The Diary of a Communist Schoolboy*. Trans Dan Ling. Shanghai: Guanghua Books Company. [Ognyov, Nikolai 著. 丹苓译 (1929b).《新俄学生日记》. 上海: 光华书局.]

— Ognyov, Nikolai (1929c). *The Diary of a Communist Schoolboy*. Trans. Cha Shiji. Shanghai: Beixin Books Company. [查士骥译 (1929c).《苏俄中学生日记》. 上海: 北新书局.]

Pearsall, Judy (1998). *The New Oxford Dictionary of English*. Oxford: Clarendon Press, reprinted by the Shanghai Foreign Language Education Press, 2001.

Pu, Songling (1997). *Liao Zhai Zhi Yi (1)*. Jinan: Shandong Youyi Press. [蒲松龄 (1997).《聊斋志异 (上册)》. 济南: 山东友谊出版社. (1997).]

Pym, Anthony (2000). *Negotiating the Frontier: Translators and Intercultures in Hispanic History*. Manchester: St. Jerome.

Qian, Jun (1996). "Lin Yutang: Negotiating Modernity between East and West." Thesis Ph D in Comparative Literature. University of California Berkeley May, 1996.

Qin, Linfang (1997). On Translated Drama in the 1930s. *Journal of Nantong Teachers College (Social Science Edition)* (04): 28 -32. [秦林芳 (1997). 论三十年代的翻译话剧.《南通师范学院学报(哲学社会科学版)》(04): 28—32.]

Ransome, Arthur (1927). *The Chinese Puzzle*. London: George Allen & Unwin Ltd.

— (1929). *The Chinese Puzzle*. Trans. Shi Nong (Lin Yutang). Shanghai: Beixin Books Company. [兰塞姆著 (1929).《国民革命外纪》. 石农译. 上海: 北新书局.]

Robinson, Douglas, and NetLibrary Inc. (2001). *Who Translates? Translator Subjectivities beyond Reason*. Albany: State University of New York Press.

Russell, Dora (1925). *Hypatia, or Woman and Knowledge*. New York: E. P. Dutton & Company.

— (1929). *Hypatia, or Woman and Knowledge*. Trans. Lin Yutang. Shanghai: Beixin Books Company. 罗素夫人著, 林玉堂译 (1929).《女子与知识》. 上海: 北新书局.

Shaw, Bernard (1929). *Pygmalion*. Shanghai: Kaiming Bookstore. [肖伯纳著, 林语堂译 (1929).《卖花女》. 上海: 开明书店.]

— (1945). *Pygmalion in English and Chinese*. Trans. Lin Yutang. Shanghai: Kaiming Bookstore. [萧伯纳著 (1945).《卖花女 英汉对照》. 林语堂译. 开明书店.]

— (1982). *Pygmalion, A Drama in Five Acts*. Trans. Yang Xianyi. Beijing: China Translation & Publishing Corporation. [肖伯纳著, 杨宪益译 (1982).《卖花女 五幕传奇剧》. 北京: 中国对外翻译出版公司.]

Shen, Fu (1983). *Six Records of a Floating Life*. Trans. Leonard Pratt and Chiang Su-Hui. London: Penguin Books.

— (1999). *Six Chapters of a Floating Life*. Trans. Lin Yutang. Beijing: Foreign Language Teaching and Research Press. [沈复著.(1999). 浮生六记. 林语堂译. 北京: 外语教学与研究出版社.]

Shen, Yanbing (1984). A Discussion of the Methods of Literary Translation. In The Editorial Board of *Translation Newsletter* of the China Translators Association (Ed.). *Articles on Translation (1894 -1948)*. Beijing: Foreign Language Teaching and Research Press. [沈雁冰 (1984). 译文学书方法的讨论. 中国翻译工作者协会《翻译通讯》编辑部编.《翻译研究论文集(1894—1948)》. 北京:外语教学与研究出版社.]

Shi, Ping (2005). A Revolutionist but Not a Revolutionary — On Lin Yutang's Position as an Intellectual. *Social Sciences* (11): 99 - 104. [施萍 (2005). "革命", 非"革命家"——论林语堂的知识分子立场.《社会科学》(11): 99—104.]

Simpson, Allen (1998). "Henrik Ibsen." *Encyclopedia of World Biography*, 2nd Ed. 17 Vols. Gale Research. Reproduced in History Resource Center. Farmington Hills, MI: Gale Group. http://galenet.galegroup.com/servlet/History.

Sohigian, Diran John (1991). *The Life and Times of Lin Yutang*. Columbia University. Ph. D..

Spingarn, J. E. (1917). *Creative Criticism: Essays on the Unity of Genius and Taste*. New York: Henry Holt and Company.

Tang, Tao (2003). On Lin Yutang. In Zitong (Ed.). *Seventy Years of Comments on Lin Yutang*. Beijing: China Huaqiao Press: 261—268. [唐弢 (2003). 林语堂论. 载子通编.《林语堂评说七十年》. 北京: 中国华侨出版社: 261—268.]

— (Ed.) (1993). *History of Modern Chinese Literature*. Beijing: Foreign Languages Press.

Venuti, Lawrence (2000). Translation, Community, Utopia. In *The Translation Studies Reader*. London & New York: Routledge.

— (2004). *The Translator's Invisibility: A History of Translation*. Shanghai: Shanghai Foreign Language Education Press.

Wan, Pingjin (1987). *On Lin Yutang*. Xi'an: Shaanxi People's Press. [万平近 (1987).《林语堂论》. 西安: 陕西人民出版社.]

— (1993). *A Critical Biography of Lin Yutang*. Chongqing: Chongqin Press. [万平近 (1993).《林语堂评传》. 重庆: 重庆出版社.]

Wang, Yougui (2001). *Zhou Zuoren as Translator*. Chengdu: Sichuan People's Press. [王友贵 (2001).《翻译家周作人》. 成都: 四川人民出版社.]

— (2004). *Translation East and West: Six Chinese Translators*. Chengdu: Sichuan People's Press. [王友贵 (2004).《翻译西方与东方: 中国六位翻译家》. 成都: 四川人民出版社.]

— (2005). *Lu Xun as Translator*. Tianjin: Nankai University Press. [王友贵 (2005).《翻

译家鲁迅》. 南开大学出版社.]

Wang, Zhaosheng (2003). Approximating the Truth of Life — Lin Yutang's Philosophy of Life. In Zitong (Ed.). *Seventy Years of Comments on Lin Yutang*. Beijing: China Huaqiao Press. [王兆胜 (2003). 紧紧贴近人生本相—林语堂的人生哲学. 子通(主编).《林语堂评说七十年》. 中国华侨出版社.]

Wilss, Wolfram (1976). "Perspectives and limitations of a didactic framework for the teaching of translation". In *Translation*. Ed. by Richard W. Brislin.

Xu, Yuanzhong (1999). On the Importance of Courage in Translation Studies. *China Translators Journal* (02): 4 -9. [许渊冲 (1999). "译学要敢为天下先".《中国翻译》(02): 4—9.]

— (2003). On the Chinese School of Translation — Is Translation Studies in China Lagging Behind? *Foreign Languages and Their Teaching* (01): 52—59. [许渊冲 (2003). "谈中国学派的翻译理论——中国翻译学落后于西方吗?"《外语与外语教学》(01): 52—59.]

Yang, Hong and Wang Gang (1997). *Zhongyong with Modern Chinese Translation and Annotations*. Lanzhou: Gansu Minzu Press. [杨洪,王刚注译 (1997).《中庸》. 甘肃民族出版社.]

Yang, Liu (2004). *On the Aesthetic Modernity of Lin Yutang's Translation*. Nanjing University. Ph. D.. [杨柳 (2004).《论林语堂翻译中的审美现代性》(博士论文). 南京大学.]

— (2005). *A Study of Lin Yutang's Translations — From the Perspective of Aesthetic Modernity*. Changsha: Hunan People's Press. [杨柳 (2005).《林语堂翻译研究——审美现代性透视》. 长沙: 湖南人民出版社.]

Ye, Ming (1991). Lin Yutang: From the Perspective of the Merging of Chinese and Western Cultures. *Journal of Huaqiao University (Philosophy and Social Sciences)* (02): 99 -105. [叶鸣 (1991). 林语堂:从"中西文化溶合"破题.《华侨大学学报(哲学社会科学版)》(02): 99—105.]

Yuan, Jinxiang (1990). *Studies and Appreciation of Translations by Famous Translators*. Wuhan: Hubei Education Press. [袁锦翔. (1990.《名家翻译研究与赏析》. 武汉: 湖北教育出版社.]

Zhang, Shizhao (1984). Answer to Rong Tinggong's Letter on the Translation of Names, written in 1914. In The Editorial Board of *Translation Newsletter* of the China Translators Association (Ed.). *Articles on Translation (1894 - 1948)*. Beijing: Foreign Language Teaching and Research Press. [章士钊 (1984). 答容挺公论译名书 (1914). 载中国翻译工作者协会《翻译. 通讯》编辑部编.《翻译研究论文集(1894—1948)》. 北京:外语教学与研究出版社.]

Zhou, Shibao (2004). Lin Yutang's Idea of Translation. *Foreign Language Research* (02): 107 -110. [周仕宝 (2004). 林语堂的翻译观.《外语学刊》(02): 107—110.]

Zhu, Chuanyu (Ed.) (1981). *Lin Yutang: Biographical Documents (Photocopied, Five*

Volumes). Taipei: Tianyi Publishing House. [朱传誉主编(1981).《林语堂传记资料影印本(共五册)》. 台北: 天一出版社.]

Zhu, Xi (1987). *The Four Books Annotated*. Changsha: Yuelu Publishing Society. [朱熹集注 (1987).《四书集注》. 长沙: 岳麓书社.]

Zhu, Ziqing (1919). On the Translation of Names, first published in 1919. In The Editorial Board of *Translation Newsletter* of the China Translators Association (Ed.). *Articles on Translation (1894 –1948)*. Beijing: Foreign Language Teaching and Research Press. [朱自清. 论译名 (1919). (1984. 载中国翻译工作者协会《翻译. 通讯》编辑部编.《翻译研究论文集(1894—1948)》. 北京:外语教学与研究出版社.]

Zhuang Zi (1998). *Zhuang Zi*. Trans. Sun Yongchang. Guangzhou: Huacheng Press. [庄子著 (1998).《庄子》. 孙雍长注译. 广州: 花城出版社.]